Freedom of Speech

Recent Titles in Reference Guides to the United States Constitution
Jack Stark, Series Editor

The Right to the Assistance of Counsel
James J. Tomkovicz

Prohibited Government Acts
Jack Stark

State Sovereign Immunity
Melvyn R. Durchslag

Constitutional Remedies
Michael Wells and Thomas A. Eaton

Privileges and Immunities
David Skillen Bogen

Searches, Seizures, and Warrants
Robert M. Brown

The Supremacy Clause
Christopher R. Drahozal

Procedural Due Process
Rhonda Wasserman

Double Jeopardy
David S. Rudstein

Freedom of the Press
Lyrissa Barnett Lidsky and R. George Wright

The Taxing Power
Erik M. Jensen

Freedom of Speech

A Reference Guide to the United States Constitution

Keith Werhan

Foreword by the Honorable
Jacques L. Wiener, Jr.

REFERENCE GUIDES TO THE
UNITED STATES CONSTITUTION, NUMBER 12
Jack Stark, *Series Editor*

PRAEGER

Westport, Connecticut
London

Library of Congress Cataloging-in-Publication Data

Werhan, Keith, 1950–
Freedom of speech : a reference guide to the United States Constitution / Keith Werhan; foreword by Jacques L. Wiener, Jr.
p. cm. —(Reference guides to the United States Constitution, ISSN 1539-8986 ; no. 12)
Includes bibliographical references and index.
ISBN 0-313-31997-9 (alk. paper)
1. Freedom of speech—United States. I. Title. II. Series.

KF4772.W465 2004
342.7308'53—dc22 2004017678

British Library Cataloguing in Publication Data is available.

Library of Congress Catalog Card Number: 2004017678
ISBN: 0-313-31997-9
ISSN: 1539-8986

First published in 2004

Praeger Publishers, 88 Post Road West, Westport, CT 06881
An imprint of Greenwood Publishing Group, Inc.
www.praeger.com

Printed in the United States of America

The paper used in this book complies with the Permanent Paper Standard issued by the National Information Standards Organization (Z39.48–1984).

10 9 8 7 6 5 4 3 2 1

To Lo and Ben, with love and gratitude for their support and patience

Contents

Series Foreword

Jack Stark

One can conceive of the United States Constitution in many ways. For example, noting the reverence in which it has been held, one can think of it as equivalent to a sacred text. Unfortunately, most of its devotees have had less knowledge and even less understanding of the document than they have had reverence for it. Sometimes it is treated as primarily a political document and on that basis has been subjected to analysis, such as Charles Beard's *An Economic Interpretation of the Constitution of the United States.* One can plausibly argue that the Constitution seems most astounding when it is seen in the light of the intellectual effort that has been associated with it. Three brief but highly intense bursts of intellectual energy produced, and established as organic law, most of the Constitution as it now exists. Two of these efforts, sustained over a long period of time, have enabled us better to understand that document.

The first burst of energy occurred at the Constitutional Convention. Although some of the delegates' business, such as the struggle between populous and nonpopulous states about their representation in Congress, was political, much of it was about fundamental issues of political theory. A few of the delegates had or later achieved international eminence for their intellects. Among them were Benjamin Franklin, Alexander Hamilton, and James Madison. Others, although less well known, had first-rate minds. That group includes George Mason and George Wythe. Many of the delegates contributed intelligently. Although the Convention's records are less than satisfactory, they indicate clearly enough that the delegates worked mightily to constitute not merely a polity but a rational polity—one that would rise to the standards envisioned by the delegates' intellectual ancestors. Their product, though brief, is amazing. William Gladstone called it "the most wonderful work ever struck off."

Despite the delegates' eminence and the Constitution's excellence as seen from our place in history, its ratification was far from certain. That state of affairs necessitated the second burst of intellectual energy associated with that document: the debate over ratification. Soon after the Convention adjourned, articles and speeches—some supporting the Constitution and some attacking it—began to proliferate. A national debate commenced, not only about the document itself, but also about the nature of the polity that ought to exist in this country. Both sides included many writers and speakers who were verbally adroit and steeped in the relevant political and philosophical literature. The result was an accumulation of material that is remarkable for both its quantity and its quality. At its apex is *The Federalist Papers,* a production of Alexander Hamilton, James Madison, and John Jay that deserves a place among the great books of Western culture.

Another burst, not as impressive as the first two but highly respectable, occurred when the Bill of Rights was proposed. Some delegates to the Constitutional Convention had vigorously asserted that such guarantees should be included in the original document. George Mason, the principal drafter of the Virginia Declaration of Rights, so held, and he walked out of the Convention when he failed to achieve his purpose. Even those who had argued that the rights in question were implicit recognized the value of adding protection of them to the Constitution. The debate was thus focused on the rights that were to be explicitly granted, not on whether any rights *ought* to be explicitly granted. Again many writers and speakers entered the fray, and again the debate was solidly grounded in theory and was conducted on a high intellectual level.

Thus, within a few years a statement of organic law and a vital coda to it had been produced. However, the meaning and effect of many of that document's provisions were far from certain; the debates on ratification of the Constitution and the Bill of Rights had demonstrated that. In addition, the document existed in a vacuum, because statutes and actions had not been assessed by its standards. The attempt to resolve these problems began after Chief Justice John Marshall, in Marbury v. Madison, asserted the right of the U.S. Supreme Court to interpret and apply the Constitution. Judicial interpretation and application of the Constitution, beginning with the first constitutional case and persisting until the most recent, is one of the sustained exertions of intellectual energy associated with the Constitution. The framers would be surprised by some of the results of those activities. References in the document to "due process," which seems to refer only to procedures, have been held also to have a substantive dimension. A right to privacy has been found lurking among the penumbras of various parts of the text. A requirement that states grant the same "privileges and immunities" to citizens of other states that they granted to their own citizens, which seemed to guarantee important rights, was held not to be particularly important. The corpus of judicial interpretations of the Constitution is now as voluminous as that document is terse.

As the judicial interpretations multiplied, another layer—interpretations of interpretations—appeared, and also multiplied. This layer, the other sustained intellectual effort associated with the Constitution, consists of articles, most of them published in law reviews, and books on the Constitution. This material varies in quality and significance. Some of these works of scholarship result from meticulous examination and incisive thought. Others repeat earlier work, or apply a fine-tooth comb to matters that are too minute even for such a comb. Somewhere in that welter of tertiary material is the answer to almost every question that one could ask about constitutional law. The problem is finding the answer that one wants. The difficulty of locating useful guidance is exacerbated by the bifurcation of most constitutional scholarship into two kinds. In "Two Styles of Social Science Research," C. Wright Mills delineates macroscopic and molecular research. The former deals with huge issues, the latter with tiny issues. Virtually all of the scholarship on the Constitution is of one of those two types. Little of it is macroscopic, but that category does include some first-rate syntheses such as Jack Rakove's *Original Meanings*. Most constitutional scholarship is molecular and, again, some fine work is included in that category.

In his essay, Mills bemoans the inability of social scientists to combine the two kinds of research that he describes to create a third category that will be more generally useful. This series of books is an attempt to do for constitutional law the intellectual work that Mills proposed for social science. The author of each book has dealt carefully and at reasonable length with a topic that lies in the middle range of generality. Upon completion, this series will consist of thirty-seven books, each on a constitutional law topic. Some of the books, such as the book on freedom of the press, explicate one portion of the Constitution's text. Others, such as the volume on federalism, treat a topic that has several anchors in the Constitution. The books on constitutional history and constitutional interpretation range over the entire document, but each does so from one perspective. Except for a very few of the books, for which special circumstances dictate minor changes in format, each book includes the same components: a brief history of the topic, a lengthy and sophisticated analysis of the current state of the law on that topic, a bibliographical essay that organizes and evaluates scholarly material in order to facilitate further research, a table of cases, and an index. The books are intellectually rigorous—in fact, authorities have written them—but, due to their clarity and to brief definitions of terms that are unfamiliar to laypersons, each is comprehensible and useful to a wide audience, one that ranges from other experts on the book's subject to intelligent nonlawyers.

In short, this series provides an extremely valuable service to the legal community and to others who are interested in constitutional law, as every citizen should be. Each book is a map of part of the U.S. Constitution. Together they map all of that document's territory that is worth mapping. When this series is complete, each book will be a third kind of scholarly work that combines the macroscopic and the molecular. Together they will explicate all of the important constitutional topics. Anyone who wants assistance in understanding either a topic in constitutional law or the Constitution as a whole can easily find it in these books.

Foreword

THE HONORABLE JACQUES L. WIENER, JR.
CIRCUIT JUDGE
UNITED STATES COURT OF APPEALS FOR THE FIFTH CIRCUIT

As the latest addition to this burgeoning multivolume set, Professor Keith Werhan's historical treatment of free speech in the United States assumes its rightful place in *Reference Guides to the United States Constitution*. His book underscores the preeminence of expression among the individual freedoms protected by the Constitution, enshrined as it is in the second clause (following only freedom of and from religion) of the first of the Bill of Rights' 10 amendments. In recounting the history of the Supreme Court's development of free speech doctrine, the author also makes quite clear that this bedrock individual liberty is not, and has never been, absolute or without exception.[1] It is nevertheless this fundamental freedom's historical journey, with its twists, turns, and "speed bumps," culminating in the Court's present (but still evolving) speech doctrine, that is the foundation of the matrix proffered by Professor Werhan for comprehending the current status of free speech and testing present and future iterations for possible abridgments.

When I accepted the author's gracious and complimentary invitation to write this foreword, I expected to find his research impeccable, his coverage of the topic comprehensive, and his presentation of this series' overarching historical perspective scholarly—which of course I did. I was not prepared, however, for the delightful discovery that Professor Werhan's writing style is not just "simple and direct,"[2] but that his crisp and uncomplicated prose would provide a reading adventure unique in my experience: a learned treatise on an historically complex and legally technical subject that is nonetheless a can't-put-it-down "page turner." I soon found myself racing through the Werhan manuscript in rapt attention, all the while resenting the inevitable interruptions that kept me from completing his book without turning aside to less enjoyable but more pressing chores. It truly is a "reader's read."

Complementing the Professor's enviable style is the straightforward structure that he employs for explicating his topic. This author gently takes the hand of his reader—whether lawyer, judge, or law professor; undergraduate or law student; well-versed layman or neophyte—and leads him from the starting point of broad and general history, down the ever-narrowing and increasingly specific (but never hypertechnical) path that is the Supreme Court's case-by-case development of modern free speech doctrine. The genius of the Professor's approach is reflected in the care with which he avoids the universal temptation to cite an excessive number of Supreme Court precedents. In holding down the quantity of cases referenced, he makes his points without obscuring the propositions for which his charily selected Court precedents, and dissents, are cited and discussed. Using only the most significant of the Court's free-speech landmarks, Professor Werhan erects a developmental framework of speech categories, both contrasting and complementary, that even the most underexposed reader will follow comfortably, understand readily, and recall easily in years to come.

For openers, I anticipate that quite a few readers will be at least mildly surprised to learn that, in immortalizing freedom of expression in the First Amendment, the framers were concerned almost exclusively with the *printed* word rather than *oral* utterances. This likely accounts for their combining the freedoms of speech, press, and assembly to present the global concept of free expression. It also explains the framers' pairing of expression with religion—the preeminent topic of the speech that the framers were determined to protect.

Even more unexpected might be the less familiar readers' discovery that the framers—and indeed, virtually all Eighteenth Century legal thinkers—focused almost exclusively on the evils of prior restraint as manifested in the despised licensing or permitting practices of the Crown, both in England and in Colonial America. Harking back to Blackstone himself, Professor Werhan's historical account of the early development of free speech—paralleling as it did the proliferation of the printing press and thus the increased dissemination of newspapers and pamphlets critical of government—confirms that free speech doctrine as we know it today is a creature of Twentieth (and now, Twenty-First) Century Supreme Court jurisprudence.

I find Professor Werhan's choice of "subversive advocacy" or seditious libel for his historical tracer of the doctrine's development to be an excellent thematic choice.[3] Whether his readers visualize this evolution as a sine curve graph or an irregular but ever-ascending stairway, the emergence of free speech doctrine in the Supreme Court, from the First World War to the post-9/11 present, follows in lock-step the pendular swings of popular and emotional concern with antigovernment expression. As seen through the lens of historical hindsight, these concerns ebbed and flowed in sync with the minuet of wartime patriotic fervor and post-war concerns about antidemocratic ideologies such as socialism and communism. The Professor's identification of the two most prominent examples of the latter genre as "Red Scares"—one occurring between the World Wars and the other following World

War II—sets the stage for his presentation of the justices' most significant free speech pronouncements. Tracking the Court's treatment of subversive advocacy also introduces the reader to Justices Holmes and Brandeis as the early giants in free speech development, and Justices Cardozo, Frankfurter, Black, and Douglas as their worthy (if not always like-minded) successors.

After thus setting the table for his reader in the first three chapters of this book, Professor Werhan proceeds to crystallize by categories a number of manifestations of constitutional protection afforded, or denied, to the various subspecies of expression. It is this cataloging that produces the cubbyholes into which discrete types of free speech should be segregated. This in turn gives the researcher a leg up in identifying the specific speech issue to be analyzed. It also aids in the narrowing process by first excluding speech that does not enjoy constitutional protection and then assigning appropriate labels to the categories of speech that enjoy some degree of protection, as well as the extent of protection afforded to the particular class of speech. Here the reader will encounter such contrapuntal pairings as content-based vis-à-vis content-neutral restrictions and the concomitant testing standards of strict scrutiny vis-à-vis intermediate scrutiny. This leads to the identification of such niches as "fighting words," hate speech, sexual expressions of obscenity and child pornography—each, incidentally, increasingly more visual and less verbal—until the emergence of "symbolic expression." (Who can forget the non-verbal message conveyed by the sight of two African-American athletes standing on the medals-award podium at the Mexico City Olympics, heads bowed, right arms upthrust, and gloved fists clenched?)

Professor Werhan continues his analytical taxonomy by identifying the modern concepts of commercial speech, the public forum doctrine, prior restraint (coming full circle historically) and the modern version of governmental licensing (another full circle) of such expression as obscenity and access to public fora. And, finally, there appear the relatively recent concepts of overbreadth and vagueness.

For those of us to whom free speech issues are presented in the real-world context of court challenges, the categorical grid that Professor Werhan presents is particularly helpful in visualizing the issue and cabining the inquiry. The author's diagnostic construct—a sort of constitutional CAT scan—is sure to prove both enlightening and useful, not just to practicing lawyers and serving judges, but to instructors and students alike, whether the setting be law school or some other university discipline such as political science, American history, or constitutional law. Moreover, even the random reader with but a passing interest in the Bill of Rights and free speech is sure to find the later analytical sections of this book as compelling as the historical underpinnings of free speech doctrine that the author explores first.

In sum, Professor Werhan's contribution to the *Reference Guides* set presents to the disparate audience that it targets, a finely melded, history-based approach to the Supreme Court's modern free speech doctrine. And, it does so in a style that makes his book both a fun read and a valuable pedagogical and analytical tool.

Finally, I suggest that the readers of the book that follows this Foreword will be well served to heed its Afterword, an unimpassioned reminder that attacks on free speech, such as those occurring during the Red Scares that followed closely on the heels of major military conflicts, are not exempt from repetition. The Professor's closing admonition ("There is no reason to believe that the continued development of free speech doctrine will be possible without [courageous litigants, lawyers, and judges willing to challenge the majority sentiment] in the future") is less theoretical than it is real and timely, coming as it does while our War on Terrorism is ongoing. There is no better time for a history lesson than when history has the very real potential for repeating itself. From this perspective, none can do better than to heed the lessons of Professor Werhan's book *now*—and keep it handy, not only as an excellent reference but also as a reminder of Santayana's caution, "Those who cannot remember the past are condemned to repeat it."[4] Enjoy!

NOTES

1. The professor spares us the tautology of Holmes's "falsely-shouting-fire-in-a-theatre" analogy from Schenck v. United States, 249 U.S. 47, 52 (1919) (Holmes, J), a sure sign of the professor's level of comfort with his subject, as well as with his status as a recognized constitutional scholar. *But see*, Konigsberg v. State Bar of California, 366 U.S. 36, 56 (1961) (Black, J, dissenting).
2. Jacques Barzun, *Simple & Direct, A Rhetoric for Writing*, Harper & Row (1975).
3. "The saga of subversive advocacy provides the central narrative of the meaning of freedom of speech in the United States. . . . [T]he Court finally aligned First Amendment doctrine with the constitutional standing of freedom of speech as a fundamental right that courts must protect in all but the narrowest of circumstances." Werhan, *Freedom of Speech*, *66 (2005).
4. George Santayana, *The Life of Reason*, Vol. 1 (1905).

Acknowledgments

This book reflects my synthesis of the core jurisprudence of the First Amendment's protection of freedom of speech, which I have distilled over the past twenty years or so of teaching and writing in this field. I must gratefully acknowledge the many fine scholars whose work has helped to shape my understanding of free speech issues. Much of their scholarship is cited in the bibliographic essay included in this book. I hope that I have done their work justice.

I also wish to express my appreciation to the many law students who have taken my classes on freedom of speech over the years. I have gained, and continue to gain, insight into these rich materials through our class discussions. Many are the classes that I have left thinking differently about a free speech case or issue than when I had entered. That has always been my definition of a good class, and I am very grateful to my students for having giving me many such classes.

Finally, I wish to thank Gail Nelson for her contribution to this project. She is responsible for transforming my drawing of the chart depicting free speech methodology on page 79 into its present form. She also spent more hours than she cares to remember incorporating many of my manuscript revisions. I also would like to thank Stephanie Mitchell for her help in incorporating manuscript revisions as well.

Keith Werhan
New Orleans, Louisiana
November 2004

1

A History of Freedom of Speech in the United States

Strong judicial protection of speech is a worthy tradition. It is also a comparatively recent one. For much of American history, . . . many judges have been less protective of free speech. . . ., [and] at crucial times in American history the nation has failed to live up to its free speech and democratic ideals.

*Michael Kent Curtis**

THE ENGLISH BACKGROUND

It is one of the great paradoxes of the American Revolution that the revolutionaries fought for independence in the name of liberties that they owed to their mother country. Americans of the Revolutionary Era cherished individual liberty as their special birthright as English subjects. They turned against England only when they became convinced that their liberty had become imperiled by the corruption of imperial power over them. American revolutionaries believed they were fighting for, not against, the true principles of British constitutionalism.

In order to understand the origins of the American commitment to freedom of speech, then, it is profitable to first take a quick look at England before the American Revolution.[1] For virtually all of the seventeenth and eighteenth centuries, what the English called "freedom of speech" referred to the hard-won immunity from prosecution enjoyed by members of Parliament for the statements they made during floor debate. Freedom of speech, in this original English understanding, was thus a parliamentary privilege rather than an individual right. Open debate on the issues of the day was reserved for the people's representatives. The people themselves, as subjects of the realm, were expected to content themselves with listening—silently—to that debate. The United States Constitution incorporated this early

English understanding of the freedom of speech in the Constitution's speech-or-debate clause, which immunizes members of Congress for their "Speech or Debate in either House" (Article I, section 6, clause 1). The recognition—and protection—of free expression in the U.S. Constitution, as originally drafted, rested largely with this provision of immunity for the members of Congress. (As mentioned below, however, the original Constitution's strict definition of treason also provided meaningful protection for freedom of speech.)

The "freedom of speech" protected in the First Amendment to the U.S. Constitution applies to all individuals. Its English origins lie in two complementary freedoms—the freedom of conscience on matters of religious belief and the freedom of the press. Those who demanded broad freedom of expression for individuals in England before the American Revolution usually did so while debating religious questions. Because of the establishment of religious belief and practice in England, such questions were matters of state. This was especially so in the seventeenth century, when the country divided, sharply and violently, along religious lines. The participants in this religious debate "spoke" through the presses. From the beginning, freedom of the press—that is, the freedom of writers and printers to publish information and ideas for the general public—was bound together with a broader right of all individuals to express themselves freely on matters of public importance.

Any American of the twenty-first century who takes for granted the broad right of individuals to speak freely would be shocked by the customary constraints on that freedom which existed in England before the American Revolution. The introduction in England of the printing press in 1476 triggered a quick reaction from the Crown. In the view of the Tudors, the peace and stability of the realm required the silencing of dissenting voices, which in turn demanded strict governmental control over the content of the texts that could be printed, published and thus made available to their subjects. The Tudors created a complex and pervasive regulatory regime that enabled the government to identify and to discipline those printers who had published, in the official language, "seditious words" or "evil opinions."[2]

Beginning in 1538, England embarked on a licensing system that required printers to gain the permission of the government (called an *imprimatur*) before publishing any text. Government censors possessed authority to remove any passages that offended their sensibilities. State censorship under the licensing system never approached its full potential, however. Many printers published without the government's *imprimatur*, even though it was a crime to do so. When the monarchy was overthrown in 1640, printers were freed from the licensing system, but only until 1643 when licensing was resurrected by Parliament. The effect of the revolution, as Parliament saw it, had not been to advance individual or press freedom, but rather to transfer governmental prerogative to control expression from the Crown to Parliament, acting as the people's representative.

That self-serving view was not fully shared outside Parliament, however. For the first time, publications began to appear in England that challenged the legitimacy of *any* governmental entity assuming the power to license individual expression. The most famous of these publications is John Milton's pamphlet, *Areopagitica*, which he published in 1644, the year after Parliament re-instituted the press-licensing system. The pamphlet, which appropriately enough lacked an *imprimatur*, attacked governmental licensing of the presses as a denial of the freedoms of thought, conscience and expression, which Milton eloquently portrayed as paramount human rights, rather than as points of parliamentary privilege. Milton wrote, "Give me the liberty to know, to utter, and to argue freely according to conscience, above all liberties." While falling strikingly short of a wholesale endorsement of free expression (Milton, for example, would deny that liberty to Roman Catholic publications), he welcomed the contentiousness of open debate on public issues, which English authorities reflexively feared. He expressed confidence not only in the power of truth and rational argument, but also in the capacity of the people to see and to act on the truth. In the most frequently quoted passage from *Areopagitica*, Milton wrote, "[T]hough all the winds of doctrine were let loose to play upon the earth, so Truth be in the field, we do injuriously by licensing and prohibiting, to misdoubt her strength. Let her and Falsehood grapple; who ever knew Truth put to the worse, in a free and open encounter?" Milton applauded societal disagreement and argument as a sign of social vigor, not vulnerability. He wrote, "Where there is much desire to learn, there of necessity will be much arguing, much writing, many opinions; for opinions in good men is but knowledge in the making." To those who were dubious—this, after all, was a period of civil war in England—Milton argued that official censorship, in any event, was ineffectual. Governmental licensors were not competent to serve as the arbiters of truth and wisdom. Even if they possessed such an ability, competing ideas would surface and circulate among the public regardless of their efforts. Although Milton was not persuasive to his contemporaries, we will see in the following chapter that his arguments in *Areopagitica* contributed considerable grounding for the American theory of free speech.

Licensing survived another fifty years, until 1695, when the House of Commons declined to renew the latest iteration of the statute that enabled the system. Although that (non)action would be remembered as a great victory for free expression in England, the demise of the licensing system was caused by its practical failings as a regulatory regime, rather than by any sudden embrace of free expression by Parliament. As the number of presses proliferated, publications grew exponentially. Licensing officials could not hope to review, let alone edit, every text before public release. Nor could the government realistically aspire to prosecute the constant stream of printers who evaded the requirement of pre-publication review altogether.

When Parliament abandoned the licensing system, the government redirected its efforts to control the presses by relying on the criminal laws of treason and seditious libel to punish writers and printers who published material that officials considered objectionable. The English law of treason, which dates to a statute enacted by Parliament in 1352, made it a crime, punishable by death, to take up arms against the Crown, to align with the enemies of the Crown, or even to imagine the death of the king. As written, the act required more than a defendant simply having spoken out against the government. To obtain a conviction, the government was required to prove that a defendant had taken some overt action against the state. In the seventeenth century, however, the English judiciary adopted the concept of "constructive treason," which subjected those who had simply written or spoken against the Crown to treason prosecutions. Although enforcement of the law against treason, actual as well as constructive, was rare, Frederick Seaton Siebert concluded in his exhaustive study of the subject that the mere threat of prosecution for treason, which was a capital offense, constituted a "real and present threat to freedom of expression" in England until about the time of the drafting of the United States Constitution in 1787.[3] At the least, the law of constructive treason must have encouraged dissidents to think twice before expressing opposition to the Crown.

The delegates to the U.S. Constitutional Convention drew from the English experience and took great care to rein in the law of treason. The judicial article of the Constitution provides, "Treason against the United States, shall consist only in levying War against them, or in adhering to their Enemies, giving them Aid and Comfort. No person shall be convicted of Treason unless on the Testimony of two Witnesses to the same overt Act, or on Confession in open Court" (Article III, section 3, clause 1). Like the original English statute, the U.S. Constitution focuses on hostile "overt Act[s]," not on hostile speech. There is no place for the crime of constructive treason in the American constitutional system.

The common law of seditious libel—that is, a statement that defames the government or its officials—proved to be the English government's method of choice for controlling dissident speech after the demise of the licensing system. The crime of seditious libel originated in a statute that Parliament enacted in 1275 to outlaw the telling of falsehoods concerning the king, the nobility, and other "great men of the Realm."[4] It was not until the seventeenth century that the law assumed an important role in controlling the presses. By the eighteenth century, the English courts regarded seditious libel as a distinctively serious offense. In the language of a leading treatise of the time, seditious libel not only "endanger[ed] the public peace," as did other kinds of libel, but also it created "a direct tendency to breed in the people a dislike of their governors, and [to] incline them to faction and sedition."[5] The penalties for committing seditious libel in eighteenth-century England, accordingly, could be quite harsh.

The English common law concept of seditious libel, in operation, was notoriously broad. In historian Leonard Levy's description, "Judged by actual prosecutions, the crime consisted of defaming or contemning [sic] or ridiculing the government: its form, constitution, officers, laws, conduct, or policies, to the jeopardy of the public peace. In effect, any malicious criticism about the government that could be construed to have the bad tendency of lowering it in the public's esteem, holding it up to contempt or hatred, or of disturbing the peace was seditious libel, exposing the speaker or writer to criminal prosecution."[6] Beginning in the seventeenth century, the courts broadened the offense by refusing to recognize the truth of a statement as a defense to a charge of seditious libel. Indeed, because the truth was more likely to gain traction than a falsehood, English law regarded truthful criticisms of the government and of its officials as more harmful than false ones. Judges did not trust juries to decide whether a defendant's statement qualified as seditious libel. They kept that determination for themselves.

William Blackstone, who authoritatively distilled the common law in 1769 in his *Commentaries on the Laws of England*, crystallized English law regarding free expression at the time of the American Revolution. He exalted "liberty of the press" as "essential to the nature of a free state," but he limited the reach of that liberty, "properly understood," to a freedom from "*previous* restraints upon publications [i.e., licensing], and not in freedom from censure for criminal matter when published [e.g., seditious libel]." (Emphasis in original.) Blackstone explained,

> Every freeman has an undoubted right to lay what sentiments he pleases before the public: to forbid this, is to destroy the freedom of the press; but if he publishes what is improper, mischievous, or illegal, he must take the consequences of his own temerity. . . . [T]o punish (as the law does at present) any dangerous or offensive writings, which, when published, shall on a fair and impartial trial be adjudged of a pernicious tendency, is necessary for the preservation of peace and good order, of government and religion, the only solid foundations of civil liberty. Thus the will of individuals is still left free; the abuse only of that free will is the object of legal punishment.[7]

English common law at the time of the American Revolution thus protected freedom of expression only from pre-publication review. Otherwise, speakers exercised their "undoubted right" to express their views in the shadow created by the prerogative of prosecutors and judges to invoke the power of the state if those views struck the authorities as "improper, mischievous, or illegal."

In light of the rather unforgiving stance of the common law, perhaps the most remarkable fact about freedom of speech in eighteenth-century England was that English subjects, at home and abroad in the American colonies, did not keep quiet. Just as the licensing system proved unsuccessful in blocking publication of texts that strayed from official orthodoxy, the law of seditious libel, while it certainly constricted free expression, nevertheless failed to insulate the government and its officials from public criticism. The practice of freedom of speech in eighteenth-century England was freer than the common law would have it.

THE AMERICAN COLONIAL BACKGROUND

"The persistent image of colonial America as a society in which freedom of expression was cherished is an hallucination of sentiment that ignores history."[8,9] So writes Leonard Levy in *Emergence of a Free Press*, the leading history of the early evolution of free expression in the United States. Although stated provocatively, Levy's conclusion should come as no great surprise. American colonials were English subjects, and their collective conception of individual rights, naturally enough, was shaped by their understanding of common law. Mainstream legal thought in the American colonies, as in England, assumed not only that individuals were free to speak their minds, but also that they were legally accountable for the harmful tendencies of their speech. As one legal scholar has put it, "There simply never existed any golden age of free speech in England or the colonies."[10]

But there is a brighter side to American colonial history. Just as in eighteenth-century England, the *practice* of free speech outpaced the *right* of free speech in the American colonies. Levy himself noted "the most extraordinary diversity of opinion on religion, politics, social structure, and other vital subjects" that the colonists apparently felt free to discuss.[11] If anything, free speech in the American colonies was far freer than in the mother country. Because of the geographical distance separating London from the colonies, English authority in America was never pervasive. Indeed, the American Revolution was triggered by England's belated and clumsy efforts in the 1760s to assert sovereign control over its colonials. American colonists over time developed a sense of their distinctiveness as a people, which separated them from their fellow Englishmen living in the mother country. That sense of distinctiveness helps to account for the colonists' refusal to accept England's position that they were "virtually" represented in Parliament by the votes of English commoners. A central element of the distinctive American identity was the celebration of liberty. Historian Eric Foner has observed, "The American Revolution was fought in the name of liberty."[12]

Legal historian Michael Kent Curtis has identified the dueling narratives that dominate the early Anglo-American history of free expression before the American Revolution. On one hand, as we have seen, legal recognition of a right of free expression was sharply limited. On the other hand, beginning in the seventeenth century, what Curtis described as a "a robust . . . popular tradition" demanded recognition and protection of free speech that extended considerably beyond what the law of the time allowed. This tension between the legal and popular traditions produced a kind of dialogue that has continued ever since, between those who fear free speech for the threat that it appears to pose to the order and stability of society, and those who champion that freedom as a constituent element of a free and just society.[13] As we have seen, John Milton helped launch this debate in England in the middle of the seventeenth century when he wrote *Areopagitica.* And as we shall see in Chapter 3 concerning subversive advocacy, it would not be until the second half of the twentieth century that the popular tradition can be said to have reformed the legal tradition in America.

The capacity of the popular tradition to liberalize legal doctrine is the central theme of the defining free speech experience of the colonial period, the acquittal in 1735 of John Peter Zenger by a New York jury on a charge of seditious libel. Zenger was the printer of the *New-York Weekly Journal,* a newspaper controlled by political opponents of New York's governor. As the mouthpiece of the opposition, the *Weekly Journal* regularly launched verbal assaults against the governor and his administration, which retaliated by resort to the common law. The governor received early warning of what lay ahead when a grand jury refused to indict Zenger for seditious libel. The state attorney general nevertheless plunged ahead, filing his own criminal charge against Zenger for having published "false, scandalous, malicious, and seditious" libels.[14]

Zenger staked all on the defense that his newspaper's criticisms were true, and that the state could not legitimately make truthful commentary illegal. The strategy was innovative but risky, because the English courts had long ago eliminated truth as a defense to seditious libel at common law. Thus, even though the attorney general had charged that Zenger's publications were "false," the trial judge ruled that he need not submit evidence in support of that allegation in order to obtain a conviction. The judge also prohibited the defense from proving the truth of the *Weekly Journal*'s attacks. Zenger's lawyer ignored that ruling, bypassed the common law, and tapped into a rich vein of the popular tradition of free speech. He turned his attention from the judge to the jurors, telling them, contrary to common law, that *they* were the proper judges of the case. Zenger's lawyer urged the jurors to ignore the rulings and instructions of the trial judge, and to acquit Zenger unless *they* were convinced that his publications were false. He argued, "[T]he laws of our country have given us the right—the liberty—both of exposing and opposing arbitrary power . . . by speaking and writing truth."[15]

The jurors were convinced, and they acquitted Zenger after brief deliberations. In doing so, the *Zenger* jury reformed the common law of seditious libel in America. Their acquittal, as a practical matter, shifted from the trial judge to the jury the ultimate authority to determine whether a defendant's criticism of government officials constituted seditious libel. In addition, after the *Zenger* verdict, no American jury convicted anyone of seditious libel unless the jurors found the defendant's criticism to have been false. As a result of the *Zenger* reformation of the common law, government officials—whether prosecutor or judge—no longer possessed the power to punish individuals for expression that *they* regarded as seditious. The government was required to convince a popular jury that its critics had abused their right of free speech.

While *Zenger*'s reformation of the common law of seditious libel was woefully deficient by today's First Amendment standards, which do not countenance any crime of seditious libel, the jury acquittal in that case nevertheless marks an important break with the past. Moreover, the symbolic and practical effects of the *Zenger* verdict, which were widely reported throughout the colonies, were greater than its legal impact. Not only had the colonists, in the form of the *Zenger* jury, assumed the power to define and to control seditious libel prosecutions, but also they had refused to do the government's bidding by silencing its critics. Thus, as revolutionary fervor took hold during the 1760s and 1770s, popular juries stood as bulwarks safeguarding American presses by refusing to convict patriots for seditious libel. Colonial governments stood by helplessly during a rhetorical onslaught that most English judges would have punished severely. As a result of its connection with the revolutionary experience, the *Zenger* verdict ultimately had the effect of fostering among American colonists a general celebration of individual liberty, as well as a deep recognition of the connection between their liberty and their freedom of expression.

Yet, after the Revolution the American understanding of, and commitment to, freedom of expression remained incomplete. While public officials recognized the freedom of patriots to criticize and to challenge the fledgling state governments, they did not tolerate the dissenting voices of those who remained loyal to the mother country. The Tories shouted, "Hypocrisy!" American patriots purported to see no inconsistency, however. As historian Arthur Schlesinger observed, "They simply contended that liberty of speech belonged solely to those who spoke the speech of liberty."[16]

THE FIRST AMENDMENT

The crosscurrents between law and practice that buffeted free expression in Colonial America did not suddenly disappear with the Declaration of Independence. During the extraordinarily creative period between the American Revolution and ratification of the First Amendment,[17] the years 1776 through 1791, free speech in America was freer than anywhere else in the world. Throughout the United States, Leonard Levy writes, Americans "habitually lambasted their leaders, excoriated public policies, and acted as if their governments were their servants"—which in the new revolutionary ideology, they were.[18] But while the historical record makes clear that the early Americans felt free to express themselves on the issues of their time, it does not tell us how they defined their right to free expression. States commonly protected free expression in their new constitutions (typically in the form of a free press clause, rather than a free speech clause) even as they adopted the common law of England as their governing law. There is no evidence that any state consciously reconciled the common law of seditious libel with a constitutional protection of free expression. No state specifically adopted or rejected the common law of seditious libel. Nor did any state offer specific guidance on the meaning it ascribed to the freedom of expression that it constitutionalized. This ambiguity likely did not matter much at the time. The practice of free expression thrived: the American press remained vital and outspoken, and prosecutions for seditious libel were rare.

Unlike the state constitutions in existence at the time, the U. S. Constitution of 1787 contained no provision generally protecting an individual right of free expression. Although the original Constitution demonstrated sensitivity to free speech values in the treason and speech-or-debate clauses, the framers, in the final days of the Constitutional Convention, defeated a motion by Charles Pinckney and Elbridge Gerry to include a provision "that the liberty of the press should be inviolably observed." The only recorded statement from the debate on this proposal was by Roger Sherman, who felt that the language was "unnecessary" because "[t]he power of the Congress does not extend to the press."[19] Although one statement provides too fragile a foundation upon which to settle a conclusive interpretation, the delegates may have been satisfied that their proposed constitution left the press free from federal control without explicitly so providing. Because the Constitution did not explicitly provide legislative power to regulate the presses (a conspicuous absence in the light of English history), the framers may have believed it would be clear to readers that Congress lacked such power.

Sherman's response to the Pinckney/Gerry proposal betrays an atypical myopia on the part of the framers, who managed to convince themselves that a bill of rights, which was a common feature in state constitutions, was unnecessary for the federal charter. They were unable to convince the nation, however. Anti-Federalists (the label assigned to those who opposed ratification of the Constitution) excoriated the convention delegates for their misstep. They particularly criticized the absence of explicit protection for the "grand palladium of freedom, the liberty of the press."[20] On this point, at least, the Anti-Federalists understood better than the drafters of the Constitution the potential power that resided in the interplay of provisions that prescribed the legislative authority of Congress. Public opposition to the framers' decision to omit a bill of rights in the Constitution was adamant, and the Federalists (the name taken by those who supported the Constitution) were able to secure ratification only on the understanding that Congress would propose for public consideration a bill of rights as one of its first orders of business.

As adopted in 1791, the Bill of Rights prominently provides in the First Amendment to the Constitution of the United States: "Congress shall make no law . . . abridging the freedom of speech, or of the press." What at first may seem to be a simple, straightforward declaration—"no law"—assumes a more delphic quality if one lingers over the phrase "abridging the freedom of speech." The surviving paper trail of the drafting of the First Amendment does not illuminate the meaning that such key terms as "abridging" or "freedom of speech" had for the framers. For example, use of the word "abridging" in the speech clause contrasts with the language of the religion clauses of the First Amendment, which provide, "Congress shall make no law *respecting* an establishment of religion, or *prohibiting* the free exercise thereof." (Emphasis added.) Do the different word choices signify that the framers intended to impose different limits on the regulatory power of Congress with respect to the First Amendment rights of free expression, nonestablishment, and free exercise of religion? The language suggests that "abridging" might stake out a middle ground, so that Congress would have no power to legislate the establishment of a state religion, but it would have some power to regulate free speech (short of "abridging" that right), and it would have even greater power to regulate the free exercise of religion (short of "prohibiting" that right). There is no evidence in the historical record, however, that the framers of the First Amendment intended such a nuanced interpretation.

Similar uncertainties cloud the phrase "freedom of speech." As originally proposed by James Madison, the speech clause protected a "right to speak." That phrase is hardly more illuminating than "freedom of speech," and in any event, there is no indication whether the framers intended a different meaning when they opted for the latter, more polished phrase. The Senate considered, and rejected, qualifying constitutional protection of free speech and of a free press by including the clause, "in as ample a manner as hath at any time been secured by the common law." The written record contains no explanation of the qualification, but the language seems to signal an intent to extend constitutional protection for free expression to the full extent provided by the common law, but no further. There is no explanation for the Senate's rejection of the proposal, either. Senators may have intended that the constitutional protection of free expression be liberated from the familiar constraints of the common law. But it is also possible that senators omitted the qualifying phrase as surplusage. They may have assumed, in other words, that readers naturally would ascribe to "freedom of speech" its common law meaning.

A definitive answer on the original meaning of the speech clause of the First Amendment is not possible because there is virtually no recorded debate of the drafting and ratification of that provision. The only recorded statement in the congressional debate directly concerning the speech and press clauses occurred on June 8, 1789, the very day that James Madison introduced his proposed Bill of Rights on the floor of the House of Representatives. Echoing Roger Sherman's position during the Constitutional Convention, the statement *opposed* constitutional protection of the freedom of press as unnecessary. The only hint of the meaning of free speech to the founders came during discussion of the assembly clause of the First Amendment, which protects "the right of the people peaceably to assemble." Madison linked freedom of assembly with freedom of speech and freedom of the press as alternative means by which the people "may communicate their will" to their representatives in government.[21] While such communication is an important component of the meaning of free speech, it cannot plausibly have supplied the full meaning of that guarantee for the founding generation.

It is likely, as Leonard Levy has suggested, that the founding generation reached no consensus on any specific meaning of "freedom of speech."[22] Levy also may be correct that the absence of recorded debate on the speech clause signals that the framers did not intend for the provision "to institute broad reform."[23] The priority at the time may have been less to define the precise contours of expressive freedom than to declare the constitutional principle that the new national legislature would lack power to silence the American people. Such a declaration would have brought constitutional comfort to former revolutionaries, who cherished individual freedom, as well as to present-day localists, who feared the power of the federal government.

This much is clear: The new republican governments in the United States, state and federal, required a commitment to freedom of speech by individuals on public issues and about public officials that extended far beyond Blackstone's description of the common law injunction against prior restraints. Individuals no longer were subjects of the realm; they were now citizens. But if the requirements of free speech in the United States necessarily had moved beyond the traditional common law understanding, the First Amendment did not clearly demarcate the boundaries of the new constitutional right. As would be true of so much of the Constitution, the meaning of freedom of speech, of necessity, would be worked out in the course of the American experiment in constitutional self-government.

THE "DARK AGE" OF FREE SPEECH JURISPRUDENCE: FROM THE EARLY NATIONAL PERIOD TO WORLD WAR I

The considerable period of time that extends from the formation of the federal government shortly before the close of the eighteenth century to the First World War shortly after the beginning of the twentieth century was the "dark age" for the constitutional jurisprudence of free expression in the United States. It is only in a series of cases involving opposition to U.S. involvement in the First World War that the Supreme Court of the United States began to develop any sense of a *protective* free speech jurisprudence. This is not to say that there were no constitutional controversies over the meaning of free expression until World War I. Far from it. But the issues that arose typically ran their course with the justices playing little or no role in their resolution. In a way that is difficult to fathom for those accustomed to the contemporary judicial dominance in the elaboration of constitutional rights, the Court during this dark age largely took a back seat to the political process.

The two major controversies over freedom of expression before World War I were generated, first, by Congress's enactment of the Sedition Act of 1798, and several decades later, by the national crises of slavery and the Civil War. Each of these controversies raised the most fundamental question posed by freedom of speech: Whether and to what extent may individuals speak out in opposition to the legal and societal commitments of their communities when community leaders believe that their doing so threatens the public order? This question lay at the core of the earlier controversies over the English licensing system and the common law crime of seditious libel. And as we shall see, this same question remains central to many modern free speech problems as well.

The Sedition Act of 1798

If members of the founding generation finessed the opportunity to define the meaning of free expression when they adopted the First Amendment, their day of reckoning was not long in coming.[24] The occasion was what historians Stanley Elkins and Eric McKitrick have described as the "Fever of 1798."[25] Midway during the administration of John Adams, the nation's second president, a diplomatic flare-up pushed the United States to the brink of war with France, its erstwhile ally during the War for Independence. Leading members of the Federalist Party, which controlled Congress at the time, already were agitated by the rhetoric and maneuverings of the rival Republican Party, led by Adams's vice president, Thomas Jefferson. The Republicans strongly opposed Federalist policy on a number of fronts, including the perceived tilt of the administration toward England, at the expense of France. Believing, with Adams, that it was necessary to maintain national unity during the crisis, the Federalists pushed through Congress the first national law of seditious libel in U.S. history. The Sedition Act of 1798 made it a federal crime for any person to make "any false, scandalous, and malicious" statement about the government of the United States, Congress or the President, "with intent to defame [them] . . . or to bring them . . . into contempt or disrepute; or to excite against them . . . the hatred of the good people of the United States." The Act observed the *Zenger* reformation of seditious libel. It allowed as a defense to any claimed libel "the truth of the matter contained in the publication." The statue provided, moreover, that at trial, "the jury . . . shall have the right to determine the law and the fact, under the directions of the court, as in other cases."[26]

With the passage of the Sedition Act in Congress, the founding generation failed the "first, crucial test" of the Bill of Rights.[27] Paradoxically, however, this sobering event provided the constitutional service of generating a documentary record on the meaning of free speech for the founding generation that adoption of the First Amendment itself had failed to produce. The Sedition Act was closely contested in Congress along partisan lines, and it generated sharp debate. Republicans made two principal constitutional arguments against the Act, which were in significant tension with each other. They argued, first, that the First Amendment denied Congress any regulatory authority over speech or press. This absolutist interpretation appeared to owe more to the principle of federalism then to that of free expression, however, because those who advanced this claim often indicated that it was the role of the states, rather than the federal government, to control individual expression. The second Republican argument in opposition to the Act was squarely based on the value of free expression, and if successful, it would have discredited state as well as federal regulation of speech. This claim held that the First Amendment's protection of free speech represented constitutional recognition that in a republican government premised on the concept of popular sovereignty, the people, by definition, remain free to express themselves on the performance of public officials and on matters of public policy. For the government to restrict such speech, in the Republican argument, was to deny citizens the information they needed to perform their primary public duty, that of voting their representatives into and out of office. Such restrictions, the argument continued, subverted the constitutional order because they overturned the principal-agent relationship between the sovereign people and *their* officials, returning republican citizens to their pre-Revolutionary status as mere subjects of a sovereign government. As Madison put the argument several years before the Sedition Act controversy, "Opinions are not the objects of legislation. . . . If we advert to the nature of Republican Government, we shall find that the censorial power is in the people over the Government, and not in the Government over the people."[28]

While the Republicans' second argument charted the future meaning of the First Amendment, the Federalist defense of the Sedition Act was steeped in the English common law tradition. In their Old World thinking, Federalists regarded the organized political opposition of the Republicans to the policies of the Adams administration as subversive of the United States government. Their outrage over Republican opposition was fueled by the war fever of 1798 and by the public support that flowed their way. During House debate, one Federalist congressman described the Republican opposition as nothing less than a "conspiracy against the Constitution, the Government, the peace and safety of this country."[29] Federalists saw the criticism that came their way from Republican-controlled newspapers not as an exercise of expressive freedom, but as an abuse of that liberty.

Just as Republicans had built their challenge to Old World assumptions about freedom of speech on what they believed to be the cornerstone of republican government, Federalists based their traditionalist reaction to the Republican challenge on their own understanding of republican government. Because the people elected their officials, Federalists argued, popular sovereignty was undermined by individuals who challenged the actions of the people's representatives. These opponents, having lost in free and fair elections, appeared to the Federalists as being intent on thwarting the will of the people as expressed by the government of their choosing. Republican opposition, according to the Federalists, was not just misguided as a matter of policy, but was also dangerously anti-democratic. And thus, Federalists argued, such oppositional speech need not—indeed, it could not—be tolerated.

The Federalists nestled their interpretation of the First Amendment's protection of freedom of speech in the English common law, which stated that while such freedom relieved speakers of prior restraints on their expression, it did not immunize them from subsequent punishment for any harmful effects threatened by their speech. Republican opponents of the Sedition Act responded in the only way they could, by questioning whether the common law of free expression had survived the First Amendment. Could the sole aim of the speech clause, they asked, have been to prevent a licensing system that no American advocated or even believed possible? Indeed, could that have been any part of its purpose? Was not the very idea of requiring individuals to obtain a government license before *speaking* (rather than *printing*) absurd? James Madison, writing in 1799, concluded more broadly that it was nonsensical to limit the First Amendment protection of freedom of speech to a freedom from prior restraints. "It would seem a mockery to say," he wrote, "that no law should be passed, preventing publications from being made, but that laws might be passed for punishing them in case they should be made."[30]

Although the Federalists prevailed in Congress, their victory should not canonize their traditionalist conception of free expression as the "framers' intent" of the speech clause. The debate in Congress was deeply partisan, and it proceeded almost exclusively along party lines. Federalists and Republicans advanced constitutional arguments for tactical gain. Members of Congress were keenly aware that the purpose of the Sedition Act was to provide the Federalist-controlled government a means of silencing Republican dissent even as Federalists remained free to attack their Republican opponents. The partisan dimension of the Sedition Act surfaces on a couple of occasions in the text. For example, the Act prohibited seditious libel of the Federalist president and Congress, but not of the Republican vice president, Thomas Jefferson. In addition, the Act contained a sunset provision that extinguished its provisions on March 3, 1801, which just happened to be the final day of President Adams's term of office. Congress passed the Sedition Act of 1798 not because the Federalist reading of the First Amendment was correct, but because the Federalists controlled Congress.

Having fought so hard to secure passage of the Sedition Act, the Federalists were hardly hesitant to enforce its previsions. The federal government brought fourteen prosecutions under the Act in the two and one-half years of its existence. All of the prosecutions targeted Republicans, with a special emphasis on the editors of leading Republican newspapers. Convictions were routine (there was only one acquittal), and federal judges (including Supreme Court justices sitting as members of circuit courts) just as routinely dismissed constitutional challenges to the Act.

Events began to turn against the Federalists in 1800. The threat of war subsided, as did the sense of crisis. In January of that year, the Republicans nearly succeeded in repealing the Sedition Act. Even though the Federalists retained sufficient muscle to beat back that attempt, they could not prevent the constitutional legitimacy of the Act from becoming an issue in the presidential election of 1800. The American public, which had supported the push for the Sedition Act in 1798, now turned against the Federalists and elected Thomas Jefferson the nation's third president. Adams was left to claim the distinction of being the first American president to be turned from office by losing a bid for re-election.

When Jefferson took office on March 4, 1801, the Sedition Act expired in accordance with its terms. Jefferson was not content to rest there, however. He pardoned those who had been convicted under the Act, and Congress, now under Republican control, authorized the government to repay their fines. Both President Jefferson and Congress justified their actions on the ground that the Sedition Act was unconstitutional. And the modern Supreme Court, in looking back on the "great controversy over the Sedition Act of 1798," has seen in these actions a judgment "in the court of history" that the Act had violated the First Amendment (New York Times Co. v. Sullivan, 1964). But historical judgments often are not as tidy as we suppose. After the Republican takeover in the "Revolution of 1800," Republican prosecutors in the states, with the knowing acquiescence of President Jefferson, used state laws against seditious libel to silence their Federalist opponents. By the arrival of the Civil War, according to Leonard Levy, most states had in place criminal seditious libel laws along the lines of the supposedly discredited Sedition Act of 1798.

From the Sedition Act to the Civil War

As had been characteristic of Anglo-American history since the seventeenth century, the first half of the nineteenth century witnessed individuals who vigorously exercised their freedom of speech together with government officials who were determined to silence them once their rhetoric threatened to upset the status quo. The dominant public issue of the antebellum period, of course, was slavery and its abolition. Controversy over free speech inevitably became intertwined with that increasingly intractable problem.[31]

The election of 1800 registered the view that the Sedition Act was an unconstitutional exercise of congressional power, but as Republican enforcement of state laws against seditious libel showed, the election had not resolved the question of the legitimacy of state authority to punish dissident speech. In 1833, the Supreme Court ruled that the Bill of Rights, in its entirety, controlled only the actions of the national government, and not those of the states (Barron v. Baltimore). At about the same time, the long simmering controversy over slavery began to erupt. Abolitionists coupled an intensification of their activities with a demand for an immediate end to slavery. They organized associations, held public rallies, and conducted public meetings. They extended their assault on slavery through a variety of written media. The abolitionists hoped that putting slavery on the national political agenda would swing public opinion in their favor, which in turn would lead slaveholders to emancipation. Indeed, believing they could directly persuade slaveholders to abandon the practice, they sent antislavery publications to members of the Southern elite in a series of mass mailings. Abolitionists invested all of these efforts with the faith that mobilizing their freedom of expression would hasten the end of slavery.[32]

The legal response to the abolitionists in the Southern slave states was as decisive as it was predictable: most Southern states banned antislavery speech. A number of Southern legislatures made it a crime for anyone to advocate against slavery, or indeed, to say anything that might arouse disaffection or rebellion within slave communities. North Carolina, for example, outlawed the publication or circulation of material, "the evident tendency whereof is to cause slaves to become discontented with the bondage in which they are held by their masters and the laws regulating the same, and free negroes to be dissatisfied with their social condition and the denial to them of political privileges, and thereby to excite among the said slaves and free negroes a disposition to make conspiracies, insurrections, or resistance."[33] Michael Kent Curtis summarized the effect of this "Southern quarantine"[34] of antislavery speech:

> Most Southerners did not own slaves, and some opposed slavery. The restriction of antislavery speech by Southern statutes tended to keep slavery off the political agenda in those states. Legal and extralegal suppression of antislavery speech protected an entrenched economic elite from the democratic process and silenced those who wanted to speak against the horrors of slavery and for the humanity of the slave.[35]

Southern states were determined not to repeat the "mistake" of the Virginia legislature, which in 1832 considered a proposal to abolish slavery. Although the legislature ultimately rejected abolition, the proposal generated a degree of legislative support that pro-slavery forces found disquieting.

The Southern states were not satisfied with halting the importation of antislavery advocacy. They also wished to eliminate the abolitionist threat at its source. They demanded that Northern states outlaw abolitionist organizations and antislavery publications operating within their borders, and that Congress prohibit the mailing of antislavery publications to Southern destinations. Many Northerners violently disagreed with the abolitionists, as evidenced by the recurrent mob actions against them in a number of Northern cities. Moreover, there was considerable agreement in the North that it was legitimate for the Southern states to suppress antislavery rhetoric because of the threat it posed to public order. Even so, legislatures of the Northern states resisted the call to suppress abolitionist advocacy at home. To do so, they concluded, would stifle freedom of speech on a question of pressing public importance.

Congress was more equivocal. It refused to adopt a legislative proposal by President Andrew Jackson that, in Jackson's language, would have "prohibit[ed], under severe penalties, the circulation in the Southern States, through the mail, of incendiary publications intended to instigate the slaves to insurrection."[36] But in the Post Office Act of 1836, Congress supported the Southern quarantine by allowing federal postmasters to refuse delivery of antislavery writings in states that had outlawed such material. The Act did not require postmasters to refuse delivery; it just did not require them to make the delivery. Congress, in other words, punted the decision whether to provide federal reinforcement of the Southern quarantine to postmasters who lived in the South.

In the same year, Congress attempted to establish a similar, hands-off approach to the entire controversy over slavery. Staggering from a torrent of abolitionist petitions, the U.S. House of Representatives in 1836 adopted a rule that permanently tabled consideration of "all petitions, memorials, resolutions, propositions, or papers, relating in any way, or to any extent whatever, to the subject of slavery, or the abolition of slavery." According to the House resolution that imposed the rule, resort to a wholesale tabling of the slavery issue was necessary to "restor[e] tranquility to the public mind" by "arrest[ing]" the "agitation" of the subject of abolition.[37] This infamous "gag rule" was in severe tension, to say the least, with the First Amendment right of individuals to "petition the Government for a redress of grievances." The gag rule also was unrealistic. It proved impossible for Congress to maintain its own quarantine of the slavery problem. The House acknowledged that political reality when it repealed the gag rule in 1844.

The repeal of the gag rule symbolized a cultural reality as well: the nation's appreciation of the value of free expression had grown in the decades of abolitionist agitation against slavery. Michael Kent Curtis, in his detailed study of free expression in antebellum America, identified the death of Elijah P. Lovejoy as a transformative event for many Northerners. Lovejoy was a Presbyterian minister and abolitionist editor in Alton, Illinois. Mobs destroyed, in succession, three of his printing presses. When local authorities declined to provide him protection, Lovejoy, together with a group of supporters, stood armed guard over his fourth press. Lovejoy was shot and killed trying to hold off yet another mob, this one intent on burning the warehouse in which he had secured the press. While this kind of mob action against abolitionists hardly was a unique occurrence, the event, Curtis recounts, produced "an immense public reaction" that in turn, contributed to "a remarkable transformation of public opinion."[38]

Northerners, many of whom remained unsympathetic to the abolitionist agenda, saw in the Lovejoy incident an illegitimate and dangerous attack not just on abolitionists, but also, in the language of the time, on the general "right" of free expression that all Americans shared as a "privilege" and "immunity" of their citizenship. Curtis describes the evolving public understanding of the freedom of speech, at least in the North:

> Northerners increasingly saw free speech as a right of all Americans not to have speech restrained except according to regularly enacted laws that comported with constitutional limitations. Some things were paradigmatic examples of free speech: the right to espouse opinions on all political, moral, religious, and scientific subjects and the right to criticize laws and institutions of one's own or another state. Many suggested that free speech, though not unlimited, was a principle of general application that must be available even to evil views. Jefferson's statement [in his first inaugural address] that error of opinion could be tolerated where truth was left free to combat it was reiterated again and again.[39]

By the 1850s, the new antislavery Republican Party would place the call for free expression at the core of its political agenda.

But as always in the history of free expression, there was counterpoint. In the wake of the Lovejoy killing, the antislavery Unitarian minister William Ellery Channing asked to use Faneuil Hall in Boston in order to hold a meeting to protest mob violence and to promote free speech. The city refused, citing its fear of mob violence. And indeed, when Philadelphia abolitionists and others opened Pennsylvania Hall in 1838 as a forum dedicated to freedom of expression, with a special emphasis on the slavery issue, a mob promptly burned it to the ground. As the slavery controversy propelled the United States toward Civil War, the cup of free expression was both half-full and half-empty.

The Civil War

Notwithstanding the many issues that divided them, the North and the South agreed on one thing—that freedom of expression must give way to wartime necessity. Throughout the Civil War, President Abraham Lincoln believed that his primary obligation was to hold the country together. He faced formidable obstacles in doing so. The Southern states seceded from the Union, and there was outspoken resistance to Lincoln's war policy in the states that remained. In addition,

Southern spies were active in the North. Lincoln took seriously the internal threat posed by the collection of war resisters and Southern sympathizers in his midst. A couple of years into the war, he authorized the military to arrest, try, and imprison civilians for "discouraging volunteer enlistments," "resisting militia drafts," "affording aid and comfort to Rebels," or more generally, for engaging in "any disloyal practice." Lincoln consolidated that authority by suspending the writ of habeas corpus for anyone arrested or held by the military "during the rebellion." Congress followed up by affirming the authority of the President "to suspend the privilege of habeas corpus in any case throughout the United States, or any part thereof," albeit with several strings attached.[40]

The Union's actions controlling wartime dissent, however, were more measured than the breadth of Lincoln's conferral of authority to the military might suggest. In his careful and often critical study of Lincoln's handling of civil liberties during the Civil War, historian Mark Neely found that arrests of dissidents in the North for criticizing the war proved to be the exception, rather than the rule.[41] Lincoln explained that he attempted to walk a fine line, permitting expression that threatened "the political prospects of the administration," while silencing those who directed their antiwar advocacy toward discouraging enlistment into and encouraging desertion from the armed forces of the Union. The Supreme Court would struggle for much of the twentieth century to define a satisfactory First Amendment principle for this kind of "subversive advocacy." But at the time, Lincoln harbored no doubt that such speech was beyond First Amendment protection. He explained, "Must I shoot a simple-minded soldier boy who deserts, while I must not touch a hair of a wily agitator who induces him to desert? . . . I think that in such a case, to silence the agitator, and save the boy, is not only constitutional, but, withal, a great mercy."[42]

Experience teaches, however, that it is difficult during wartime for government officials to separate subversive speech from legitimate political dissent. And indeed, it is doubtful that the government of the Union was able to walk Lincoln's line. Arrest records from early in the Civil War testify to the military's jailing of a significant number of individuals for such offenses as using "treasonable language," manifesting "disloyalty," or "threatening Unionists." The most celebrated case of military excess occurred in 1863, when General Ambrose Burnside ordered the arrest of Clement Vallandigham, a well-known Democratic leader and antiwar activist. Vallandigham's crime was a speech attacking the legitimacy of the Union's war effort, but without calling for any resistance to military or civil law. Just one day after the arrest, a military commission ordered Vallandigham imprisoned for the remainder of the war. The military's action caused an uproar among Northern Democrats and embarrassed Lincoln, who apparently had known nothing about Vallandigham's arrest until he read about it in the newspapers. In the end, Lincoln countermanded the military order of imprisonment, and instead exiled Vallandigham to the Confederacy.

From the Civil War to World War I

The conclusion of the Civil War not only ensured the perpetuation of the Union, but also generated a constitutional revolution that redrew the relationships among the nation, the states, and the people of the United States. The core of that revolution is to be found in the succession of amendments to the Constitution that followed the war, a latter-day Bill of Rights. The Thirteenth Amendment (1865) handled the first order of business by constitutionalizing the interment of slavery, which had expired on the battlefields of the Civil War. The final piece of the postwar constitutional agenda, the Fifteenth Amendment (1870), provided constitutional assurance (at least in theory) that former slaves would be able to participate in all elections as full members of the political community. It prohibited the nation and the states from curtailing the right of citizens to vote "on account of race, color, or previous condition of servitude." Sandwiched between was the most powerful of the postwar amendments, the Fourteenth Amendment (1868), which attended to the former slaves' transition into the civic life of the United States.

The Fourteenth Amendment began by extending national as well as state citizenship to the former slaves, providing generally, "[a]ll persons born or naturalized in the United States, and subject to the jurisdiction thereof, are citizens of the United States and of the State wherein they reside." The Fourteenth Amendment added some muscle to national citizenship status by prohibiting the states from "abridg[ing] the privileges or immunities of citizens of the United States." Although the question remains controversial, the framers of the Fourteenth Amendment may have intended that the privileges-or-immunities clause require state governments to respect the fundamental rights of their citizens, as delineated in the Bill of Rights. In an opinion well known among the Congress that proposed the Fourteenth Amendment, Supreme Court Justice Bushrod Washington, sitting on a circuit court, had equated the constitutional phrase "Privileges and Immunities of Citizens" (Article IV, section 2, clause 1), with the "fundamental rights" that belong to the "citizens of all free governments" (Corfield v. Coryall, 1823). A number of participants in the congressional debate on the Fourteenth Amendment followed suit, making clear their understanding of the phrase "privileges or immunities of citizens" as a constitutional term of art encompassing all individual rights they generally regarded as fundamental. Moreover, as has been noted, there was a pronounced tendency in antebellum political rhetoric to characterize freedom of speech as, interchangeably, a "right," "privilege," or "immunity" of U.S. citizens. A leading historian of the Reconstruction era, Eric Foner, has thus concluded, "it is abundantly clear that [supporters of the Fourteenth Amendment] wished to give constitutional sanction to states' obligations to respect such key provisions [of the Bill of Rights] as freedom of speech . . . ."[43] Many historians share Foner's view.

The Supreme Court, however, eviscerated the privileges-or-immunities clause of the Fourteenth Amendment at its earliest opportunity (Slaughter-House Cases,

1873). The Court distinguished between the privileges or immunities of *national* citizenship and the privileges and immunities of *state* citizenship, which were at issue in *Corfield*, holding that individuals held such fundamental rights as the freedom of speech in their capacity as citizens of the state in which they lived, and not as U.S. citizens. The protection of fundamental rights, the Court held, "lay within the constitutional and legislative power of the States, and without that of the Federal government." The justices in 1873 simply could not accept that the framers of the Fourteenth Amendment had intended to make it a federal responsibility to protect the fundamental rights of American citizens from actions taken by state governments. They were intent on preserving the antebellum constitutionalism of Barron v. Baltimore to the maximum extent possible.

It would be fifty years before the Court would apply the free speech guarantee of the First Amendment to the actions of state governments (Gitlow v. New York, 1925). (Under the "incorporation doctrine," the Court has held that virtually every provision of the Bill of Rights protects fundamental rights and thus constitutes part of the individual "liberty" that the Fourteenth Amendment prohibits states from depriving without "due process of law.") But the reign of *Slaughter-House* from 1873 until 1925 helped retard the development of free speech jurisprudence by immunizing the actions by state governments abridging freedom of speech from Supreme Court review. Free speech issues arose between the Civil War and World War I, to be sure, but for the most part they ran their course without the participation of the High Court.

The contested terrain of freedom of speech during this period, not surprisingly, centered primarily on two areas of social conflict that at times riveted national attention: the control of obscenity and the organizing activity and rhetoric of radical labor unions.[44] The focus on sexual expression in the years following the Civil War was part of a larger "movement for social purity" that drew on the energy, idealism, and organizing skills of some former abolitionists.[45] The crusade against obscenity and other forms of sexual expression thus was allied with a variety of causes, including labor reform, the women's rights movement, prison reform, the temperance movement, and the attacks on prostitution and gambling. The leader of the movement to control sexual expression was Anthony Comstock, who in league with the New York chapter of the Young Men's Christian Association (YMCA), was largely responsible for enlisting Congress in the cause. The "Comstock Act" of 1873 made it a federal crime to knowingly send obscene materials, as well as information or advertisements concerning contraception or abortion, through the U.S. mail. Within days of his statute's enactment, Comstock became a special agent of the Post Office with authority to enforce the new restrictions. He served in that capacity until his death in 1915.

According to David Rabban, who has written the leading history of free speech in the United States from the Civil War to World War I, "Comstock focused most of his prodigious energy against a wide range of sexually related material that he considered immoral."[46] His targets included literary classics that Comstock believed had been marketed for their sexual content, as well as writings that provided medical information to the general public. He especially went after works that challenged conventional sexual mores, such as those that advocated free love. Comstock's crusade was popular with the public, and he obtained convictions for three of every four individuals he arrested.

The Supreme Court upheld the constitutionality of the Comstock Act in 1877 (Ex Parte Jackson). It says much about the unformed nature of free speech jurisprudence during this dark age that the Court focused much of its brief opinion on the scope of Congress's power "[t]o establish Post Offices and post Roads" (U.S. Constitution, Article I, section 8, clause 7). The justices rebuffed the First Amendment challenge with one sentence at the conclusion of the opinion. The Court wrote, "In excluding various articles from the mail, the object of Congress has not been to interfere with the freedom of the press, or with any other rights of the people; but to refuse its facilities for the distribution of matter deemed injurious to the public morals." As was true in Blackstone's time, the government's assessment that a particular type of expression was harmful justified its suppression.

The following year, a group called the National Liberal League brought the First Amendment question to Congress. The League submitted a petition, with between fifty and seventy thousand signatures, urging Congress to repeal, or at least to trim, the prohibitions of sexual expression in the Comstock Act so that the law no longer would serve as an implement "to abridge the freedom of the press or of conscience."[47] Congress refused, explaining, "The Post Office was not established to carry instruments of vice, or obscene writings, indecent pictures, or lewd books."[48] Whatever freedom of speech might have meant to Congress at the time, it seemed clearly to exclude sexual expression that the legislators regarded as obscene or otherwise improper.

As America entered the twentieth century, national attention shifted from sexual expression to radical unionism. Between 1906 and 1913, the Industrial Workers of the World (IWW), nicknamed the Wobblies, waged a number of "free speech fights" against local officials who had resisted the efforts of union leaders to organize and to advocate radical labor ideology in their communities.[49] It is no wonder that community leaders across America did not welcome the IWW message. While the mainstream labor movement attempted to improve the economic lot of its members by seeking to bargain collectively with their employers, the IWW believed that securing the rights of working people required nothing less than the overthrow of the economic system of the United States. They thus eschewed collective bargaining in favor of such "direct actions" as sabotage, work slowdowns, spontaneous strikes, picketing, and mass demonstrations. This activity ultimately would lead, they hoped, to a general strike that would discredit and bring down capitalism once and for all.

The Wobblies compared themselves to the abolitionists of antebellum America. And indeed, like the abolitionists before them, the IWW encountered widespread public opposition, accompanied at times by acts of vigilante violence. To many of their opponents, the Wobblies abused, rather than exercised, the right of free expression. But again, as had been the case with the abolitionists, while many Americans disagreed wholeheartedly with the IWW message, some nevertheless supported the freedom of radical unionists to attempt to persuade workers to their point of view.

The Wobblies won some of their free speech fights when local authorities gave in to their demands and allowed them to proselytize on public property. They lost, however, in the two fights with the highest profile, those in Paterson, New Jersey, and in San Diego, California. In the courts, the experience was more uniform: the IWW's assertion of the right to express their point of view in public met with a "mechanistic rejection."[50]

The cold shoulder from the Supreme Court that the challengers to the Comstock Act received, as well as the routine judicial rejection of the Wobblies' free speech claims, were emblematic of the courts' general approach to freedom of speech during this period. David Rabban writes:

> Throughout the period from the Civil War to World War I, the overwhelming majority of [judicial] decisions in all jurisdictions rejected free speech claims, often by ignoring their existence. . . . No court was more unsympathetic to freedom of expression than the Supreme Court, which rarely produced even a dissenting opinion in a First Amendment case. Most decisions by lower federal courts and state courts were also restrictive. Radicals fared particularly poorly, but the widespread judicial hostility to free speech claims transcended any individual issue or litigant.[51]

The state of free speech jurisprudence on the eve of the First World War would have looked strikingly familiar to Anglo-American lawyers on the eve of the American Revolution. Blackstone's *Commentaries* on the common law of eighteenth-century England remained the touchstone of the Supreme Court's understanding of free expression. Shortly after the turn of the twentieth century, Justice Oliver Wendell Holmes, Jr., writing for a majority of his colleagues, aligned the freedom of speech protected by the First Amendment with the common law rule which limited that right to a freedom from prior restraints on publication (Patterson v. Colorado, 1907). As had Blackstone, Holmes excluded from constitutional concern "the subsequent punishment of [speech that] may be deemed contrary to the public welfare." Consistent with the old common law of England, the Supreme Court, along with the vast majority of American courts, was comfortable with governmental restrictions on any speech that legislators believed had a "bad tendency," that is, a tendency to produce harmful effects (see Turner v. Williams, 1904; Patterson v. Colorado, 1907).

At the beginning of the twentieth century, the only Supreme Court justice who was prepared to move beyond Blackstone and to demand a more substantial justification for governmental restrictions on freedom of speech was the first Justice John Marshall Harlan (Patterson v. Colorado, 1907, dissenting opinion). "The public welfare," Harlan insisted, "cannot override constitutional privileges." To

Harlan, freedom of speech, together with freedom of press, formed "essential parts of every man's liberty" that the Constitution protected against encroachment by governmental action, state or federal. The justices eventually came around to Harlan's view that the speech clause of the First Amendment could not be reduced to a freedom from prior restraints when they began to construct modern free speech jurisprudence after World War I, but it would not be until the 1930s that the Court would acknowledge any special constitutional protection for freedom of speech.

Although Justice Harlan was not prepared in his brief dissenting opinion in *Patterson* to explicate the nature and extent of the protection that he believed to be required by the First Amendment, he was ahead of his colleagues in seeing that freedom of speech should be assigned a special status in constitutional jurisprudence. The then-dominant judicial adherence to the so-called "bad tendency" test for assessing speech restrictions implied that free speech claims were no different than other, more pedestrian claims to individual liberty, which were overridden whenever the government had a reasonable and legitimate policy reason for doing so. In order for the courts to require special protection for the freedom of speech, and therefore impose special restrictions on the government's authority to control expression, they must believe that speech is special. One of the haunting facts of American constitutional history is that for most of its existence, the Supreme Court of the United States did not act as though it believed that to be the case.

NOTES

* Michael Kent Curtis, *Free Speech, "The People's Darling Privilege": Struggles for Freedom of Expression in American History* (Durham: Duke University Press, 2000): pp. 9, 19.

1. This section draws generally from Fredrick Seaton Siebert, *Freedom of the Press in England, 1476–1776: The Rise and Decline of Government Control* (Urbana: University of Illinois Press, 1952), as well from Leonard W. Levy, *Emergence of a Free Press* (New York: Oxford University Press, 1985): 3–15.
2. Quoted in Siebert, *Freedom of the Press in England*, pp. 28–29.
3. *Id.*, p. 265.
4. Quoted in *id.*, pp. 118–19.
5. Sergeant William Hawkins, "A Treatise of the Pleas of the Crown" (London, 1716), quoted in Levy, *Emergence of a Free Press*, p. 8.
6. Levy, *Emergence of a Free Press*, p. 8.
7. *Blackstone's Commentaries on the Laws of England*, Bk. IV, Ch. XI, Wayne Morrison, ed., (London: Cavendish Publishing Ltd., 2001): 151–52.
8. This section draws generally from Levy, *Emergence of a Free Press*, pp. 16–61.
9. *Id.*, p. 16.
10. Mark P. Denbeaux, "The First Word of the First Amendment," *Northwestern University Law Review* 80 (1986): 1156–1220, p. 1173.

11. Levy, *Emergence of a Free Press*, p. 16.

12. Eric Foner, *The Story of American Freedom* (New York: W.W. Norton & Co., 1998), p. 12.

13. Curtis, *Free Speech*, p. 12.

14. Quoted in Levy, *Emergence of a Free Press*, p. 40.

15. Quoted in *id.*, p. 44.

16. Arthur M. Schlesinger, *Prelude to Independence: The Newspaper War on Britain, 1764–1776* (New York: Alfred A. Knopf, 1971): p.189.

17. This section draws generally from Levy, *Emergence of a Free Press*, pp. 220–74.

18. *Id.*, p. 188.

19. Neil H. Cogan, ed., *The Complete Bill of Rights: The Drafts, Debates, Sources, & Origins* (New York: Oxford University Press, 1997): p. 101.

20. Centinel, No. 2, Oct. 24, 1787, excerpted in Cogan, *Complete Bill of Rights*, p. 103.

21. Cogan, *Complete Bill of Rights*, p. 150.

22. Levy, *Emergence of a Free Press*, p. 268.

23. *Id.*, p. 220.

24. This section draws generally from Curtis, *Free Speech*, pp. 52–116, as well as from Levy, *Emergence of a Free Press*, pp. 279–349.

25. Stanley Elkins and Eric McKitrick, *The Age of Federalism* (New York: Oxford University Press, 1993): p. 581.

26. Act of July 14, 1798, §§ 2–3, ch. 74, 1 Stat. 596.

27. Curtis, *Free Speech*, p. 58.

28. Quoted in Levy, *Emergence of a Free Press*, p. 322.

29. Remarks of Rep. John Allen, quoted in Curtis, *Free Speech*, p. 64.

30. Quoted in Curtis, *Free Speech*, p. 94.

31. This section draws generally from Curtis, *Free Speech*, pp. 117–356.

32. *Id.*, p. 127.

33. Quoted in *id.*, pp. 125–26.

34. *Id.*, p. 125.

35. *Id.*, p. 10.

36. Quoted in *id.*, p. 159.

37. Quoted in *id.*, pp. 177–78.

38. *Id.*, pp. 227, 242.

39. *Id.*, p. 255.

40. Quoted in *id.*, p. 306–07.

41. Mark E. Neely, Jr., *The Fate of Liberty: Abraham Lincoln and Civil Liberties* (New York: Oxford University Press, 1991): p. 223.

42. Quoted in *id.*, p. 68.

43. Eric Foner, *Reconstruction: America's Unfinished Revolution, 1863–1877* (New York: Harper & Roe, Publishers, 1988): p. 258.

44. The remainder of this section draws generally from David M. Rabban, *Free Speech in Its Forgotten Years* (Cambridge: Cambridge University Press, 1997).

45. *Id.*, p. 27.

46. *Id.*, p. 30.
47. Quoted in *id.*, p. 38.
48. Quoted in *id.*, p. 38.
49. *Id.*, p. 77.
50. *Id.*, p. 78.
51. *Id.*, p. 131.

2

What Makes Freedom of Speech Special?

[N]o really adequate or comprehensive theory of the first amendment has been enunciated, much less agreed upon.

Thomas I. Emerson*

Writing for the Supreme Court in 1937, Justice Benjamin N. Cardozo described freedom of speech as a charter member of the pantheon of fundamental rights without which "neither liberty nor justice would exist" (Palko v. Connecticut, 1937). Indeed, free speech occupied a special seat in that august group, Justice Cardozo explained, because "freedom of thought and speech . . . is the matrix, the indispensable condition, of nearly every other form of freedom." Cardozo staked these claims to the privileged position of free speech with the confidence of a booster who could imagine no disagreement among his readers. His one-sentence justification for the special status of freedom of speech among constitutional rights was grounded on his reading of the political and legal history of the United States, which revealed, albeit with "rare aberrations," a "pervasive recognition" among Americans of the necessity of free speech. But that interpretation of American history, as we saw in the preceding chapter, is overly sanguine. Justice Cardozo's reliance on the popular tradition of free speech in America ignored the dishearteningly consistent legal tradition that subordinated freedom of speech to the interest of preserving public order and the comfort of the status quo.

In order to support a special status for freedom of speech in American constitutionalism, it is necessary to turn from history to theory. Is there something in the nature or function of free speech in the United States that justifies affording it special protection under the Constitution? Commentators who have considered that question generally have answered in the affirmative, but their justifications have varied. Amid the theoretical debate, several justifications for the privileged position of free speech remain prevalent. These justifications are that freedom of speech (1) is necessary for self-government, (2) facilitates the societal search for truth, and (3) is an essential element of individual autonomy. Each of these claims is positive in nature, positing that freedom of speech either furthers some desirable end or is itself desirable. A negative case also has been made. The negative justification highlights the special dangers presented by government regulation of expression, rather than any special value served by free speech. In this chapter, I introduce and discuss briefly each of these commonly advanced justifications for the special constitutional protection of freedom of speech provided by the First Amendment.

POSITIVE JUSTIFICATIONS FOR THE FREEDOM OF SPEECH

Those who have defended a special status for freedom of speech more often have emphasized the positive rather than the negative case for that position. The three leading positive justifications differ in their emphases, but they are not mutually exclusive. It therefore is possible to hold that each justification offers a partial support for special constitutional protection of freedom of speech and that each requires reinforcement by the other justifications. The three positive justifications also differ in their scope. The self-government rationale provides the narrowest support for freedom of speech. The search-for-truth justification is broader, and the autonomy argument is broader still. Paradoxically, it may well be that the strength of the three justifications are inversely related to their scope, with the narrowest account grounded on the nature of self-government providing the strongest and most limited support for special free speech protections.

Self-government

The linkage among the ideas of democracy, popular sovereignty, and freedom of speech is as old as those ideas themselves, and they are very old indeed. Freedom of speech was a constituent element of the world's first democracy, that which prevailed in Athens during the Classical Era (508 BCE–323 BCE).[1] Classical Athenians believed that authentic public debate was a prerequisite for the creation and refinement of public policy in a democracy. They nurtured a political culture that encouraged common citizens not only to participate fully in political institutions, but also to speak forthrightly on issues of public concern.

Athenians embraced two concepts of free speech during the classical democracy: *isēgoria*, which meant the "equal freedom of speech," and *parrhēsia*, which classical scholars usually translate simply as "freedom of speech." *Isēgoria* had a more determinate meaning for Classical Athenians than did *parrhēsia*. *Isēgoria* gave each Athenian citizen an equal right to speak in the Assembly, which was the principal governing institution of the democracy. *Isēgoria* ensured that common citizens, sitting in the Assembly, could speak as well as listen, and thus could become active and not just passive participants in the formation of public policy. As the word suggests (the prefix *iso* meant "equal"), *isēgoria* effectuated, even as it symbolized, the equal political status of all citizens, who regardless of wealth or family, were sovereign at Athens. The opportunity *isēgoria* offered for broad, active inclusion of the entire citizenry in the decision making of the Assembly also reinforced the legitimacy of that institution to "speak" as the authoritative voice of the *dēmos*, the "people" of Athens.

Parrhēsia referred to the general freedom of speech that Athenians enjoyed as an aspect of their "liberty" (*eleutheria*). Classical scholar Sara Monoson emphasized the more nuanced meaning of *parrhēsia* as "frank speaking," which, she argued, captures the nature of the democratic practice better than the more conventional, but bland translation, "freedom of speech." Monoson explained, "Speaking with parrhesia meant, broadly, 'saying everything.' More specifically, it meant speaking one's mind, that is, frankly saying what one thinks, and especially uttering a deserved reproach." For Athenians, *parrhēsia* implied critical speech by one who expressed a conviction that was honestly held and deeply felt. According to Monoson, "To speak with parrhesia was to confront, oppose, or find fault with another individual or a popular view in a spirit of concern for illuminating what is right and best."[2]

Athenian *parrhēsia* was not limited to the political institutions of the *polis*. It was an element of "the open life promised by democracy."[3] Still, for Athenian democrats, *parrhēsia* conveyed their ideal conception of Assembly debate. Because *parrhēsia* encouraged a sharp airing of competing points of view, Athenians believed that the practice enabled the *dēmos* to choose wisely from among alternative policy proposals. More subtly, Athenians valued *parrhēsia* because it tested, and thereby affirmed, the *arēte* (virtue, excellence) of citizens by requiring them, for the ultimate good of the community, not only to tolerate, but also to consider, criticism from their fellow citizens. And as with *isēgoria*, *parrhēsia* helped establish the legitimacy of decisions by the Assembly. As Sara Monoson explained, "A vote taken after speeches delivered in a spirit of parrhesia could represent not simply the preferences of the majority, but the considered judgment of the demos."[4]

The ancient understanding of the nature and function *isēgoria* and *parrhēsia* resonates powerfully with the contemporary understanding of the role of free speech in American self-government. As the debate over the Sedition Act of 1798 showed, the earliest American claims for strongly protecting freedom of speech under the First Amendment were grounded on the idea that democracy requires that all citizens be permitted to speak freely on matters of public concern. Americans understand free speech, as did the Athenians more than two thousand years before them, as a form of political participation to which all citizens are entitled simply because they are citizens. The connection between free speech and self-government provides a prominent theme in the Supreme Court's First Amendment jurisprudence as well. As Justice Hugo L. Black, writing for the Court, observed, "Whatever differences may exist about interpretations of the First Amendment, there is practically universal agreement that a major purpose of that Amendment was to protect the free discussion of governmental affairs" (Mills v. Alabama, 1966).

Alexander Meiklejohn is the leading proponent of the linkage between freedom of speech and democracy.[5] Meiklejohn modeled his theory of free speech on "the traditional American town meeting," the American political institution that most closely resembles the ancient Athenian Assembly. It was in the town meeting that Meiklejohn found "self-government in its simplest, most obvious form." His description of a town meeting makes clear the connection he posited between the fundamental principles of democracy and freedom of speech, as well as that freedom's Classical Athenian roots. Meiklejohn wrote:

> In the town meeting the people of a community assemble to discuss and act upon matters of public concern . . . . Every man is free to come. They meet as political equals. Each has a right and duty to think his own thoughts, to express them, and to listen to the arguments of others. The basic principle is that freedom of speech shall be unabridged.

For Meiklejohn, the "basic principle" of free speech succeeded for the very reason it had prevailed in Athens: It was necessary for *effective* self-government. "The final aim of the meeting," he wrote, "is the voting of wise decisions."[6]

In Meiklejohn's theory, freedom of speech is subject to limitation in accordance with rules of order that facilitate debate, deliberation, and decision making in a public assembly. "The First Amendment," he argued, "is not the guardian of unregulated talkativeness." This was because the "ultimate interest" served by freedom of speech is not to be found in the "the words of the speakers, but in the minds of the hearers." Meiklejohn explained. "What is essential is not that everyone shall speak," he wrote, "but that everything worth saying shall be said." From these premises, Meiklejohn derived his understanding of the right of free speech in a self-governing community. He wrote, "[T]he vital point, stated negatively, is that no suggestion of policy shall be denied a hearing because it is on one side of the issue rather than another." For Meiklejohn, as for Athenian democrats, "equality of status in the field of ideas lies deep in the very foundation of the self-governing process." For the government to breach that democratic commitment to equality, Meiklejohn argued, was to mutilate "the thinking process of the community."[7]

The democratic justification for freedom of speech put forward by Meiklejohn, notwithstanding its intuitive appeal for most Americans, is subject to several criticisms. For one thing, the very resonance of Meiklejohn's account of free speech with the experience of Classical Athens raises the question of whether his portrayal of self-government is idealized. A town meeting might embody democracy in its "simplest, most obvious form," but it does not adequately capture the reality of contemporary American politics, particularly on a national scale. One also wonders how helpful Meiklejohn's account is when political discourse occurs, as it frequently does, in a setting that lacks the decorum of a town meeting operating under Robert's Rules of Order.

These shortcomings, of course, might be peculiar to Meiklejohn's reliance on the metaphor of the town meeting. Not every argument from democracy so relies.

But all theories that justify the special protection of speech because of its linkage to the process of self-government are vulnerable, with Meiklejohn's argument, to the criticism that they are incomplete. Meiklejohn's suggestion that free speech exists more for the audience than for the speaker provides one symptom of the incompleteness of his account. More generally, though, anyone who, as Justice Black put it in *Mills*, locates "the free discussion of governmental affairs" at the core of the First Amendment must confront the problem of accounting for speech that is not political in nature. In *Mills*, for example, the Court defined the speech it had in mind as including "discussions of candidates, structures and forms of government, the manner in which government is operated or should be operated, and all such matters relating to political processes." That definition seemingly excludes a considerable amount of expression that many Americans assume is fully protected by the First Amendment, such as art, literature, philosophy, entertainment, and science. Does the self-government justification locate such expression on the periphery of First Amendment concern, and is thus subject to lesser constitutional protection than political speech? Is nonpolitical speech to be cast wholly outside constitutional protection and is thus at the complete mercy of government censorship?

Meiklejohn responded to this final set of objections by broadly defining the "public" speech that he regarded as a central First Amendment concern. As he reconsidered and elaborated his theory in later years, Meiklejohn included all forms of education, philosophy, science, arts, and literature in his conception of public speech, because self-government was possible only if "voters acquire the intelligence, integrity, sensitivity, and generous devotion to the general welfare that, in theory, casting a ballot is assumed to express."[8] But one might legitimately question whether such an inclusive definition of public speech obliterates any meaningful boundary between speech that is related to self-government and speech that lacks such a relationship. Judge Robert H. Bork, who like Meiklejohn grounded the protection of freedom of speech on its relationship to self-government, distinguished sharply between the political expression that he would include within First Amendment protection and the nonpolitical speech he would exclude. To Bork, "Constitutional protection should be accorded only to speech that is explicitly political. There is no basis for judicial intervention to protect any other form of expression, be it scientific [or] literary . . . ."[9] Indeed, Judge Bork was so attached to the relationship between free speech and democracy that he also would deny constitutional protection to explicitly political speech that advocates governmental change by nondemocratic means. Other scholars who have advocated the self-government justification for the First Amendment's protection of free speech have drawn different lines between the political and the nonpolitical, but all were required by the logic of this justification to make some such separation. Many scholars have responded to the boundary problem presented by Meiklejohn's theory by concluding that the promotion of self-government can be but one element of a comprehensive justification for the special status enjoyed by freedom of speech.

The Search for Truth

Another prominent justification for special constitutional recognition of freedom of speech holds that such a right is necessary for a society's collective search for truth. The claim here is that the function of the First Amendment is to create a hospitable environment for open inquiry, rigorous critique, and the free exchange of ideas, all of which enable a society to progress in a never-ending quest for truth. The search-for-truth justification has dominated the literature on freedom of speech, with a lineage that reaches back at least to the publication in 1644 of John Milton's pamphlet, *Areopagitica*. Milton's eloquent statement—"Let [Truth] and Falsehood grapple; who ever knew Truth put to the worse, in a free and open encounter?"—remains a cornerstone of American free speech theory. Milton's influence can be glimpsed in early American history as well. For example, in 1786, the year before the Constitutional Convention met in Philadelphia, the state of Virginia enacted Thomas Jefferson's "Bill for Establishing Religious Freedom," which included the assurance that "truth is great and will prevail if left to herself."

The classic statement justifying freedom of speech as necessary for a society's search for truth, like Milton's pamphlet, is an English product. In *On Liberty*, John Stuart Mill argued, "[T]he peculiar evil of silencing the expression of an opinion is, that it is robbing the human race; posterity as well as the existing generation; those who dissent from the opinion, still more than those who hold it. If the opinion is right, they are deprived of the opportunity of exchanging error for truth: if wrong, they lose, what is almost as great a benefit, the clearer perception and livelier impression of truth, produced by its collision with error." Mill observed that all efforts to silence discussion are tainted by "an assumption of infallibility." Indulging that assumption, he believed, was a human frailty. While individuals acknowledge their own fallibility, they remain blind to the possibility of error in the opinions they held dearest.[10]

At the core of Mill's argument was a paradox: He believed that individuals could be confident in the truth of their opinions only if those opinions remained open to challenge. He wrote, "Complete liberty of contradicting and disproving our opinion, is the very condition which justifies us in assuming its truth for purposes of action; and on no other terms can a being with human faculties have any rational assurance of being right." This was the case for societies as well. The "only stable foundation for a just reliance" on societal opinion rested on the "steady habit of correcting and completing [its] own opinion by collating it with those of others." Indeed, Mill correlated the soundness of societal opinion with the society's facility in correcting its mistakes. "Wrong opinions and practice," he argued, "gradually yield to fact and argument."[11]

The search-for-truth justification for free speech seems especially vulnerable in a postmodern age. Is there any such thing as truth, especially in the realm of ideas? This is not just a postmodern question. Opponents of the Sedition Act of 1798 raised this very question when insisting that truth not be considered a criterion for assessing free speech claims, especially in the realm of political critique. But Mill does not provide such an easy target. Unlike Milton and Jefferson, Mill never claimed that truth invariably triumphed over falsehood, and thus that societal opinions that emerge from freedom of speech necessarily would be true. He considered that notion "a piece of idle speculation," for he noticed, "[m]en are not more zealous for truth than they often are for error." Mill's goal was not that societies obtain objective truth, but rather "truth for purposes of action," that is, that societies have sufficient confidence in their opinions to legitimate their actions. Mill argued, "The beliefs which we have most warrant for, have no safeguard to rest on, but a standing invitation to the whole world to prove them unfounded. If the challenge is not accepted, or is accepted and the attempt fails, we are far enough from certainty still; but we have done the best that the existing state of human reason admits of." Mill's "truth" resembles a scientific proposition, which provides a legitimate basis for experimentation until it is successfully challenged and replaced by another proposition that better fits the data. That process of challenge and replacement, Mill hinted, was perpetual.[12]

For Mill, societies do not search for truth because they will attain it in any complete or permanent sense. Even if a society believes that it has attained truth (indeed, even if a society *has* attained truth), according to Mill, it cannot know with certainty that it has done so. Mill enjoins societies to act on the basis of a search for truth as a second-best alternative to acting on the basis of truth itself: It is the best they can do. The opinions that emerge from that search are always provisional, and they remain subject to refinement or rejection as a result of constant critique and re-examination. Freedom of speech, in this view, is necessary because it is indispensable to critique, and thus to the improvement of societal opinions over time. Free speech cannot bring societies to an understanding of ultimate truth, for such is not the human condition. But it can expose at least some errors in their collective thinking, and thereby help societies progress.

Justice Oliver Wendell Holmes, Jr., embraced Mill's theory of free speech in his breakthrough argument for affording strong First Amendment protection to dissident speakers. Holmes's statement is one of the most eloquent, and enduring, justifications for freedom of speech. He wrote:

> Persecution for the expression of opinions seems to me perfectly logical. If you have no doubt of your premises or your power and want a certain result with all your heart you naturally express your wishes in law and sweep away all opposition. . . . But when men have realized that time has upset many fighting faiths, they may come to believe even more than they believe the very foundations of their own conduct that the ultimate good desired is better reached by free trade in ideas — that the best test of truth is the power of the thought to get itself accepted in the competition of the market, and that truth is the only ground upon which their wishes safely can be carried out. (Abrams v. United States, 1919, dissenting opinion).

Holmes, following Mill, believed that truth provides legitimacy for societal action. But also like Mill, he did not claim that a "free trade in ideas" inexorably leads a community to truth in any objective sense. When Holmes argued, "the best test of truth is the power of the thought to get itself accepted in the competition of the market," he did not endorse the reductionist position that societal consensus on a proposition is a marker of truth. Such orthodoxies, he warned, often are displaced over time. Holmes's "best test of truth" is Mills's second-best solution to the imperfection of human knowledge and reason. Collective acceptance or rejection of any idea after free debate is the best that any society can do in approximating truth at any given time.

Properly understood, the search-for-truth justification for free speech proffered by Mill and Holmes does not suffer from a naïve belief that unfettered discussion leads a society to the objectively correct social organization or policy. Quite to the contrary, their brief for free speech is premised on a thorough skepticism of all societal orthodoxies of the moment. Indeed, Holmes's skepticism extended even to the case he had made for free speech itself. Immediately following the above-quoted passage, Holmes added, "[t]hat at any rate is the theory of our Constitution. It is an experiment, as all life is an experiment. Every year if not every day we have to wager our salvation upon some prophecy based upon imperfect knowledge."

If Meiklejohn's democratic justification for free speech resonates with Classical Athenian democracy, Mills's and Holmes's grounding of that freedom in a search for truth evokes the most famous critic of the ancient democracy, Socrates. The Socrates we know is based largely on Plato's portrayal of him as "the ideal philosopher,"[13] a seeker of truth who questioned the orthodoxies of his time by engaging the reputed wise men of Athens in adversarial dialogue. When he was done, Socrates invariably had exposed the pretensions of those who cling unskeptically to conventional wisdom. He also had gained some measure of wisdom by exposing the errors and inconsistencies of the ideas and beliefs those men had defended. But Platos's Socratic dialogues typically end inconclusively: Having unraveled some orthodoxy, Socrates showed little interest in replacing it with another. He continued his search for true wisdom by searching out other wise men to deflate. That lifelong quest, in fact, is the defining element of Socratic wisdom—the acceptance, as Socrates put it, that one does not "know[] anything worthwhile,"[14] coupled with the commitment to pursue a wisdom that is unattainable (the search for truth) as the essence of a life well lived. Because Athens was a democracy, Socrates's critical stance inevitably put him on a collision course with the people of Athens. When, in the crucible of societal stress, the Athenians judged Socrates to be a deeply subversive and destabilizing threat to their community, they had him executed. His crime, at bottom, was nothing more than practicing freedom of speech.

Although the Socratic echo adds to the allure of the search for truth as a justification for freedom of speech by dramatically illustrating the nobility of that quest, the linkage also reveals the most telling weakness of this rationale. Although Socrates had set out to lead his fellow Athenians to truth, they responded by killing him. By placing faith in the "process of rational thinking,"[15] the search-for-truth justification is subject to the charge that it presents a false, or at least a simplistic, account of the development of public opinion in a society. Mill grounded his theory on the assumption that societies are characterized by "rational opinions and rational conduct."[16] Holmes's economic metaphor, which over time evolved into the famous "marketplace of ideas," built on Mill's assumption by depicting ideas as discrete entities that offer themselves up for societal acceptance or rejection, presumably on the basis of rational consumer choice. Holmes suggested that society is a collective *homo economicus*, which rationally and dispassionately selects the best product (idea) from a full selection of alternatives based on complete and unbiased information about them. But this is hardly an accurate portrayal of how opinions become dominant in a society. It is not necessarily the case that an idea prevails because it is better or truer than the alternatives. Ideas are not products that compete on a supermarket shelf. They often are agenda items of competing social and political groups, which differ substantially in their makeup, rhetorical ability, and financial resources. Societal acceptance might be traced less to the correctness of an idea than to the power and skill of the group advocating it. At times an idea may prevail over the competition because it best serves the interests of a dominant group or most clearly resonates with the pre-existing beliefs of a society. And as all marketers know, whether they specialize in products or ideas, acceptance in the marketplace often is determined more by the frequency and form of message than by its logical persuasiveness, by the allure of the packaging more than by the quality of the contents.

Ironically, at least one reason for the success of the search-for-truth justification in the literature of freedom of speech has been its packaging, that is, the eloquence and persuasiveness of the pens of Mill and Holmes. But a persistent unease over the plausibility of Mills's and Holmes's claims about the rationality of societal belief formation has led many contemporary commentators to discount this justification.

Individual Autonomy

The third commonly cited justification for freedom of speech supports this right as central to the general American commitments to individual liberty, personal autonomy, and self-realization. As is the case with the first two justifications, the autonomy rationale has its roots in Classical Athens, particularly in the writings of Aristotle. In his *Politics*, Aristotle argued that the end (*telos*) of the state was to enable each of its citizens to live the good life (*eudaimonia*, commonly, but inadequately, translated as "happiness"). By "good life," Aristotle meant the ultimate realization by an individual of his or her essential self as a distinctively rational human being. In order to attain *eudaimonia*, Aristotle believed that individuals must develop their intellects and use their powers of reason wisely. It thus followed for him that the state was obligated to create an environment that allowed individual citizens to develop their rational capacities in a way that enabled them to realize their full potential as human beings.

Justice Louis D. Brandeis, in his classic justification of free speech, connected Aristotle to the American experience with his observation, "Those who won our independence believed that the final end of the state was to make men free to develop their faculties" (Whitney v. California, 1927, concurring opinion). The founding documents of the United States support Brandeis's claim that Americans, from the beginning, endorsed Aristotle's prescription for the good state. In the Declaration of Independence, for instance, the United States asserted as a "self-evident" truth that individuals create governments as a means of securing such "unalienable Rights" as "Life, Liberty and the pursuit of Happiness." And today, those who ground the First Amendment's protection of freedom of speech on individual autonomy tend to argue, with Justice Cardozo (Palko v. Connecticut, 1937), that freedom of speech is an indispensable element of "the Blessings of Liberty" that the preamble to the Constitution obligates the government of the United States to "secure" for its citizens.

Thomas Emerson, a leading First Amendment scholar, advanced an influential argument that the autonomy rationale should be considered the leading justification for freedom of speech. Emerson believed that freedom of speech should be protected as an inherent human right. "The right to freedom of expression," he claimed, "is justified first of all as the right of an individual purely in his capacity as an individual." Emerson's premises were Aristotle's. He wrote, "[T]he proper end of man is the realization of his character and potentialities as a human being," and "the purpose of society, and of its more formal aspect the state, is to promote the welfare of the individual." Following Aristotle, Emerson argued, "Man is distinguished from other animals principally by the qualities of his mind. . . . It is through development of these powers that man finds his meaning and his place in the world."[17]

That is where freedom of speech comes in. Emerson began, "The achievement of self-realization commences with development of the mind." Although individuals, he conceded, are influenced in their thinking by many factors, in the end, he claimed, their minds are their own, and "its functioning is necessarily an individual affair." For Emerson, it was fundamental that each individual member of society possesses "the right to form his own beliefs and opinions," as well as the right to express them. He explained, "[E]xpression is an integral part of the development of ideas, of mental elaboration and of the affirmation of self. The power to realize his potentiality as a human being begins at this point and must extend at least this far if the whole nature of man is not to be thwarted." From this perspective, Emerson argued, the "suppression of belief, opinion and expression is an affront to the dignity of man, a negation of man's essential nature."[18] The state, paradoxically, fulfills its highest purpose by consciously adopting a course of *in*action, thereby creating zones of personal autonomy that individuals need in order to flourish.

The autonomy rationale differs in a crucial respect from the first two justifications of free speech. While the democracy and search-for-truth rationales generally situate freedom of speech as a means towards desirable ends, most autonomy justifications embrace that right as an end in itself. Thus, unlike Meiklejohn, one who understands freedom of speech as an aspect of personal autonomy sees that right as serving the speaker more than the audience. Here again is Emerson: "[I]t is not a general measure of the individual's right to freedom of expression that any particular exercise of the right may be thought to promote or retard other goals of the society," such as serving self-government or facilitating the search for truth. Rather, Emerson explained, "The [autonomy] theory asserts that freedom of expression, while not the sole or sufficient end of society, is a good in itself, or at least an essential element of a good society." And because free speech is a constituent element of the good that society exists to promote, it is as self-defeating as it is wrong for governments to pursue their other goals or to solve their problems "by suppressing the beliefs or opinions of individual members." By definition, doing so makes "a good society" impossible.[19]

Because it conceives of freedom of speech *per se* as an inherent human right, the autonomy rationale is the broadest of the three most common justifications for that freedom. There is no limit implied here that speech must be political or otherwise public in nature, as with the self-government rationale, or that speech must serve the marketplace of ideas, as with the search-for-truth rationale. All the autonomy justification asks is that expression be *self*-expression. This breadth of coverage is the *yin* and the *yang* of the autonomy rationale; it is appealing to some scholars, but disconcerting to others. Is it indeed fair to ask whether it is sensible, or sustainable, to hold that the First Amendment indiscriminately protects all expression as an essential societal good?

The principal boundary limit on First Amendment protection according to the autonomy justification is not between protected and unprotected speech, but rather, as Emerson argued, between speech and action.[20] While that limiting principle might seem firm, on inspection it is subject to serious question. If freedom of speech is essential to individual liberty and self-realization, why is not freedom of action? As Frederick Schauer has observed, "virtually any activity may be a form of self-expression."[21] The central problem with the autonomy rationale, according to this criticism, is its failure to demonstrate why speech should be singled out for special constitutional solicitude from among all of the other activities in which individuals engage in order to develop and to express themselves.

* * *

While it is probably fair to conclude that the search-for-truth rationale has enjoyed a prominence of place over the other two positive justifications for freedom of speech, that rationale has not fully carried the day over its two competitors. If there is any consensus among scholars on free speech theory, it is that no single rationale is sufficient to explain or to justify the special status of free speech in American constitutionalism. Most scholars appreciate the appeal, as well as the limitations, of each of the three major justifications. And by and large, they are content with the claim that the three justifications in combination present sufficient support for special constitutional protection of freedom of speech.

Not all scholars are content to rest there, however. Some have added complementary justifications for freedom of speech. Two frequently mentioned alternatives are, first, that free speech serves a "checking value" by helping to expose the abuse of power by public officials,[22] and second, that it operates as a "safety valve" that enables society to maintain a "balance between stability and change" by encouraging dissenters to express their grievances openly rather than take them underground.[23] Two other supplemental justifications are more idiosyncratic to their authors, but nevertheless occupy a respected place in the free speech literature. These are, first, that freedom of speech nurtures the tolerance that a multicultural society requires for social harmony,[24] and second, that it plays the crucial, cultural role of nurturing healthy dissent against the status quo.[25] Each of these supplemental accounts of free speech has some explanatory force, but each remains subsidiary to the three principle justifications on which we have focused.

There remains one additional justification for specially protecting freedom of speech, and it requires special emphasis. This rationale, so-called negative theory, has assumed a particular prominence in the free speech literature in recent years, perhaps as a result of some lingering unease over the persuasiveness of the three positive justifications.

NEGATIVE JUSTIFICATIONS FOR THE FREEDOM OF SPEECH

All of the theories of justification for the First Amendment's strong protection of freedom of speech that we have canvassed so far have been "positive" in nature. They claim that free speech is of special value because it enables society to attain something that is especially valuable, namely, self-government, the discovery of truth, or self-realization. "Negative" free speech theories reverse that claim. They do not support any special value served by freedom of speech, but rather they justify the First Amendment's special protection of freedom of speech by positing that government regulation of expression is especially dysfunctional and dangerous.[26]

While positive justifications for free speech are drawn principally from Western political theory, the negative case for special hostility to government restrictions of expression derives from the painful lessons of Anglo-American political history. This history teaches that government officials are notoriously bad at regulating speech. Looking back, it is rare to conclude that speech regulations served the public interest. Perhaps the most notorious examples of this tendency toward regulatory failure in early Anglo-American history are the English licensing system and the American Sedition Act of 1798, each of which was reviewed in the preceding chapter. Both of those regulatory efforts were repressive, and both failed to achieve their objectives. Licensing was utterly ineffectual in controlling publications, and the Sedition Act helped to doom, rather than to preserve, the Federalist Party.

History also suggests that government officials, if left to their own devices, tend to overregulate speech. It is especially easy for government officials to mistake their self-interest for the public interest when regulating expression. Government officials have an inherent conflict of interest whenever they regulate commentary on their conduct in office or on the policies they favor or fear. Such conflicts, James Madison warned, "certainly bias [one's] judgment, and, not improbably, corrupt one's integrity."[27] The history of seditious libel in England and America, sketched in the previous chapter, amply illustrates the grounds for Madison's concern.

Not all government censorship proceeds from such a conflict of interest, however. Justice Brandeis long ago noticed that speech which fundamentally challenges the mainstream beliefs and prejudices of a community often stirs up "irrational fears" among "a vast majority" of the citizen body (Whitney v. California, 1927, concurring opinion). It should come as no surprise in a representative government that public officials often respond to such fears by attempting to silence the offending voices. Indeed, Madison regarded the susceptibility of representatives to sway with the fleeting passions of their constituents to be among the most intractable problems of representative government. As the experience of the Sedition Act of 1798 showed, when governmental censorship enjoys majority support, juries are unreliable defenders of the free speech rights of dissidents. Usually, only with hindsight, after the perceived danger has passed, have people been able to see that their fears had been overdrawn. Justice Brandeis captured this phenomenon with the haunting remembrance of the Salem Witch Trials, an event in American colonial history that we have difficulty understanding today. Brandeis wrote, "Men feared witches and burnt women" (Whitney v. California, 1927, concurring opinion).

Even when officials are not motivated by a desire to suppress speakers or their messages, they tend to overregulate speech. Government officials tend to be overly concerned about expressive activities that threaten to disrupt public services or the daily routine, especially if the speech is controversial or of interest to only a small segment of the community. From the perspective of a government regulator, protecting freedom of speech can appear abstract and unappealing when compared to the seemingly more concrete and pressing demands of maintaining public convenience and order. When one adds the inherent difficulty of regulating expression—deciding what can and cannot be said or selecting the circumstances in which expression is or is not appropriate—the recipe for regulatory failure is complete.

Positive and negative justifications of freedom of speech are not mutually exclusive. Indeed, it might well be that any comprehensive, theoretical account of freedom of speech in the United States must include positive and negative elements. But as Frederick Schauer, the scholar who is most closely associated with a negative theory of freedom of speech, observed, on a deeper, perhaps psychological level, the two kinds of justifications stand as opposites. While positive theories are optimistic, declaring a set of "ideal aspirations" that capture "all that we are and all that we wish to be," negative theory is infused with pessimism, reflecting our realization of the limits of our government and of ourselves. Negative theory, Schauer wrote, accepts that "neither a population nor its authoritative decision makers can even approach their society's most ideal aspirations."[28]

NOTES

* Thomas I. Emerson, "Toward a General Theory of the First Amendment," *Yale Law Journal* 72 (1963): 877–956, p. 877.

1. The discussion of freedom of speech in the Classical Athenian democracy draws generally from S. Sara Monoson, *Plato's Democratic Entanglements: Athenian Politics and the Practice of Philosophy* (Princeton: Princeton University Press, 2000): pp. 50–63.
2. *Id.*, 52–53.
3. *Id.*, 55.
4. *Id.*, 62.
5. See Alexander Meiklejohn, "Free Speech and its Relation to Self-government" (1948), as revised and reprinted in *Political Freedom: The Constitutional Powers of the People* (New York: Harper & Brothers, 1960): pp. 3–89.
6. *Id.*, pp. 24–27.
7. *Id.*, pp. 26–27.
8. Alexander Meiklejohn, "The First Amendment is an Absolute," *The Supreme Court Review* (1961): 245–66, pp. 255–57.
9. Robert H. Bork, "Neutral Principles and Some First Amendment Problems," *Indiana Law Journal* 47 (1971): 1–35, p. 20.
10. John Stuart Mill, "On Liberty" (1859), in *On Liberty and Other Writings* (Cambridge: Cambridge University Press, 1989): 5–115, pp. 20–21.
11. *Id.*, pp. 23–24.
12. *Id.*, pp. 24, 31.
13. C.C.W. Taylor, *Socrates* (Oxford: Oxford University Press, 1998): p. 1.
14. Plato, "Apology," 21d, in *Plato: Complete Works*, G.M.A. Grube, trans., (Indianapolis: Hackett Publishing Co., John M. Cooper, ed., 1997).
15. Frederick Schauer, *Free Speech: A Philosophical Enquiry* (Cambridge: Cambridge University Press, 1982): p. 30.
16. Mill, *On Liberty*, p. 23.
17. Thomas I. Emerson, "Toward a General Theory of the First Amendment," *Yale Law Journal* 72 (1963): 877–956, pp. 879–80.
18. *Id.*, p. 879.
19. *Id.*, p. 880.
20. *Id.*, pp. 880–81.
21. Schauer, *Free Speech*, p. 52.
22. See Vincent Blasi, "The Checking Value in First Amendment Theory," *American Bar Foundation Research Journal* (1977): 523–649.
23. Emerson, *General Theory*, pp. 884–86.
24. See Lee Bollinger, *The Tolerant Society: Freedom of Speech and Extremist Speech in America* (New York: Oxford University Press, 1986).
25. See Steven H. Shiffrin, *The First Amendment, Democracy, and Romance* (Cambridge: Harvard University Press, 1990).

26. The discussion in this section draws generally from my article: Keith Werhan, "The Liberalization of Freedom of Speech on a Conservative Court," *Iowa Law Review* 80 (1994): 51–100, pp. 86–94.

27. *The Federalist No. 10*, p. 44 (Indianapolis: Liberty Fund, Inc., 2001).

28. Frederick Schauer, "The Second-Best First Amendment," *William and Mary Law Review* 31 (1989): 1–23, pp. 1–2.

3

The Problem of Subversive Advocacy and the Central Meaning of Freedom of Speech

If there be any among us who would wish to dissolve this Union or to change its republican form, let them stand undisturbed as monuments of the safety with which error of opinion may be tolerated where reason is left free to combat it.

Thomas Jefferson*

It is doubly appropriate to begin this consideration of free speech jurisprudence with the problem of subversive advocacy, that is, speech which advocates that its listeners violate the law. It is appropriate, first, because modern free speech doctrine began where this chapter begins, with the Supreme Court's review of federal prosecutions of dissidents for various forms of subversive advocacy during the national unrest that accompanied America's entry into the First World War. The interplay of opinions among the justices in the World War I cases began a fifty-year process of doctrinal evolution that provides the central narrative of free speech jurisprudence in the United States. These cases also produced the stirring defenses of freedom of speech written by Justices Holmes and Brandeis, which figured prominently in the previous chapter and which have become essential texts of the free speech tradition. Moreover, the Court developed many of the basic principles that shape contemporary free speech jurisprudence in these cases, and perhaps for that reason, the doctrine of subversive advocacy has become a benchmark against which other aspects of free speech doctrine are often measured.

Beginning this discussion with subversive advocacy is appropriate for a second reason as well. The problem of subversive advocacy raises the most fundamental of all questions concerning freedom of speech: Under what circumstances, if any, may governments restrict speech because the expression of particular ideas or information threatens some harm to society? Every controversy we canvassed when reviewing the Anglo-American history of free speech in Chapter 1—from the English licensing system that began in the sixteenth century to the free speech fights of urban America at the beginning of the twentieth century—turned on this very question. Subversive advocacy in its strongest forms, moreover, presents an excruciating democratic dilemma: Can individuals employ freedom of speech, the quintessential democratic practice, to urge the overthrow of the contemporary world's oldest democracy by force and violence, the very antithesis of democratic change? Even in its least troubling manifestations, subversive advocacy still involves speakers who exhort their listeners to oppose or violate the laws laid down by the people's representatives. In a representative democracy such as the United States, subversive advocacy thus pits political dissenters against the most basic legal and constitutional commitments of the collective citizenry, such as majority rule and the rule of law. Because subversive advocacy produces fundamental conflicts for any democracy, the degree to which democratic societies tolerate such speech is a telling barometer of the depth of their commitment to freedom of speech.

THE WORLD WAR I CASES AND THE PROBLEM OF SUBVERSIVE SPEECH

The "Great War" was a destabilizing and ultimately transformative event in world history. In the United States, the war years ushered in a sustained period of national anxiety. America entered the conflict in 1917 and for the first time experienced war on a global scale. The following year, the great influenza pandemic, which claimed forty million lives around the world, hit the United States. Through it all, the interrelated and interacting forces of industrialization, urbanization, and immigration were rapidly changing American society, reinforcing a general sense of unease in the country. And last, but certainly not least, a determined group of dissidents fiercely resisted the war effort on the home front.

Socialists and anarchists constituted a significant component of the antiwar movement. They indicted the American war effort as little more than a capitalist plot to send members of the working class to violent deaths for the enrichment of the wealthy few. This radical opposition challenged the democratic legitimacy of the congressional declaration of war, insisting on a national referendum. Their sharpest focus, however, was on the wartime draft, which antiwar rhetoric depicted as nothing less than a reintroduction of slavery in the United States. Many radical opponents of the war did not limit themselves to criticizing American war policy. A persistent theme of their agitation was a general call to action. They exhorted workers to shun enlistment into the armed forces, to resist the draft if called, and otherwise to refuse to lend a hand to the war effort.

The setting for the Court's World War I cases thus hardly could have been more volatile. Adding to the sense of drama, the justices approached these cases without the benefit of a mature, free speech jurisprudence that adequately balanced the competing claims of free expression and societal self-defense. As we saw in Chapter 1, constitutional jurisprudence at the turn of the twentieth century afforded no special protection to the First Amendment's guarantee of freedom of speech. Conventional constitutional jurisprudence conceptualized free speech as an undifferentiated part of the general constitutional entitlement to individual liberty, which typically gave way to any governmental restriction that reasonably served a legitimate public interest. Federal courts had adapted that reasonableness requirement in the free speech area by developing the so-called "bad tendency" test, which allowed the government to restrict any speech that had a tendency to cause harm.

The Supreme Court's development of subversive advocacy doctrine, and with it modern free speech jurisprudence, began soon after the Armistice, in March of 1919. Justice Oliver Wendell Holmes, Jr., wrote for a unanimous Court in upholding convictions in three federal prosecutions brought under the Espionage Act of 1917, which Congress had passed shortly after the United States entered the war. As its title suggested, the primary target of the Espionage Act was conventional espionage activities. But the statute also made it a crime for anyone, at least during wartime, (1) to "willfully cause or attempt to cause insubordination, disloyalty, mutiny, or refusal of duty, in the military or naval forces of the Unites States," or (2) to "willfully obstruct the recruiting or enlistment services of the United States, to the injury of the services or of the United States." The maximum prison sentence for violating the Act was twenty years, with a maximum fine of $10,000.[1] Federal prosecutors seized on the quoted provisions of the statute as a method of stifling antiwar dissent. Although the Espionage Act was in effect only for the final two years of the war, the federal government brought over 2,000 prosecutions under its provisions. The prosecutors obtained convictions in nearly all of them.

The defendants in each of the three cases of March 1919 had been convicted of violating the Act's prohibitions against actions that caused, or were attempts to cause, insubordination in the armed forces or obstruction of military recruitment. The defendants' actions in each case consisted of their strongly expressed criticism of the American war effort. Each spoke in his own way, and in a distinct medium. Schenck, the defendant in the first case, was a socialist party leader in Philadelphia. He received a prison term of six months for his role in printing and circulating to draftees about fifteen thousand copies of a leaflet that attacked the legitimacy of the wartime draft—in "impassioned language," according to Justice Holmes. The theme of Schenck's leaflet was that the war, and especially the draft, was illegitimate, and that draftees owed it to themselves and to their fellow citizens to refuse the call to military service. (Schenck v. United States, 1919).

Justice Holmes's opinion for the Court in *Schenck* reflected both continuity and change regarding both the pre-modern judicial understanding of freedom of speech and the many lower court decisions that upheld Espionage Act convictions of antiwar dissidents. The lower courts had generally followed the "bad tendency" test. And the Supreme Court, in *Schenck* as well as in all of its free speech decisions of March 1919, accepted the position that the First Amendment did not protect speech that had a "tendency" to cause action that Congress had legitimately outlawed (here, causing insubordination in the military or obstruction to military recruitment). This reasoning, as we have seen, has a common law lineage that traces back to Blackstone and beyond. It also has impressive American roots. Recall that Abraham Lincoln had argued during the Civil War that, if Congress could punish a bad actor, it likewise could punish a speaker who had persuaded the actor to violate the law. This reasoning might be shown in the following causal chain:

speech → persuasion → belief → illegal action → societal harm

The Court used this causal chain in each of the World War I cases to justify its refusal to protect antiwar speech.

Although the Court in *Schenck* followed the logic of "bad tendency" in upholding the conviction, Justice Holmes's opinion cloaked that rationale in language that seemed to promise a more speech-protective orientation. "The question in every case," Holmes wrote, "is whether the words used are used in such circumstances and are of such a nature as to create a clear and present danger that they will bring about the substantive evils that Congress has a right to prevent." The *Schenck* requirement that speech pose "a clear and present danger" seemed to ratchet up considerably both the "proximity and degree" of actual harm that the Court would require to legitimate prosecutions against individuals because of the harmful tendency of their speech. But the Court in *Schenck* provided no doctrinal content for the ringing rhetoric of "clear and present danger." Holmes, as if by habit, explained the Court's constitutional comfort with Schenck's conviction by falling back on the "tendency and intent" that the justices discerned in his circulation of an antidraft circular to draftees, namely, that the draftees resist their draft call. One possible reading of *Schenck*, then, is that Holmes's clear and present danger test was more a rhetorical flourish than the prescription of a new First Amendment standard.

Justice Holmes's opinion for the Court the following week in the second of the World War I cases, however, suggests that the clear and present danger formulation may have been more than simply a constitutional cover for the bad tendency routine (Frohwerk v. United States, 1919). Frohwerk faced a ten-year sentence, as well as a fine, for a series of twelve articles that he wrote over a five-month period for *Staats Zeitung* ("The State's Newspaper"), a German language periodical with a very small circulation that was published in Missouri. Frohwerk's articles, in Holmes's language, praised "the unconquerable spirit and undiminished strength of the German people," and warned that the United States had made a mistake that its people would come to regret by entering the war against them. Frohwerk disingenuously bemoaned the unfortunate "sufferings" of American draftees, suggesting that they could hardly be blamed if they escaped service and thereby heeded "the first impulse of nature: self-preservation."

Holmes used his opinion for the Court in *Frohwerk* to elaborate on *Schenck*. In *Schenck*, the Court had evaluated the "nature" of and "circumstances" surrounding the speech in order to determine whether it presented a clear and present danger of generating unlawful action. In *Frohwerk*, Holmes characterized the nature of the speech in both cases as "words of persuasion." But the more revealing comparison was in the set of circumstances that the two cases shared. The speech by Schenck and Frohwerk, Justice Holmes explained in *Frohwerk*, had been targeted at an audience that was especially susceptible to being persuaded to action. Schenck, Holmes emphasized a week later in *Frohwerk*, had made "a special effort to reach men who were subject to the draft." In *Frohwerk*, the circulation of *Staats Zeitung*, although small, was largely limited to those of German descent, and thus the antiwar articles, Holmes wrote, entered "quarters where a little breath would be enough to kindle a flame."

Justice Holmes's refinement in *Frohwerk* of the nature and circumstances of speech that ran afoul of the clear and present danger test, however, seemed to evaporate in the third of the March 1919 decisions (Debs v. United States, 1919). *Debs*, which was announced on the same day as *Frohwerk*, was the most enigmatic of this first wave of World War I cases. Eugene Debs, like Schenck, was a Socialist leader, but unlike Schenck, he was *the* leader, and frequent presidential candidate, of the national Socialist Party. Debs was convicted for a speech he gave to the Ohio state convention of the Socialist Party, not for circulating antiwar leaflets among draftees. According to Holmes, the primary theme of Debs's speech centered not on the war, but rather on the general tenets and promise of socialism. When he did address the war, Debs, unlike Schenck and Frohwerk, did not address "words of persuasion" to his audience in order to motivate them to illegal acts of war resistance. Debs's speech became actionable, Holmes explained, when Debs "expressed sympathy and admiration" for those who had been convicted for "obstructing the recruiting services." Debs, like Frohwerk, was sentenced to ten years in prison.

While in many ways *Debs* was the most far-reaching of the March Three, Holmes's opinion for the Court in *Debs* was the most peremptory of that group. He dismissed Debs's First Amendment challenge to his conviction as having been "disposed of in *Schenck*." Holmes was content to observe that "one purpose of [Debs's] speech" had been "to oppose" the war, and that "the opposition was so expressed that its natural and intended effect would be to obstruct recruiting." Holmes did not explain why this was so. Debs might be said to have targeted an especially persuadable audience by addressing fellow party members who shared his opposition to the war and to the draft, and who thus were likely to engage in acts of resistance. But Holmes did not advance such a rationale. Intent rather than tendency may have been the key. Debs had not helped himself (at least legally) when, at trial, he told the jury, "I have been accused of obstructing the war. I admit it. Gentlemen, I abhor war. I would oppose the war if I stood alone." Holmes seized on that "admission" in affirming Debs' conviction.

The intention of each of the speakers in the March 1919 cases had been to obstruct the war, and this may have been the common ingredient that explains the Court's rejection of their free speech claims. Or perhaps, the three decisions are best explained by the Court's allegiance to the logic of "bad tendency." In this view, strongly expressed opposition to the war was not constitutionally protected because it was inherently threatening to the war effort. In the end, the best reading of *Schenck*, *Frohwerk*, and *Debs* might simply be that the justices, led by Holmes, recognized that subversive advocacy raised a distinct and troubling First Amendment problem, but they failed to grasp the problem fully. The March Three perhaps are best read as a first, faltering step down a long road.

The justices' journey reached a fork in that road the following fall in Abrams v. United States (1919). *Abrams* involved a federal prosecution under the 1918 Amendments to the Espionage Act, which Congress had enacted precisely in order to target those who spoke out against the American war effort. Abrams and several co-defendants were convicted for printing leaflets that advocated a general strike and then distributing them in the garment district of New York City. Unlike the defendants in the March Three, the intent of the *Abrams* defendants had not been to undermine the war effort against Germany, but rather to protest the abbreviated attempt by the United States in 1918 to overturn the Bolshevik Revolution. Thus, one of the leaflets directly addressed "[w]orkers in the ammunition factories," informing them that they were "producing bullets, bayonets, cannon, to murder not only the Germans, but also [their] dearest, best, who are in Russia and are fighting for freedom." The leaflet also discouraged workers and "Russian emigrants" from purchasing war bonds, because the United States would use that revenue to "make bullets not only for the Germans, but also for the Workers Soviets of Russia." Although the general strike they advocated, if it materialized, would have derailed the war effort, their objective was to protect the Russian Revolution, not to stop the war. One of the *Abrams* leaflets included the following postscript: "It is absurd to call us pro-German. We hate and despise German militarism more than do your hypocritical tyrants."[2]

Abrams is distinguishable from *Schenck*, *Frohwerk*, and *Debs* not only because the defendants had lacked the intent to persuade their audience to resist American participation in the war against Germany, but also because they had not targeted their leaflets at an especially persuadable audience. Although their leaflets directly addressed "[w]orkers in ammunition factories" and "Russian emigrants," they had indiscriminately distributed their leaflets in the garment district. Nor was there any suggestion that either group was especially susceptible to the *Abrams* defendants' call to action, and any such susceptibility seems especially far-fetched on the part of workers in munitions plants. These distinctions between *Abrams* and the March Three did not register with a majority of the justices, but they did with Holmes. The majority noted that the leaflets had "circulated in the greatest port of our land, from which great numbers of soldiers were at the time taking ship daily, and in which great quantities of war supplies of every kind were at the time being manufactured and transported overseas," but even after that insinuation, they did not find any hint of danger as a result of the circulation. For the majority, the crucial point was that "the defendants, in terms, plainly used and advocated a resort to a general strike of workers in ammunition factories for the purpose of curtailing the production of ordinance and munitions necessary and essential to the prosecution of the war." It was the content of the leaflets that excluded the *Abrams* defendants from First Amendment protection. Although there was no realistic threat of the *Abrams* leaflets resulting in a general strike, the majority, true to the spirit of the decisions of March 1919, remained concerned that such revolutionary rhetoric during wartime was inherently dangerous.

While the majority remained entranced by the logic of "bad tendency," Holmes had broken free. Although it is conventional to date the origins of modern free speech doctrine to Holmes's introduction of the clear and present danger test in *Schenck*, the soul of free speech jurisprudence did not appear until Holmes's dissenting opinion in *Abrams*. It is in his *Abrams* dissent that Holmes found his First Amendment voice. He succinctly laid out his case for the special protection of free speech, grounded on the search for truth in the marketplace of ideas, which we reviewed in the preceding chapter. Viewed through that lens, Holmes now saw what had been invisible to him in March: the first three elements of the bad tendency causal chain (*speech → persuasion → belief*) described the marketplace of ideas that he believed was necessary for society's search for "the ultimate good." It was illegitimate for the government to penalize persuasive speech simply because it threatened "to change the mind of the country." A "free trade in ideas," Holmes argued, meant that "opposition by speech" must be nurtured, not stymied.

While Holmes refused to allow government officials to prohibit mere "opposition by speech," he recognized, as he had in *Schenck*, that it was legitimate for the state to prohibit *actions* that harm society. He rejected the logic of bad tendency because he now realized that the permissiveness of that doctrine allowed the state's concern over harmful action to silence too much speech. Having moved beyond bad tendency, he now saw the speech-protective potential of the clear and present danger formulation of *Schenck*—language that Holmes had not repeated in *Frohwerk* or *Debs* and that the *Abrams* majority likewise had ignored. Holmes's rigorous application of the clear and present danger test in his *Abrams* dissent bore little resemblance to his halfhearted effort in *Schenck*. Holmes animated the requirement of immediacy that had heretofore lain dormant in the test. "It is only the present danger of immediate evil or an intent to bring it about," Holmes wrote in *Abrams*, that justified the state in limiting "the expression of opinion." For Holmes, "only the emergency that makes it immediately dangerous to leave the correction of evil counsels to time warrants making any exception to the sweeping command [of the First Amendment]." In other words, the First Amendment disabled the government from restricting speech based on any fear of its eventual persuasive power in the marketplace of ideas. The legitimate sphere of government regulation was the realm of action. The government could extend its reach to restrict speech only when the circumstances indicated that an audience might act before thinking, or when a speaker intended to incite them to do so. As Judge Learned Hand had observed a couple of years earlier, words can operate not only as "keys of persuasion," but also as "triggers of action" (Masses Publishing Co. v. Patten, 1917). Holmes would protect the former use of speech, but not the latter. Having opened the marketplace of ideas to political dissidents, Holmes would require that they use it. In order to change the nation, they would have to "change the mind of the country."

From this new understanding of the clear and present danger test, Holmes argued that the *Abrams* defendants remained protected by the First Amendment because "the surreptitious publishing of a silly leaflet by an unknown man" posed no "immediate danger" of illegal action against which the government had been obligated to respond. There is something odd, even disconcerting, about Holmes's emphasis on the inefficacy of the *Abrams* defendants' leaflets as justification for their constitutional protection, and Holmes has been criticized on the ground that he would protect free speech merely as a "luxury civil liberty."[3] Is it not perverse to hold that a speaker will be protected only so long as the speech is unlikely to persuade others, and thus remain harmless? That, in other words, unpersuasive speech is protected, but speech likely to persuade an audience to action is itself actionable? That Abrams would be protected, but not Debs? But it is doubtful that this was Holmes's meaning. This criticism ignores Holmes's stress on the absence of *immediate* danger. His justification in *Abrams* for a special protection of the freedom of speech was an argument against enforcing the orthodoxy of the status quo, not for preserving it by force of law.

Holmes's disparaging description of the *Abrams* defendants as "poor and puny anonymities" revealed his core understanding of the First Amendment violation of the conviction. Why, he asked, had the *Abrams* defendants received the maximum sentence of twenty years' imprisonment for expression that seemed so unlikely to cause any measurable harm? He answered, "[T]he most nominal punishment seems to me all that possibly could be inflicted, unless the defendants are to be made to suffer not for what the indictment alleges [that is, threatening the curtailment of production of war materials] but for the creed they avow." By demanding a close—that is, immediate—causal connection between subversive advocacy and harmful action, Holmes would ensure that government prosecutions are grounded on the harmful *actions* that the government legitimacy can punish, and not on the mere *expression* of threatening ideas and unorthodox opinion, which it cannot.

Holmes's First Amendment approach to subversive advocacy illuminated a new path, but he had left most of the justices behind. He no longer wrote for a unanimous Court, but only for himself and Justice Louis D. Brandeis.

THE FIRST "RED SCARE" AND THE PROBLEM OF SUBVERSIVE ORGANIZATIONS

After World War I, American anxiety caused by opponents to the war made a fairly smooth transition to a broader concern over radical opposition to American democracy itself. The affinity between antiwar and revolutionary sentiments had been a powerful subtext in *Abrams*, the last of the Court's World War I cases. Holmes had been driven to dissent in *Abrams* because he was convinced that the defendants had been punished for "the creed that they avow" (three were anarchists; one was a socialist) rather than for any harm that their advocacy realistically threatened to produce. But the consolidation of Bolshevik control in Russia, coupled with the creation there of the Comintern (Communist International), an institution with the mission of fostering a worldwide Communist movement, stoked American anxiety over revolutionary ideology and activity anew. The fear of domestic subversive activity reached its boiling point with the formation in the United States of Revolutionary Communist Parties advocating violent revolution on the Bolshevik model.

The governmental response to the postwar radical activity was both swift and widespread. By 1920, thirty-five states had enacted anti-sedition laws to combat the new wave of revolutionary organizations and their rhetoric. These laws took two complementary forms. "Criminal anarchy" laws were directed at communist parties. They made it a crime to advocate overthrow of the government by force or to organize a group that so advocated. "Criminal syndicalism" statutes targeted radical labor unions, such as the Industrial Workers of the World (IWW). They made it unlawful to advocate industrial change by force or to organize a group that so advocated. In addition to enacting anti-sedition laws, about two-thirds of the states adopted so-called "red flag" laws, which made it unlawful to display a red flag with seditious intent. Although Congress declined a request by the United States Department of Justice to follow suit and enact a peacetime anti-sedition law (the Espionage Act took effect only during wartime), it did pass a law in October of 1918 that authorized the deportation of aliens who advocated anarchism, syndicalism, or violent revolution, or who joined organizations that so advocated. The United States had entered its first "Red Scare," a condition that would linger into the 1930s.[4]

The convictions that state prosecutors obtained under their anti-sedition laws inexorably worked their way to the Supreme Court, braced by the powerful momentum of widespread public support. And the Court responded as it had in *Abrams*: Comfortable majorities of the justices brushed aside First Amendment challenges to the convictions over the dissent of Holmes and Brandeis. The Court first reviewed an appeal from Benjamin Gitlow, an organizer and leader of the Revolutionary Communist Party in New York, who had been convicted under that state's criminal anarchy statute. The New York legislature had enacted that statute in 1902 in response to the assassination of President McKinley by an anarchist, and thus long before the concern over communism that had driven the prosecution of Gitlow. The basis for the state's criminal anarchy charge was Gitlow's role in writing and distributing the "Left Wing Manifesto," a document that, according to the indictment, advocated overthrowing the government by violent and unlawful means. (Gitlow v. New York, 1925).

Gitlow claimed that his revolutionary rhetoric had never crossed the boundary of First Amendment protection marked by the clear and present danger test, because the prosecutors had failed to prove that any illegal or harmful action had resulted, or had been likely to result, from his writing. Gitlow portrayed himself, in other words, as the *Abrams*-type, harmless inciter that Justice Holmes would insulate from prosecution. As in *Abrams*, a seven-justice majority rejected Gitlow's defense, but with this difference: The Court did not even consider the tendency of Gitlow's writing to deliver the revolution he advocated, or indeed, to cause any violent or illegal action whatsoever. The majority instead announced a new constitutional distinction. According to the majority, Gitlow's conviction satisfied the First Amendment because the New York law and the indictment had not targeted protected speech, which the justices limited to advocacy of "abstract doctrine." The government instead had proceeded solely against the advocacy of "concrete [violent and unlawful] action," which, the court held, was not within the freedom of speech.

The *Gitlow* Court's version of the distinction between speech and action might be read as a concession to Holmes's dissenting opinion in *Abrams*. By protecting the advocacy of abstract doctrine, presumably regardless of its content, the Court might have seen itself as preserving Holmes's vision of an open marketplace for the "expression of opinion." So long as speakers simply advocated ideas, they retained their constitutional protection, regardless of the creed they espoused. Speakers left behind that protection if, but only if, they began to advocate unlawful or violent action. While society could tolerate the expression of mere opinion, even subversive opinion, advocacy of subversive action crossed the line because it was inherently dangerous. The Court explained, "[U]tterances inciting to the overthrow of organized government by unlawful means . . . , by their very nature, involve danger to the public peace and to the security of the State. They threaten breaches of the peace and ultimate revolution."

The Court's stated willingness in *Gitlow* to protect advocacy of any doctrine represents an important, if limited, step forward in the evolution of free speech protection. The decisions in *Frohwerk* and *Debs*, and perhaps that in *Schenck* as well, would have come out differently under the *Gitlow* approach because the speakers in those cases did not advocate any "concrete" action that was either violent or unlawful. But the *Gitlow* alternative to the clear and present danger test introduced its own difficulty, because it is not always easy to distinguish between advocacy of doctrine and advocacy of action. The *Gitlow* Court added the qualifiers of "abstract" doctrine and "concrete" action in order to sharpen the distinction, but radical rhetoric often falls between those descriptions on the doctrine-action continuum. Gitlow's manifesto illustrates the difficulty. It argued for the "necessity" of a "Communist Revolution" to "destroy the parliamentary state" in order to save humanity. According to the manifesto, only "Revolutionary Socialism" could "mobilize the proletariat . . . for the conquest of the power of the state, by means of revolutionary mass action," culminating in "the mass political strike against Capitalism and the state." Was this advocacy of abstract doctrine or advocacy of concrete action? Are not the two varieties of advocacy hopelessly intertwined in Gitlow's manifesto?

Justice Holmes, again in dissent and again joined only by Justice Brandeis, exploded the majority's new distinction. Holmes wrote, "Every idea is an incitement. It offers itself for belief and if believed it is acted on unless some other belief outweighs it or some failure of energy stifles the movement at its birth." Reasserting the strong version of the clear and present danger test that he had introduced in his *Abrams* dissent, Holmes would have allowed all advocacy, whether of doctrine or of action, unless the speech threatened to cause, or the speaker intended to cause, immediate unlawful action. Holmes clarified in *Gitlow* what he had left unclear in *Abrams*: The clear and present danger test was not limited to the protection of harmless inciters. It facilitates even the most profound efforts to overturn the status quo, so long as those efforts are confined to persuasive speech within the marketplace of ideas. Holmes wrote, "If in the long run the beliefs expressed in proletarian dictatorship are destined to be accepted by the dominant forces of the community, the only meaning of free speech is that they should be given their chance and have their way."

Once again, however, Holmes's eloquent rhetoric did not sway the majority of his colleagues. And they passed up the opportunity to rethink their *Gitlow* decision a couple of years later when they upheld the conviction of Anita Whitney under California's criminal syndicalism statute (Whitney v. California, 1927). Whitney, like Gitlow, was prosecuted because of her involvement in the creation of a state Revolutionary Communist Party. But there was a subtle difference in the two prosecutions. New York's case against Gitlow focused on his advocacy of violent overthrow in the Left Wing Manifesto. Whitney apparently left no such paper trail. She argued in her defense that she had tried, albeit unsuccessfully, to convince the California communist party to pursue its radical agenda solely through democratic means. She remained a member of the group, but, she claimed, without the intent that the party engage in terrorism or violence.

This factual difference between Gitlow's and Whitney's involvement in the organization of their respective communist parties likely accounts for the different legal posture of the two prosecutions. *Gitlow* was a conventional subversive advocacy case; he was punished for what he had written. California, by contrast, had not convicted Whitney for subversive advocacy, for it may well have been that she had engaged in no such advocacy. Rather, she was punished for her role in organizing and then joining a so-called "subversive organization," that is, an association that was formed to engage in subversive advocacy. This wrinkle introduced by the *Whitney* prosecution might be registered by adding a link at the beginning of the standard, causal chain proffered by governmental prosecutors in subversive advocacy cases:

association → speech → persuasion → belief → action → harm

This amendment to the causal chain illustrates that the government's showing of harm in the *Whitney* case was more attenuated that that presented in *Gitlow*. The proximity of the criminalized activity—the organization of a group formed to engage in subversive advocacy—is one step further removed from any eventual harmful action.

But at least according to the Court, this difference in the two cases did not distinguish them. If the advocacy of subversive action is criminalized, the Court in *Whitney* reasoned, an association formed for the purpose of engaging in such advocacy, by definition, is a criminal conspiracy. Indeed, in the Court's eyes, the difference between the two cases cut against Whitney. Although the formation of an association to engage in speech is further removed from any ultimate harm resulting from that speech, the act of forming a group is also separated from the group's expression. Whitney's role in organizing the party, on this reasoning, was more action than speech. And to make matters worse, the Court found that an individual's actions in forming an organization to engage in subversive advocacy was more harmful than an individual's actually engaging in such advocacy, rather than less. This was because, the Court explained, the formation of a subversive organization threatened to produce "united and joint action," which posed an "even greater danger than the isolated utterances and acts of individuals."

This time Justice Brandeis, joined by Justice Holmes, wrote separately. He did so because of his discomfort with the majority's easy assumption that the First Amendment licensed states to criminalize the mere organization of groups that engage in subversive advocacy. Just as the majority's affirmance of Whitney's conviction had followed from the majority decision in *Gitlow*, Brandeis's disagreement built on the Holmes's dissents. Brandeis regarded freedom of speech as a "fundamental right," and he agreed with Holmes that only a clear and present danger could justify its suppression. Yet he voted to uphold, rather than to reverse, the conviction of Whitney, because he read the trial record to support a finding that the California party was engaged in "a conspiracy . . . to commit present serious crimes." Brandeis, like Holmes, believed that the clear and present danger test was satisfied by a defendant's *intent* to foment immediate lawless action, even if there was no immediate danger of any such action. But Brandeis, along with every other member of the Court, failed to consider whether making Whitney criminally responsible for an intent held by some party members, but not by her, compromised her rights under the First Amendment—whether, in other words, guilt by association was compatible with freedom of association. Thus Brandeis's concurring opinion in *Whitney*, which contains perhaps the most eloquent judicial justification for affording strong constitutional protection for the *freedom of speech*, failed to perceive the *freedom of association* problem that was at the heart of Whitney's case. Just as Holmes and Brandeis were not fully prepared to assimilate the free speech values at stake in the first wave of World War I cases, it appears that in this early test they also were unable to fully appreciate the implications of Whitney's conviction for free association.

Brandeis's concurring opinion in *Whitney*, which figured prominently in our consideration of the theoretical justifications for freedom of speech, nevertheless marks a turning point in the development of First Amendment jurisprudence. His eloquent and powerful *apologia* for a strong protection of freedom of speech as a fundamental constitutional right overshadowed his acceptance of Whitney's conviction. Indeed, it is hardly uncommon for people to refer to Brandeis's opinion in *Whitney* as a dissent rather than as a concurrence. This phenomenon was manifest almost as soon as the *Whitney* opinions appeared. The governor of California, quoting extensively from Brandeis's opinion, pardoned Whitney about a month after the Supreme Court announced its decision.

It would take several years for Brandeis's concurring opinion in *Whitney* and for Holmes's dissents in *Abrams* and *Gitlow* to prevail on the Court. But the justices eventually came around, and when they did, the Supreme Court of the United States, for the first time in its history, began to protect freedom of speech in a manner that reflected its status as a fundamental constitutional right. Justice Cardozo made clear the thoroughness of the change in judicial attitude ten years after *Whitney* when, writing for the Court, he described freedom of speech as "the matrix, the indispensable condition, of nearly every other form of freedom" (Palko v. Connecticut, 1937). Although some may take such statements for granted now, one could hardly have imagined any such statement appearing in any of the majority opinions upholding subversive advocacy convictions from *Schenck* through *Whitney*. In the years following *Whitney*, the Court registered this newly appreciated centrality of the freedom of speech in the American constitutional system by embracing the Holmes/Brandeis understanding of the clear and present danger test. Indeed, the justices accorded the opinions of Holmes and Brandeis the authority of precedent, as if they had garnered the support of a majority of the justices instead of just themselves. By the 1940s, the Court began to use the Holmes/Brandeis version of the clear and present danger test to invalidate a wide variety of governmental restrictions on speech.

Still, the post-*Whitney* reversal of fortune experienced by the freedom of speech retained an ambiguous, ambivalent quality when it came to the problem of subversive advocacy. On one hand, *Whitney* drew a firm dividing line in the outcomes of the Supreme Court's subversive advocacy decisions. Before 1927, as we have seen, solid majorities of the justices upheld prosecutions for subversive advocacy without fail; thereafter, the Court uniformly overturned such prosecutions, at least until the Second "Red Scare" of the 1950s. On the other hand, while the justices invoked the Holmes/Brandeis clear and present danger test in a variety of First Amendment areas, they avoided doing so with respect to subversive advocacy, the very free speech problem for which Holmes had devised the principle. After 1927, the Court managed to overturn subversive advocacy convictions within the broad contours of the pre-1927 precedent. In effect, the justices applied the doctrine of the *Gitlow* and *Whitney* majority opinions with the free speech sensibility of Holmes and Brandeis. They demanded that government prosecutors prove that dissident speakers had actually crossed *Gitlow*'s boundary line of First Amendment protection by clearly advocating unlawful action. But they stopped short of requiring evidence that the speakers intended, or that their advocacy threatened, *immediate* seditious action (see Stromberg v. California, 1931; DeJonge v. Oregon, 1937; Herndon v. Lowry, 1937). Indeed, in one of the post-1927 decisions, the Supreme Court explicitly refused to apply the clear and present danger test to subversive advocacy (Herndon v. Lowry, 1937).

THE SECOND "RED SCARE" AND THE PROBLEM OF SUBVERSIVE ORGANIZATIONS REVISITED

The protective shift in subversive advocacy decisions was hardly the only change in the United States between 1927 and 1937. The Great Depression became a national preoccupation as the country and its economy slogged through the 1930s. The Depression itself was followed, and displaced, by the Second World War as Americans' most pressing public concern. Only two subversive advocacy prosecutions of wartime critics reached the Supreme Court during the war (Taylor v. Mississippi, 1943; Hartzel v. United States, 1944). The Court reversed both convictions, evincing a concern for free speech values that had been almost wholly absent in the World War I decisions. Although the Second World War would produce other violations of civil liberties—most notoriously, the internment of Japanese-Americans—the groundwork laid by Holmes and Brandeis, as well as the Court's post-1927 skepticism of subversive advocacy prosecutions, provided crucial support for a protection of freedom of speech during wartime that would have been barely imaginable during the First World War.

Ironically, it was at the conclusion of World War II that the American commitment to freedom of speech confronted what perhaps has been its most severe test. When the war ended, the United States entered a prolonged "Cold War" with its wartime ally, the Soviet Union. And with this new, metaphorical war came a Second "Red Scare." Just as had occurred after the First World War, Americans became preoccupied with the danger of subversion by internal enemies with the avowed purpose of forcibly overthrowing the government. During the First Red Scare, Americans had worried that the Revolutionary Communist Parties springing up in their midst threatened to import the instability of Europe to their homeland. When a national communist party took shape after World War II, Americans saw it as an institutional embodiment of the Soviet Union in the United States. A new front in America's worldwide struggle against communism had been established.

During the war, when the United States and the Soviet Union were allied, the communist party in the United States transformed itself into the Communist Political Association and cooperated with American interests. But in 1945, with the war successfully concluded, Moscow instructed the American communist leadership to reconstitute the Communist Party USA, and to renew the Party's commitment to organizing radical opposition to the government of the United States. In the wake of the Party's re-emergence as a subversive organization, a perception took hold among a growing number of Americans—fed by instances of actual espionage, but also exaggerated by demagogic, political leaders—that communist-sponsored spy rings had become ubiquitous in the society. They feared that communist infiltrators had dangerously compromised the key institutions of American life, including industry, labor unions, schools, the arts, and even the upper echelon of the U.S. government.

When Senator Joseph R. McCarthy spoke before the Republican Women's Club of Wheeling, West Virginia, early in 1950 and claimed to possess a list of the names of State Department officials who were members or sympathizers of the Communist Party, the Second Red Scare acquired a figurehead as well as a name—the McCarthy Era. The McCarthy Era was a time of loyalty oaths and security checks, as well as aggressive and highly publicized congressional investigations of "un-American activities." Suspicion of subversion characterized the times. To take but one example, a private coalition known as the "China Lobby" conducted its own inquiry to determine who in the government was responsible for "losing Red China." For many Americans, the world and America's place in it was threatened by a clear and present danger of communist oppression.[5]

The Second Red Scare provided the backdrop for the federal indictment of the principal leaders of the Communist Party USA in the summer of 1948 for violating the conspiracy provisions of the Smith Act, an anti-sedition statute that Congress had enacted in the run-up to U.S. entry into the Second World War (Dennis v. United States, 1951). Congress had patterned the Smith Act, naturally enough, on the state anti-sedition laws that the Supreme Court had upheld in *Gitlow* and *Whitney*. The central provision of the Act tracked *Gitlow*, making it unlawful for anyone "to knowingly and willfully advocate . . . the duty, necessity, desirability, or propriety of overthrowing or destroying any government in the United States by force or violence." Related provisions made it a crime to prepare or to distribute literature whose text reflected that prohibited advocacy, as well as to organize any group to engage in the prohibited advocacy. The Act also made it a crime to join or to affiliate with such a group "knowing the purposes thereof."[6] As in *Whitney*, Dennis and his co-defendants were charged with violating the Smith Act by organizing the Party as an organization whose goal was "the overthrow and destruction of the United States by force and violence." The government also charged, as in *Gitlow*, that the defendants themselves had advocated the overthrow and destruction of the U.S. Government. A jury convicted the defendants after a lengthy and turbulent trial in New York City. For the most part, they were sentenced to five-year prison terms. The Second Circuit Court of Appeals upheld the convictions.

Dennis returned the justices to the problem of subversive organizations, which essentially had lain dormant since 1937. The justices had entered a perfect storm. First, there was the inherent difficulty of the subversive organization problem itself, which none of the justices had satisfactorily recognized in *Whitney* and which the Court had not reopened thereafter. Second, the decision-making environment surrounding the Court hardly was conducive to a sober, second look at that problem.

Dennis was a high profile prosecution arising in the midst of deep national anxiety. The confluence of these pressures atomized the Court. Five of the eight justices who sat for the case wrote opinions; no opinion commanded a majority. In the end, for the first time since 1927, a solid majority of the Court voted to uphold convictions for sedition. And in an ironic echo of the pre-1927 cases, only two justices dissented.

The reversion to pre-1927 form should not obscure the significant step forward in First Amendment jurisprudence registered in *Dennis*. The two leading judicial statements in the case—the lead opinion by Chief Justice Fred M. Vinson for a four-justice plurality and the dissenting opinion by Justice William O. Douglas—rejected the *Gitlow/Whitney* position that legislatures could outlaw the simple advocacy of unlawful conduct. Vinson and Douglas agreed that something more was needed. They agreed as well on the additional element, namely, a showing by the government that the expressive activity in question created a clear and present danger of substantial harm. Their disagreement centered on the meaning of "clear and present danger." While Douglas insisted on the strong version of the test championed by Holmes and Brandeis, the Vinson plurality opted for a definition that eliminated the requirement of immediacy, and thus drained the test of its central meaning.

Chief Justice Vinson adopted Chief Judge Learned Hand's restatement of the clear and present danger test in the opinion for the court of appeals affirming the conviction of the *Dennis* defendants (United States v. Dennis, 1950). Judge Hand described the test as a "shorthand statement" for the following calculation, "whether the gravity of the 'evil,' discounted by its improbability, justifies such invasion of free speech as is necessary to avoid the danger." Although that restatement of the clear and present danger test followed what Hand described as a "wearisome analysis" of the Supreme Court's free speech jurisprudence, Hand did not purport to trace his formula to that precedent. Indeed, it is doubtful that Hand derived his redefinition of "clear and present danger" from any analysis of the First Amendment. Rather, Hand looked to tort law (the law concerning wrongful actions harmful to others). The formula Hand invented followed precisely from his then recent and influential restatement of the scope of an individual's duty to prevent accidents caused by instrumentalities under his or her control (see United States v. Carroll Towing Co., 1947). Nowhere in his opinion did Hand justify the importation of this tort law standard into free speech jurisprudence. Any analogy between an individual's civil liability for accidents caused by his or her property and a speaker's criminal responsibility for subversive advocacy is obscure at best. One thing seems clear, however. There is little room, if any, for free speech values in such a comparison.

Hand's redefinition of "clear and present danger" was appealing to the Vinson plurality notwithstanding its questionable First Amendment pedigree. Hand's approach enabled Vinson to retain the language of Holmes and Brandeis, which by this time had become imbedded in American culture as well as in free speech jurisprudence, while avoiding the meaning of that language. Moreover, Hand's elimination of the immediacy requirement in favor of a prosecutorial showing that the occurrence of subversive action was probable sometime in the future, fit the trial jury's finding in *Dennis* like a glove. While the jurors were unable to conclude that the defendants were likely to, or had intended to, attempt an overthrow of the government in the immediate future, they believed that the defendants had intended to do so "as speedily as circumstances would permit." Hand's revision also accommodated Vinson's conclusion that the very "existence" of the Communist Party in the United States, in light of the "inflammable nature of world conditions" during the Cold War, was itself a clear and present danger to national security. The Chief Justice did not see the Communist Party USA as a legitimate political party, but rather as a "highly organized conspiracy." He emphasized that the Party was "highly disciplined" and "tolerate[d] no dissension" among its members. Party members were "subject to call when the leaders . . . felt that the time had come for action." Because future subversive action seemed all but inevitable, Vinson would not require the government to wait for the "putsch" to begin in order to intervene to save the country.

Chief Justice Vinson's plurality opinion reflected, as it reinforced, the fear of communist subversion that riddled American society during the McCarthy Era. It is worth considering whether any other decision might have been expected from the Court during a time of such extraordinary social stress. Would the Court have been able to withstand the political firestorm that surely would have followed an alternative ruling that the First Amendment protected the Communist Party as it seemingly worked toward the violent overthrow of constitutional government in the United States? Such an outcome would have seemed unimaginable to many Americans. Yet, Justice Douglas advocated just such a ruling, and although he was unable to attract any of his colleagues to his opinion, his dissenting opinion in *Dennis* charted the path toward the Court's contemporary approach to subversive advocacy.

Justice Douglas began with a default principle that individuals, singly or in association with others, have a First Amendment right to advocate anything they please, even the violent overthrow of the world's oldest existing democracy. "[F]ree speech is the rule," he reminded, in the spirit of Holmes and Brandeis, "not the exception." Douglas identified two elements, however, that might transform an association's advocacy of unlawful action into something more sinister, thus making it a legitimate target of law enforcement. The first element occurs if an organization moves beyond advocacy of revolution to revolutionary action. In this dichotomy, an organization leaves the protective cover of the First Amendment when it begins to take specific preparatory steps towards effecting the revolution it advocates. Such preparation can take the form of speech—"teaching the techniques" of sabotage, political assassination, espionage, and the like—or it can take the form of action—acquiring weapons, building bombs, stealing government documents, and so forth. According to Douglas, it was only in either of those two events that an advocacy organization forfeited its identity as a protected political association and became a criminal conspiracy. Douglas thus objected to Vinson's characterization of the Communist Party USA as a criminal conspiracy because the government had failed to prove that the Party had done anything other than advocate a communist revolution. Their crime was teaching Marxist-Leninist doctrine, not "the techniques of terror." Although Douglas conceded that the *Dennis* defendants had "preached the creed with the hope that some day it would be acted upon," the crucial fact for him was that they only had "preached the creed."

While Justice Douglas's first element was limited to claims that the First Amendment did not protect an advocacy association itself, his second element applied generally to subversive advocacy and followed directly from the Holmes/Brandeis tradition. He allowed for the possibility that the state might silence mere revolutionary advocacy in circumstances that created an immediate danger of triggering action that would cause serious societal harm. Douglas explained, "When conditions are so critical that there will be no time to avoid the evil that the speech threatens, it is time to call a halt." For Douglas, the mere existence of Cold War anxiety was insufficient to create such critical conditions. While he conceded that communism "in the world scene [was] no bogeyman," he believed that the internal communist threat was just that. To him, American communists resembled the *Abrams* defendants; they were the "miserable merchants of unwanted ideas." Douglas observed that if the justices had retained the immediacy requirement of the clear and present danger test, they would never have allowed "senseless fear" to silence an organization that was "of little consequence."

Although Chief Justice Vinson carried the day in *Dennis*, Justice Douglas provided a glimpse of the future of subversive advocacy doctrine. Two other justices were especially prescient in their *Dennis* opinions. Justice Felix Frankfurter, who voted with the majority in *Dennis*, offered an accurate, near-term prediction. He wrote, "[I]t is self-delusion to think that we can punish [the leaders of the Communist Party] for their advocacy without adding to the risks run by loyal citizens who honestly believe in some of the reforms these defendants advance. It is a sobering fact that in sustaining the conviction before us we can hardly escape restriction on the interchange of ideas." Of the justices who voted to affirm the conviction of the *Dennis* defendants, Frankfurter was the only one to voice any sense of regret. Events vindicated Frankfurter's concern, for there is little doubt that the Court's decision in *Dennis* reinforced the fear and suspicion of the time, even as it emboldened government officials to suppress the "communist menace." Government-instigated purges of the motion-picture industry, trade unions, and higher education continued apace, fostering, in the language of one historian, a time of "intimidation and terror."[7] More to the point, following *Dennis*, the federal government launched Smith Act prosecutions against over 120 second-echelon officers of the Communist Party USA and received convictions in most of them.[8]

Hugo L. Black, the only justice other than Douglas to dissent in *Dennis*, offered an equally accurate, longer-term prediction. He wrote, "Public opinion being what it now is, few will protest the conviction of these communist petitioners. There is hope, however, that in calmer times, when present pressures, passions and fears subside, this or some later Court will restore the First Amendment liberties to the high preferred place where they belong in a free society." The restoration for which Black hoped began to take shape in 1954, when a Senate hearing investigating allegations of communist subversion among the ranks of the United States Army backfired on Senator McCarthy, the moving force behind the hearing. During McCarthy's relentless badgering of a witness, a lawyer objected memorably, "You have done enough. Have you no sense of decency, sir, at long last? Have you left no sense of decency?" When the audience in attendance at the hearing erupted into applause, McCarthy was finished as a public figure in America, as would be, before long, the era that bears his name.

The Court did not revisit its decision in *Dennis* until it took up the Smith Act prosecutions against the second-tier leaders of the Communist Party several years after Senator McCarthy's fall from grace. The justices were able to regroup in those quieter times, and in a series of decisions, they offered a unified position defining the scope of First Amendment protection of subversive organizations (Yates v. United States, 1957; Scales v. United States, 1961; Noto v. United States, 1961). Although the justices in these later decisions pronounced Chief Justice Vinson's plurality opinion in *Dennis* to be authoritative, they adopted Justice Douglas's distinction between protected political associations and unprotected criminal conspiracies. The new approach, as Douglas would have it, protected organizations whose members merely advocated subversion, without engaging in any activity towards that end.

In *Yates*, the first of the post-*Dennis* Smith Act decisions, the Court distinguished broadly between associations that engaged simply in "advocacy and teaching of forcible overthrow as an abstract principle," which were protected by the First Amendment, and organizations that coupled such advocacy with an "effort to instigate action to that end," which were unprotected. The justices elaborated the *Yates* distinction in *Scales* by identifying "at least two patterns of evidence sufficient to show illegal advocacy: (a) the teaching of forceful overthrow, accompanied by directions as to the type of illegal action which must be taken when the time for the revolution is reached; and (b) the teaching of forceful overthrow, accompanied by a contemporary, though legal, course of conduct clearly undertaken for the specific purpose of rendering effective the later illegal activity which is advocated."

The Court used *Scales* and *Noto* to tidy up *Whitney*. After its experience with litigation challenging governmental efforts to punish members of the Communist Party, an experience that ranged far beyond *Dennis* and the post-*Dennis* decisions we have discussed, the justices became convinced that it was necessary to protect those who, like Whitney, had joined subversive organizations without the intent of engaging in illegal activity. As the Court stressed in *Noto*, individual members would be judged by their actions, and not by their political affiliations. Guilt by association, at long last, was insufficient to overcome freedom of association. The cumulative weight of the Court's post-*Dennis* decisions was too much for government prosecutors to bear, and they abandoned their efforts to use the Smith Act to imprison members of the Communist Party U.S.A.

THE CONTEMPORARY DOCTRINE OF SUBVERSIVE ADVOCACY

The Court's long struggle with the subversive advocacy problem illustrates the larger challenge of accommodating the values of free speech with the other important commitments of American society. In the communist cases of the 1950s, that challenge was posed in the sharpest way imaginable: the ultimate democratic commitment—the preservation of self-government—was pitted against the central democratic commitment of freedom of expression—the right of individuals to speak out and to organize groups in order to advocate social and political change. It is little wonder that the justices could begin to approach the proper balance between those competing claims only after the Second Red Scare had receded. But while the post-*Dennis* decisions succeeded in rebalancing the distinction between protected and unprotected associations, the Court did not resolve the problem of separating protected and unprotected subversive advocacy. The Court left for another day the task of picking up the pieces of the clear and present danger test left strewn about the various *Dennis* opinions.

That day did not arrive until 1969. By that time, the Court not only had gained distance from the communist scare, but also it had acquired considerable First Amendment experience from handling a wide variety of free speech disputes arising from the civil rights movement, and to a lesser degree, from the protests against the Vietnam War. Harry Kalven, a leading free speech scholar, has connected the second Red Scare and civil rights experiences quite tellingly. He writes, "The great civil liberties issues of the postwar decade centered on national efforts to curb the domestic communist conspiracy. It is not entirely poetry to say that the NAACP [was] from the standpoint of the beleaguered South a second domestic conspiracy aiming at a revolution. And the Southern states . . . responded to the challenge by seeking to adapt the legal methods used to fight communism." That tactic, Kalven reports, was "highly unsuccessful."[9] The Court protected the civil rights movement to a degree that American communists must have envied. The contentious cases of the civil rights era, it is fair to say, convinced the justices of the potentially constructive role of dissident movements in the operation of American democracy, as well as of the vulnerability of those movements to suppression by government officials preoccupied by preserving public order and maintaining the status quo.

It was a dissident movement of a very different character that provided the justices their opportunity to finish the reformation of subversive advocacy doctrine that they had begun in the wake of *Dennis* (Brandenburg v. Ohio, 1969). Brandenburg, a Ku Klux Klan leader, had invited a local television reporter to cover a small rally at a farm in rural Ohio. At the rally, Brandenburg, perched near a burning cross, made a brief speech in which he exclaimed, "We're not a revengent organization, but if our President, our Congress, our Supreme Court, continues to suppress the white, Caucasian race, it's possible that there might have to be some revengeance taken." He closed the speech with an announcement that the Klan planned to organize a march of 400,000 on Congress on the Fourth of July, thereafter dividing into two groups, one group continuing on to Mississippi, the other to St. Augustine, Florida. Brandenburg's speech was laced with derogatory references concerning African Americans and Jews, and in a second speech he said, "Personally, I believe the nigger should be returned to Africa, the Jew to Israel."

Brandenburg was tried and convicted of violating an Ohio anti-sedition act that had been enacted in 1919 during the First Red Scare. The Ohio law resembled the California statute that the Supreme Court had upheld in *Whitney*. The statute prohibited the advocacy of "crime, . . . violence, or unlawful methods of terrorism as a means of accomplishing . . . political reform," as well as "voluntarily assembl[ing]" with others to engage in such advocacy. The trial record apparently was sparse, consisting almost entirely of the film of Brandenburg's speeches shot by the television crew he had invited to the rally. The state supreme court had dismissed Brandenburg's appeal, without opinion, on the grounds that, somehow, his First Amendment claim did not raise a "substantial constitutional question."

The United States Supreme Court reversed Brandenburg's conviction in a *per curiam* opinion (that is, an opinion issued "by the court," rather than by an individual judge). The Court began with the common ground of the Vinson and Douglas opinions in *Dennis*: advocacy of violent or illegal action, "without more," was protected. In describing the additional factor necessary for the state to restrict such advocacy, the Court in *Brandenburg* left no doubt that Douglas's solitary dissenting opinion had prevailed over Vinson's near majority. The *Brandenburg* Court wrote, "[T]he constitutional guarantees of free speech and free press do not permit a State to forbid or proscribe advocacy of the use of force or law violation [i.e., subversive advocacy] except where [1] such advocacy is directed to inciting or producing imminent lawless action and [2] is likely to incite or produce such action." Since *Brandenburg*, that two-part requirement has marked the First Amendment boundary between protected and unprotected subversive advocacy.

The Court illuminated the changed landscape of subversive advocacy doctrine in its *Brandenburg* ruling. The justices not only reversed Brandenburg's conviction; they also invalidated the Ohio anti-sedition statute in its entirety. The Court had never before invalidated any provision of an anti-sedition law. When the Court had overturned subversive advocacy convictions in the past, it had done so because the trial record was not sufficient to satisfy the First Amendment. The justices in *Brandenburg* took another unusual step: They expressly overruled *Whitney,* and thus formally laid to rest that "thoroughly discredited" decision. By its overruling of *Whitney, Brandenburg* settled an old score, vindicating not only Douglas, but also Holmes and Brandeis, whose early development of the clear and present danger test had provided the foundation for Douglas's dissent in *Dennis*.

Douglas, who was still on the Court when it decided *Brandenburg*, remained troubled, however. He wrote separately to disavow the clear and present danger test, "whether strict and tight . . . , or free-wheeling as the Court in *Dennis* rephrased it." In application, he charged, judges had "manipulated" the test in order to "crush" the fundamental right of free speech. Revolutionary rhetoric, he wrote, was "often loud but always puny and made serious only by judges so wedded to the status quo that critical analysis made them nervous." Douglas now insisted that the First Amendment insulated all speech from governmental suppression. Constitutional protection, he wrote, extended all the way to "the line between ideas and overt acts."

Douglas's lament notwithstanding, the *Brandenburg* test is best understood as a revision, rather than as an abandonment, of the Holmes/Brandeis clear and present danger test. Surprising as it may seem, *Brandenburg* marks the first time that the Court applied the strong version of that venerable test to subversive advocacy, the very free speech problem for which Holmes and Brandies had designed it. The central thrust of the *Brandenburg* test is clear: it reinstates the requirement of immediacy at the core of subversive advocacy doctrine (see Hess v. Indiana, 1973). An advocate's call for unlawful action is unprotected only if it is "directed to" producing "imminent lawless action," and is "likely" to immediately generate that action. The paradigmatic example of the advocate who would trip on the *Brandenburg* line is the demagogue who inflames an already angry mob to such a fever pitch that they lynch a victim in the heat of passion, to their deep regret once they return to their senses. Such an advocate abuses the right of free speech by manipulating the audience to act before thinking, rather than by persuading them to a course of action.

The clarity of *Brandenburg*'s imminence requirement, together with its model of demagogic abuse, obscures other ambiguities lurking in the test, however. What does it mean to say that advocacy may not be "directed to" producing imminent lawless action? And indeed, what is it that makes such action "likely"? The "directed to" language is especially puzzling, because it highlights the absence of two concepts in the *Brandenburg* formulation that had been mainstays in subversive advocacy jurisprudence—namely, the "intent" of the speaker and the "content" of the advocacy. It is possible that the Court devised the "directed to" language as a substitute for the more traditional requirements of speaker intent and explicit advocacy of illegal action. The purpose of such a substitution well may have been to incorporate a contextual flexibility into the first part of the *Brandenburg* test, by enabling courts to consider all of the surrounding circumstances in determining speaker liability for any violence or unlawful activity committed by the audience. Freed from the formal intent and content requirements, courts can simply focus on deciding whether a speaker had engaged in a good faith effort to persuade an audience to a point of view (and matters just got out of hand), or the speaker had pursed a project of prompting some spontaneous, unlawful action from the audience. But it is hardly certain that this was the Court's intention. In the thirty-plus years of *Brandenburg*'s life, the Court has yet to clarify the meaning of the "directed to" requirement.

Whatever the precise meaning assigned "directed to," it is clear that the second step of *Brandenburg*—the requirement that the advocacy be "*likely* to incite or produce [unlawful] action"—is a new and important qualifier of the clear and present danger test. In the *Brandenburg* formulation, "likelihood" substitutes for the more supercharged "danger" element of the old test. There is a subtle, but important, difference in asking whether a speaker's subversive advocacy created the "danger" of unlawful action, and in requiring a judge or jury to decide whether the advocacy actually made such action "likely" to occur. The latter formulation demands an objective showing of a real prospect of harmful action, and not simply some societal fear for what might follow from radical rhetoric. Justice Brandeis in *Whitney* had insisted that just such a move from fear to objective proof was critical in ensuring that subversive advocacy convictions not punish merely unpopular speech. While *Brandenburg*'s use of "likelihood" suggests that a showing of actual lawless action caused by the advocacy remains unnecessary, it nevertheless is difficult to prove this element if no actual harm can be traced to a speaker's advocacy (see Claiborne Hardware v. NAACP, 1982). If nothing happened after a speech, how likely could it have been that illegal action would be the immediate result? *Brandenburg* thus encourages a narrowing of the category of unprotected subversive advocacy in Douglas's direction, to speech that, in Douglas's phrase, is "brigaded with action" (Brandenburg v. Ohio, 1969, concurring opinion).

On this understanding of *Brandenburg*, the Court rotated 180 degrees from where it began in *Schenck*. There the Court's invocation of the "bad tendency" causal chain (*speech* → *persuasion* → *action* → *harm*) meant that subversive advocacy was virtually an unprotected category of speech. In *Brandenburg*, the justices treated subversive advocacy as fully protected by the First Amendment, unless the advocacy was so connected with unlawful action as to be virtually indistinguishable from it. Although it took exactly fifty years, the Court had come to the realization of Holmes and Brandeis that prosecutions for subversive advocacy almost invariably compromise the right of individuals and groups to engage in legitimate political dissent, and that such dissent, while sometimes frightening, lies at the heart of the freedom of speech protected by the First Amendment. The Court's decision in *Brandenburg* also aligned subversive advocacy doctrine with the post-*Dennis* decisions concerning subversive organizations. In either case, the state can prohibit dissent only as dissidents couple speech with action.

There is, however, an important qualification of the *Brandenburg* test that is often overlooked. In the language of *Brandenburg*, the test applies only to "*advocacy* of the use of force or law violation." (Emphasis added.) The Court's use of the word "advocacy" evokes a caveat introduced by Holmes when he first strengthened the clear and present danger test in his *Abrams* dissent. The stringent protection of that test applied, he wrote, only to "expressions of opinion and exhortation," and not to secret plotting (Abrams v. United States, 1919, dissenting opinion). Holmes thus would not have prevented the government from outlawing a private conversation in which the speaker urged another to commit an unlawful action, such as a murder or a bank robbery, at some indefinite time in the future. At least one state supreme court has ruled that the *Brandenburg* test does not immunize speech associated with a price-fixing conspiracy (State v. Blyth, 1975), and surely that conclusion is correct. The Court has only applied *Brandenburg* in cases where a public speaker has attempted to persuade an audience to a point of view or to a course of action. The protection of subversive advocacy is designed to insulate political dissent from governmental suppression, but only when such dissent takes the form of public advocacy rather than criminal conspiracy.

* * *

The saga of subversive advocacy provides the central narrative for the meaning of freedom of speech in the United States. But the meaning of that story is far from clear. For some, this is a story of progress. The Supreme Court, as well as the larger society, began with a nominal acceptance of freedom of speech as a pillar of American constitutionalism, but without a commitment to free speech values of sufficient strength to withstand the pressure exerted by government and society for restrictions on dissident speech and groups that appear truly threatening to the social order. After a long period of trial and error, of victory and defeat, in *Brandenburg* the Court finally aligned First Amendment doctrine with the constitutional standing of freedom of speech as a fundamental right that courts must protect in all but the narrowest of circumstances. In this optimistic reading, *Brandenburg* represents the culmination of an evolutionary process of societal self-realization, the result of which is the uniquely strong protection of freedom of speech that distinguishes American constitutionalism from that of every other nation.

There is truth in that reading, but it is possible that there is more validity to a less sanguine interpretation of the subversive advocacy narrative. In this reading, the story of subversive advocacy shows that courts are unwilling, or perhaps unable, to protect dissident speech except in periods of relative social tranquility. During times of stress, most notably those of the Red Scares experienced by the United States after each of the two world wars of the past century, the Court—and thus the First Amendment—was little more than a speed bump on the road to societal suppression of dissident speech and dissident associations. In this pessimistic interpretation, the central narrative for freedom of speech in the United States is not a story of progress and ultimate triumph, but rather one of strategic failure. The justices invariably were most protective of free speech when it mattered least—during times when subversive advocacy prosecutions were sporadic rather than systematic. In this light, *Brandenburg* appears as a mirage that will disappear when the next scare arrives. Freedom of speech, according to the second interpretation, is remarkable not for its unique strength, but for its fragility. This view, regrettably, has some truth to it as well.

We will not know which of these competing accounts is the more accurate interpretation of the subversive advocacy narrative until the *Brandenburg* test itself is tested during a time of intense social stress, when the citizen body, through its elected representatives, decides to confront political dissent systematically as a threat to the survival of the social order. We will not know whether *Brandenburg* (and the free speech principle that underlies it) is strong or fragile until it meets its *Dennis*.

With the tragic and traumatic terrorist attack of September 11, 2001, concern over foreign-sponsored terrorism in the United States became a major preoccupation of the American people. As the government acts to combat the terrorist threat, it is conceivable that the United States soon will enter a time of trial that echoes the experiences of the two Red Scares. If so, we will know which of the dueling narratives correctly describes the contemporary meaning of freedom of speech in the United States by gauging the success of the *Brandenburg* formula in safeguarding the opportunity for political dissent in troubled times.

NOTES

* *First Inaugural Address*, March 4, 1801.

1. Act of June 15, 1917, ch. 30, tit. I, §3, 40 Stat. 219.

2. The quotations from the *Abrams* leaflets are taken from the complete reproduction of those leaflets in Richard Polenberg, *Fighting Faiths: The Abrams Case, the Supreme Court, and Free Speech* (New York: Viking, 1987): pp. 49–52.

3. See Harry Kalven, Jr., *A Worthy Tradition: Freedom of Speech in America* (New York: Harper & Row, 1988) (Jamie Kalven, ed.): p. 156.

4. See Harold Josephson, "Political Justice during the Red Scare: The Trial of Benjamin Gitlow" in Michael R. Belknap, ed., *American Political Trials* (Westport, Conn: Greenwood Press, 1981): pp. 153–75.

5. The discussion in this paragraph draws from James MacGregor Burns, *The American Experiment: The Crosswinds of Freedom* (New York: Alfred A. Knopf, 1989): pp. 220–51; John Patrick Diggins, *The Proud Decades: America in War and Peace, 1941–1960* (New York: W. W. Norton & Co., 1988): pp. 110–17.

6. Act of June 28, 1940, ch. 439, §2, 54 Stat. 670, 671.

7. Diggins, *Proud Decades*, pp. 157–76.

8. Geoffrey Stone, et al., *The First Amendment* (Gaithersburg: Aspen Law & Business, 1999): p. 53.

9. Harry Kalven, Jr., *The Negro and the First Amendment* (Chicago & London: Phoenix Books, The University of Chicago Press, 1966): pp. 65–66.

4

The Central Organizing Principles of Free Speech Jurisprudence

The modern history of the guarantee of freedom of speech and press mainly has been one of a search for the outer limits of that right.

Justice John Marshall Harlan (Curtis Publishing Co. v. Butts and Associated Press v. Walker, 1967, plurality opinion)

Nearly every human action that the law affects, and virtually all governmental activity, involves speech. For First Amendment purposes this Court has distinguished among contexts in which speech activity might arise, applying special speech-protective rules and presumptions in some of those areas, but not in others.

Justice Stephen G. Breyer (United States v. United Foods, Inc., 2001, dissenting opinion)

"Congress shall make no law . . . abridging the freedom of speech." So reads the speech clause of the First Amendment. Justice Hugo L. Black, for one, read that text literally, insisting that its "unequivocal demand" prevented any and all efforts by the government to restrict the right of free speech in favor of competing societal interests (Konigsberg v. State Bar of California, 1961, dissenting opinion). For Justice Black, the purpose of the First Amendment, and indeed, of the Bill of Rights in general, was "to put the freedoms protected there completely out of the area of any congressional control." His emphasis on the First Amendment's clear negation of congressional power ("no law"), however, ignored the studied ambiguity of the language "abridging" and "freedom of speech." Do all laws that restrict individual expression thereby "abridg[e] the freedom of speech"? Does "freedom of speech" empower Americans to say whatever they please whenever, wherever, and however they wish?

Justice Black's absolutism has never prevailed on the Court. Constitutional law wisely avoids absolutes—whether of government power or of individual right—and the freedom of speech has been no exception. Holmes and Brandeis, in their eloquent opinions early in the Twentieth Century that laid the foundation for fortifying the First Amendment, readily conceded that freedom of speech was not an absolute right. Indeed, the entire history of the Court's struggle to reach a stable settlement of the subversive advocacy problem might be understood as an ongoing effort by the justices to find the appropriate balance between the societal imperatives of securing freedom of speech and of safeguarding the public from real harm.

The insurmountable barrier to absolute protection of speech is what one constitutional legal scholar has described as the inevitability of "irresistible counterexamples."[1] For example, laws against bribery, perjury, and price fixing all criminalize expression, but the First Amendment cannot sensibly be interpreted to provide constitutional immunity for such speech acts. To take a different kind of example, a regulation that controls sound levels near a hospital restricts expressive as well as non-expressive activity that is excessively loud. But courts likely would uphold such a regulation against a First Amendment challenge, so long as the sound threshold set by the regulation was reasonable (see Ward v. Rock Against Racism, 1989; Grayned v. City of Rockford, 1972). In other words, although perjury laws and sound-control regulations restrict speech, they do not "abridg[e] the freedom of speech" within the meaning of the First Amendment.

Just why this is so is the subject of this chapter. The two examples of permissible speech restrictions that I have described illustrate the two central organizing principles of contemporary free speech jurisprudence. The "categorization principle" denies First Amendment protection to certain categories of speech (such as bribery and perjury) by defining them out of the "freedom of speech." The "content distinction principle" allows the government greater leeway when enacting laws, such as a sound-control regulation, that restrict expressive activity without regard to the content of the expression. The remaining chapters of this book demonstrate how the categorization and content distinction principles shape the discussion of contemporary free speech doctrine. This chapter introduces these principles.

THE CATEGORIZATION PRINCIPLE

The categorization principle distinguishes between the ordinary meaning of "speech" and the constitutional meaning of "freedom of speech," thereby allowing the government to prohibit certain categories of speech without violating the First Amendment.[2] Although all speech presumptively is within the "freedom of speech" protected by the First Amendment, there are, in the Supreme Court's language, "certain well-defined and narrowly limited classes of speech, the prevention and punishment of which have never been thought to raise any Constitutional problem" (Chaplinsky v. New Hampshire, 1942). In *Chaplinsky*, the Court adopted a cost-benefit, balancing test to determine whether any particular category of speech should be outside First Amendment protection. The *Chaplinsky* test denies constitutional protection to any category of speech that constitutes "no essential part of any exposition of ideas and [is] of such slight social value as a step to truth that any benefit that may be derived from [it] is clearly outweighed by the social interest in order and morality." Thus, perjury is categorized out of the First Amendment because lying under oath, as a category of speech, causes considerable social harm without producing any offsetting communicative value.

Chaplinsky's qualification that the harm produced by an unprotected category of speech must "clearly" outweigh any benefit is an important limitation on categorization. Only a category of speech that, like perjury, provides little or no expressive value in communicating information or ideas is vulnerable to constitutional exclusion because of the social costs it imposes. For example, expressive activities such as mass demonstrations enjoy full First Amendment protection because their associated social costs in disruption of the public order, which at times are considerable, cannot be said *clearly* to outweigh their communicative value, which also is considerable. The First Amendment default position—that all speech is within the "freedom of speech"—is overcome only by an overwhelming disparity between the social risk and reward of the speech category in question. In close cases, courts err on the side of constitutional protection rather than of constitutional exclusion.

Although the categorization principle works well when explaining why some types of speech that obviously should not be protected by the Constitution are outside the First Amendment, this doctrine has never set well with many constitutional scholars. The Orwellian nature of a constitutional principle that regards some speech as "nonspeech" is, and should be, disturbing. The awkwardness of that semantic position is compounded by the First Amendment role reversal required by categorization: citizens usually are trusted to assess the value of speech for themselves, without screening by legislators or judges. In addition, some scholars are uncomfortable with the categorical nature of the doctrine, preferring that courts determine the First Amendment protection of speakers based on the factual context of individual cases, rather than on an abstract cost-benefit analysis of a category of speech per se.

Notwithstanding these criticisms, at least some version of the categorization principle has been central to free speech jurisprudence since the *Chaplinsky* decision in 1942. That year is significant, moreover, for surely it is no coincidence that the justices formalized the idea of categorization at the same time they began to invigorate First Amendment protection by adopting the Holmes/Brandeis version of the clear and present danger test for a variety of free speech problems. Faithfully applied, that test is strong medicine. The categorization principle provided a safety valve that enabled the justices to make a threshold determination whether such a strong First Amendment prescription was justified.

The categorization principle can be defended as a means of pruning First Amendment protection by excluding those types of speech that seem far removed from the values served by freedom of speech. This normative narrowing of free speech protection makes strategic sense because it husbands the credibility and strength of the courts for those occasions on which they are most needed, such as the periodic episodes of social stress illustrated by the two Red Scares of the past century. Embracing all literal speech within "freedom of speech" inevitably would force courts to dilute First Amendment protection in order to accommodate government restrictions of speech that carries low value and high costs. As a leading academic supporter of categorization has put it, "We must either water down the test for protection, . . . or conclude that certain categories of speech are to be tested under drastically different standards of protection."[3]

Even though categorization is defensible in principle, in practice drawing the line between protected and unprotected categories of speech at times, has proven to be extraordinarily difficult. In *Chaplinsky*, for example, the justices described the categories of unprotected speech they had in mind as "the lewd and obscene, the profane, the libelous, and the insulting or 'fighting' words." This was not a random sampling; these speech acts all had been prohibited at common law. A few weeks later, the Court added commercial advertising to the list (Valentine v. Christensen, 1942). As the following chapter will demonstrate, the Court's easy assumption that these categories of speech lacked any credible claim to First Amendment protection later encountered stiff resistance. Indeed, of the charter members of the *Chaplinsky* list, only fighting words and obscenity remain unprotected today. The ferment over the legitimacy of excluding particular categories of speech from First Amendment protection has ensured that the categorization principle itself has remained a continuing source of controversy. But as we shall see, notwithstanding the controversy and several post-*Chaplinsky* adjustments, the categorization principle continues to shape contemporary free speech jurisprudence.

THE CONTENT DISTINCTION PRINCIPLE

Although the doctrinal roots of the content distinction principle extend to Supreme Court decisions of the 1930s and 1940s, it did not emerge as a central organizing principle of free speech jurisprudence until several years after *Brandenburg* (Police Department v. Mosley, 1972). Since *Mosley*, the content distinction principle has come to dominate First Amendment doctrine. The content distinction principle complements the categorization principle. Just as the categorization principle posits that some types of speech are more valuable or harmful than are others, and thus more or less worthy of First Amendment protection, the content distinction principle is driven by a similar normative judgment that some types of speech restrictions are more threatening to First Amendment values than are others. The content distinction principle registers the Court's judgment that "government censorship" is the central evil against which the First Amendment is directed and that the "essence" of censorship is "content control" of speech (Mosley). Because laws that make distinctions based on the content of speech suggest a strong likelihood of censorship, they "presumptively violate the First Amendment" (City of Renton v. Playtime Theatres, Inc., 1986). The danger of censorship is reduced considerably when the government regulates expressive activity without regard to speech content. Thus, "content-neutral" restrictions, while still a subject of First Amendment concern, are far more freely allowed.

Content-based Restrictions

A "content-based" restriction is a law that the government "enacted for the purpose of restricting speech on the basis of content." (City of Renton v. Playtime Theatres, Inc., 1986). These restrictions are further divided into two subcategories: A content-based restriction turns either on the subject matter of the speech or on the viewpoint of the speaker. For example, a law that prohibited speech on the topic of terrorism (but allowed speech on other topics) would be a "subject-matter restriction," whereas a law that prohibited speech critical of the government's efforts to combat terrorism (but allowed speech that favored the government's efforts) would be a "viewpoint restriction." Although both types of content-based restrictions are constitutionally suspect and often are invalidated, they are not equally disfavored in First Amendment jurisprudence.

Many First Amendment scholars consider viewpoint discrimination to be the paradigmatic First Amendment violation,[4] and contemporary free speech jurisprudence makes it virtually impossible to justify any restriction that is based on government disapproval of the viewpoint of the speaker. This is because viewpoint restrictions, by definition, constitute government censorship. By contrast, there are times when subject-matter restrictions appear innocent of any censorial motive, and thus are permissible. For example, the First Amendment would not prohibit a school board at its meetings from limiting public discussion to the subjects included on the agenda for the meeting. Such a subject-matter restriction would organize rather than stifle debate. A school board, however, could not take the further step of limiting public comments to those supportive of school-board policies. The latter rule would constitute a viewpoint restriction that could be explained only by an official desire to silence opposition to school board policies.

When reviewing content-based restrictions of speech, whether based on subject matter or viewpoint, judges typically apply the familiar form of "strict scrutiny" that the modern Supreme Court has devised for the protection of fundamental constitutional rights. Strict scrutiny obligates the government to justify a restriction by satisfying a court that it is "necessary" to serve a "compelling governmental interest" (Simon & Schuster, Inc. v. Members of the New York State Crime Victims Board, 1991). "Necessary" is a term of art with specific doctrinal content. In order for a law to be necessary, there must be no alternative means available to the government for achieving the statutory goals in a manner less restrictive of free speech. The doctrinal meaning of a "compelling" interest is less clear. The Supreme Court has never provided, in its First Amendment decisions or elsewhere, a listing of the regulatory interests that qualify as compelling. Nor have the justices prescribed the criteria for judging whether any particular interest is compelling. The best that might be said is that a compelling interest is one that is sufficiently important to trump the fundamental right of free speech. The strict scrutiny test might therefore be expressed as requiring the government to prove that its speech restriction is the only way it can serve a public interest of overriding importance.

A content-based restriction thus is usually available to the government only as a last resort. The burden of justification is squarely on the government, and the Court has intentionally set the bar of strict scrutiny at a height that can be cleared only on rare occasions. The only exception to this strict prohibition of content-based restrictions of protected speech is for those subject-matter restrictions, such as the school-board agenda, that are benign in the First Amendment sense because they do not raise the specter of official censorship.

Content-neutral Restrictions

Contemporary free speech jurisprudence concentrates the heavy artillery of strict scrutiny on content-based restrictions, but eases up on content-neutral restrictions, that is, regulations of expressive activity that the government justifies without reference to the content of the restricted speech (City of Renton v. Playtime Theatres, 1988). Not only are content-neutral restrictions unlikely to reflect censorial purpose; they often encroach less on free speech rights than do content-based restrictions. Because content-based restrictions target particular types of speech content as harmful, they often prohibit entire categories of speech. Content-neutral restrictions never do so because they do not target any specific speech content as harmful per se. For example, while a content-based restriction might prohibit all speech opposing American involvement in the Vietnam War, a content-neutral restriction could hardly do so and remain content neutral. A content-neutral regulation might restrict antiwar speech, for example, by generally limiting the times or locations of public rallies or demonstrations, but such restrictions would fall far short of eliminating antiwar advocacy entirely from public discourse. Content-neutral restrictions thus do not *prohibit* speech. They *regulate* the time, place, or manner appropriate for speech. For this reason, courts and commentators often use the terms "time, place, and manner regulations" and "content-neutral restrictions" interchangeably.

Like content-based restrictions, content-neutral laws are subdivided into two groups: They can be either "direct" or "incidental" restrictions of speech. A restriction is "direct" if it targets an expressive activity, such as leafleting, picketing, and the like. If a regulation targets an activity that usually is not expressive in nature, any restriction on speech by that regulation on speech is considered "incidental." For example, a law that prohibits the delivery of all speeches in a public park is a speech restriction that is content-neutral (because it applies to speeches on all subjects) and direct (because it targets an expressive activity). A law that closes a public park during certain hours is not aimed directly at regulating speech, but it has the "incidental" effect of denying a venue to individuals who wish to deliver a speech in the park during the hours that it is closed.

As was the case with viewpoint and subject-matter restrictions, direct and incidental speech regulations receive different treatment in the courts. All direct regulations of speech, even if content-neutral, involve governmental targeting of expressive activity for special restriction. For that reason, although content-neutral regulations are not as troubling as are content-based restrictions, they always raise First Amendment concern. Content-neutral laws that have an incidental effect on freedom of speech only trigger First Amendment scrutiny if they operate similarly to direct regulations of speech.

The Supreme Court has identified two types of incidental restrictions that do so. The first type is a restriction that has "the inevitable effect of singling out those engaged in expressive activity" (Arcara v. Cloud Books, Inc., 1986). An example of such a law would be the imposition of a *specific* tax on the sale of large quantities of newsprint and ink (Minneapolis Star & Tribune Co. v. Minnesota Commissioner of Revenue, 1983). The second kind of incidental speech restriction that courts subject to First Amendment scrutiny is one that is applied to activity with "a significant expressive element" (Arcara). The classic example of such an application occurred in United States v. O'Brien (1968), in which a protestor who had publicly burned his draft card in protest of the Vietnam War was prosecuted for violating a federal law that generally outlawed intentional destruction of the cards. Accordingly, in the example given above, a law that required the closure of a public park during certain hours would trigger First Amendment scrutiny if it were applied to one who wished to give a speech in the park during those hours.

The Court's decision in Arcara v. Cloud Books (1986) illustrates the kind of incidental restriction on speech that the Court treats as raising no First Amendment concern. A state law authorized the closure of buildings that are used for unlawful sexual activity such as prostitution and lewdness. State authorities used that statutory authority to close a so-called "adult" bookstore. The Court held that the incidental effect of the closure in preventing the sale of adult books at the site did not implicate the First Amendment, even though, as we shall see, the First Amendment protects such sales so long as the books are not obscene. What mattered to the Court was that the regulatory target of the state was the sexual activity that occurred in the bookstore, not the sale of books. The Court explained, "[U]nlike the symbolic draft card burning in *O'Brien*, the sexual activity carried on in this case manifests absolutely no element of protected expression." Nor did the law single out bookstores or other premises dedicated to activity protected by the First Amendment: it applied generally to all buildings in which unlawful sexual activity took place. As *Arcara* illustrates, a pure incidental restriction of speech, that is, the kind of restriction that does not merit any First Amendment scrutiny, is one in which the government is neither applying the law to an expressive activity (such as symbolic draft card burning) nor restricting an activity that necessarily burdens speech (such as specific sales tax on newsprint).

Courts subject direct, content-neutral restrictions of speech—as well as the two types of incidental restrictions that essentially qualify as direct—to a form of "intermediate scrutiny." As the label suggests, intermediate scrutiny occupies a middle position between the highly demanding strict scrutiny generally afforded content-based restrictions and the highly deferential rationality review generally applied to governmental infringements of individual liberty that do not unduly burden the exercise of a fundamental, constitutional right. The Supreme Court has offered various formulations of the intermediate scrutiny appropriate for content-neutral restrictions of speech, but all prescribe a three-part test along the following lines (Ward v. Rock Against Racism, 1989). The government first must show that the restriction serves a "significant" or an "important" public interest. Although that interest need not be "compelling," it must carry more heft than the merely "legitimate" public purpose required in rationality review. Next, the restriction must be "narrowly tailored" to advance the identified public interest. The narrow tailoring requirement is less demanding for intermediate scrutiny than for strict scrutiny. The restriction need not be "necessary" for the government to serve the stated interest. It simply must not "burden substantially more speech than is necessary" to serve the government's objective. Unlike the expectation with respect to content-based restrictions, a content-neutral regulation need not be the "least restrictive or intrusive" means available to the government (Ward). While the second requirement of intermediate scrutiny, like the first, is less rigorous than strict scrutiny, it nevertheless remains considerably more demanding that the mere showing of some rational connection between governmental means and ends that is required when fundamental rights are not at stake. The third element of intermediate scrutiny for content-neutral restrictions, unlike the first two, is unique to the First Amendment. It requires the government to satisfy a reviewing court that its restriction leaves open "ample alternative avenues of communication" for a speaker to deliver his or her message to the public. If speakers are prevented from delivering their message, the law prohibits rather than regulates speech, and therefore operates more as a content-based than as a content-neutral restriction on expression.

The central question courts decide when evaluating the constitutionality of content-neutral restrictions of speech is not whether the government has engaged in censorship, but whether officials have overregulated expressive activity in their efforts to address competing social interests. The three-part test, in effect, defines three kinds of overregulation. Government officials might overregulate by inappropriately subordinating free speech to public interests that are not sufficiently important to justify the restriction. Or, they might regulate more speech than is required to accomplish their goals. Or finally, they might spread a regulatory blanket so broadly that speakers lose the capacity to express their views. In addition to providing a multifaceted consideration of the possible overregulation of speech, intermediate scrutiny of content-neutral restrictions affords considerable flexibility to reviewing courts, which are freed from the constraints of strict scrutiny and thus allowed to calibrate more finely the strength of regulatory ends and means on a case-by-case basis.[5] Context is crucial for evaluating content-neutral restrictions because they operate across terrain that is as vast and varied as is the range of government regulation itself.

Although the content distinction principle has proven to be more stable than has the categorization principle, it has not gone unchallenged. For one thing, the content distinction principle can be difficult to deploy. The line drawn between content-based and content-neutral restrictions is less treacherous than distinguishing between protected and unprotected speech, but at times the two kinds of restrictions blur. Moreover, the content neutrality of a restriction is not always a reliable guarantee that censorship is absent. United States v. O'Brien (1968) is perhaps the most striking illustration of the potential of the content distinction principle for underenforcing the anti-censorship rule of the First Amendment. In *O'Brien*, the Court used intermediate scrutiny to uphold application of the law that prohibited the intentional destruction of draft cards to an antiwar protester. Although the law was content-neutral (it prohibited all intentional destruction of draft cards), it strains credulity to view the prohibition, which Congress enacted only after war protestors began burning their draft cards, as anything other than an effort to silence a particularly provocative method of expressing dissent.

The central criticism of the content distinction principle has been more fundamental than these problems of application, however. It holds that content-neutral regulations, even if they are not the product of official censorship, are no less an "abridg[ment]" of freedom of speech than are content-based restrictions, and thus are equally deserving of strict scrutiny. In this criticism, the most important feature of content-neutral restrictions is their restrictiveness, not their neutrality. Although content-neutral laws do not prohibit the expression of entire categories of speech, as do many content-based restrictions, at times they are more restrictive than are comparable content-based restrictions.[6] For example, a content-neutral law that prohibits all speeches in a public park during certain hours is more restrictive than a viewpoint-based law that prohibits only speeches protesting the Vietnam War in the park during those hours. Why, then, should the former law be subjected to less stringent judicial review than the latter? Indeed, is it defensible that the former law likely would be upheld (assuming the hours of closure are reasonably limited) and that the latter law almost certainly would be invalidated?

The most convincing answer to this objection posits that First Amendment analysis should turn more on the *nature* of a law's restrictive effect on freedom of speech than on the *extent* of that effect. In this defense, the distinctive vice of content-based restrictions is not that they restrict speech, but that they distort public deliberation by gerrymandering the substantive boundaries of debate. Robbing public discourse of particular subjects—or worse, viewpoints—causes a "mutilation of the thinking process of the community," in the influential description of one scholar.[7] (Emphasis omitted.) This distortion is the essence of official censorship, which, the argument goes, is fundamentally inconsistent with freedom of speech. Although content-neutral regulations limit the quantum of speech, they do not, at least in the usual case, enforce official preferences for some subject matter or viewpoints over others. Content-neutral regulations limit all subjects and viewpoints indiscriminately. Moreover, all subjects and viewpoints remain equally eligible for public consideration in the speech contexts left untouched by the regulation.[8] The differing nature of the harms that flow from content-based and from content-neutral speech restrictions account for the different justification that each requires. Intermediate scrutiny is adequate for content-neutral restrictions because it enables judges to assure themselves that any particular law has not restricted too much speech. Strict scrutiny is usually necessary for content-based restrictions, however, because it requires judges to invalidate such laws unless the government can demonstrate that the restriction is not what it appears to be, an official act of censorship.

Content-neutral regulations, however, do restrict the freedom of speech, and on occasion, they disguise official censorship. The content distinction principle succeeds only to the extent judges review content-neutral restrictions, in Justice Thurgood Marshall's phrase, with a "salutary skepticism of governmental decisionmaking" (Clark v. Community for Creative Non-Violence, 1984, dissenting opinion). The most troubling difficulty associated with the content distinction principle has been that it engenders a false sense of security that content-neutral speech restrictions are trouble-free and that government officials can be trusted to balance the public's interest in free speech with other social goods. Legislators and, perhaps especially, government administrators, often overregulate expression even when they lack censorial motivation. Public officials cannot always be expected to sacrifice majoritarian demands for public order and instrumental efficiency in the name of First Amendment values. The courts must strike the final balance at intermediate scrutiny —conscientiously and independently—between speech and nonspeech interests for there to be meaningful constitutional protection.[9] Otherwise, as Justice Marshall has argued, the content distinction principle is turned on its head, "transform[ing] a ban against content distinctions from a floor that offers all persons at least equal liberty under the First Amendment into a ceiling that restricts persons to the protection of First Amendment equality—but nothing more" (Clark v. CCNV, 1984, dissenting opinion).

THE ARCHITECTURE OF FREE SPEECH ANALYSIS

Courts use the categorization principle and the content distinction principle in specific cases to create a framework within which to analyze free speech problems. The figure on p. 79 depicts the interaction of these two central organizing principles of free speech doctrine into one integrated methodology. In this most basic outline, a case that involves a content-based restriction of protected speech triggers strict scrutiny, and a court in most cases can be expected to invalidate the law. A case that involves a content-neutral restriction of protected speech is tracked to intermediate scrutiny, where a court tempers its review, thereby allowing more regulatory room for the government. Finally, a court which determines that the speech at issue falls within a category that is not protected by the First Amendment avoids any form of heightened scrutiny and simply engages in the low-level rationality review that is appropriate for cases that do not involve fundamental rights. Such regulations are routinely upheld precisely because fundamental individual rights are not at stake.

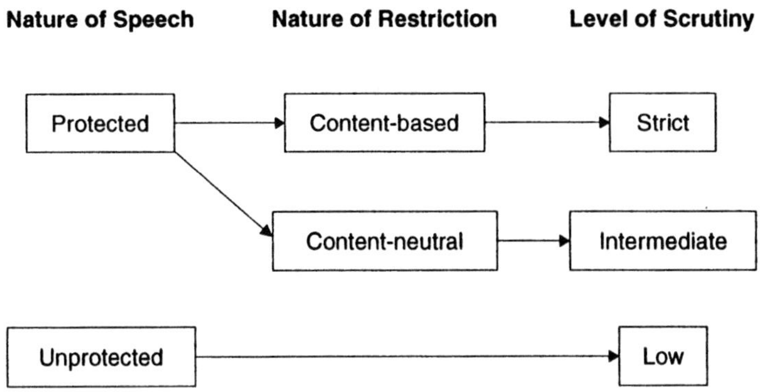

The interplay between the categorization principle and the content distinction principle helps to explain the development of subversive advocacy doctrine recounted in the preceding chapter. The Court began, in *Schenck* through *Whitney*, essentially with the view that subversive advocacy was an unprotected category of speech. For that reason, the justices routinely upheld restrictions of subversive advocacy without demanding special justifications by the state. *Brandenburg*, by contrast, represents the culmination of the Court's gradual acceptance of subversive advocacy as fully protected by the First Amendment. Laws that explicitly prohibit such advocacy, moreover, are based on the content of that speech and thus are constitutionally suspect. The *Brandenburg* test, which prescribed the strongest version of the clear and present danger test ever accepted by the Court, comes into focus as a specific application of strict scrutiny to such speech. *Brandenburg*, in short, reversed the Court's original approach to the problem of subversive advocacy because the justices finally had come to accept that category of speech as fully protected by the First Amendment.

The integration of the categorization principle and the content distinction principle have provided the framework within which the Supreme Court has developed contemporary free speech doctrine. The figure above depicts only the basic framework in free speech cases. At times, the Court's struggle to resolve free speech problems has led the justices to revise that methodology in important ways. Those revisions, in a sense, are the story of the development of contemporary free speech jurisprudence, which is the subject of the remaining chapters.[10]

NOTES

1. William Van Alstyne, "A Graphic Review of the Free Speech Clause," *California Law Review* 70 (1982): 107–50, p. 113.

2. See Frederick Schauer, "Speech and 'Speech'—Obscenity and 'Obscenity': An Exercise in the Interpretation of Constitutional Language," *The Georgetown Law Journal* 67 (1979): 899–933, pp. 902–10.

3. Frederick Schauer, "Categories and the First Amendment: A Play in Three Acts," *Vanderbilt Law Review* 34 (1981): 265–307, pp. 271–72.

4. Kathleen M. Sullivan and Gerald Gunther, *First Amendment Law* 193 (New York: Foundation Press, 1999).

5. See, e.g., Geoffrey R. Stone, "Content Regulation and the First Amendment," *William and Mary Law Review* 25 (1983): 189–252, pp. 190–93.

6. See Martin H. Redish, "The Content Distinction in First Amendment Analysis," *Stanford Law Review* 34 (1981): 113–51, pp. 128–39.

7. Alexander Meiklejohn, "Free Speech and its Relation to Self-government," in *Political Freedom: The Constitutional Powers of the People* 27 (New York: Harper & Brothers, 1960). (Emphasis omitted.)

8. The argument in this paragraph is drawn from Stone, *Content Regulation*, pp. 197–200.

9. The argument in this paragraph borrows from my article, Keith Werhan: "The O'Briening of Free Speech Methodology," *Arizona State Law Journal* 19 (1987): 635–79, pp. 657–58.

10. The discussion in this chapter has borrowed from my article, "The Liberalization of Freedom of Speech on a Conservative Court," *Iowa Law Review* 80 (1994): 51–100, pp. 53–54, 66–67.

5

The Codified First Amendment

[T]he diversity of communicative activity and governmental concerns is so wide as to make it implausible to apply the same tests or analytical tools to the entire range of First Amendment problems. This premise provides the impetus for making First Amendment doctrine more precise and at the same time more complex, developing tools and tests that are greater in number but consequently applicable to increasingly smaller categories of First Amendment issues.

Frederick Schauer*

The interplay between the categorization and content distinction principles has led the Supreme Court to codify free speech doctrine. This codification, as Frederick Schauer recognized, carries both risk and reward for the development of a workable jurisprudence. On one hand, codification promotes consistency and predictability by systemizing First Amendment doctrine. On the other hand, categorization risks over-formalizing the doctrine and thus forcing outcomes in particular cases that betray rather than further free speech values. The promises and pitfalls of codification mirror each other: Codification offers to create, as it threatens to undermine, doctrinal coherence.

This chapter surveys the primary elements of the Supreme Court's codification of free speech doctrine by speech category. According to the usual workings of the content distinction principle, a strong presumption of unconstitutionality attaches whenever the government targets a particular category of speech for any special prohibition or restraint. The best avenue of escape from the nearly certain death that awaits such a law is a demonstration that the targeted category does not merit full protection by the First Amendment. The categorization principle invites such demonstrations. The justices' use of categorization over the years has resulted in a series of special doctrinal rules applicable to particular categories of speech. On occasion, as we have seen with respect to subversive advocacy, the Court has specially tailored the strict scrutiny rule to fit a category of fully protected speech (Brandenburg). We shall now see that in other instances, as with respect to obscenity and child pornography, the justices have developed particularized definitions of certain categories of speech in order to exclude them from First Amendment protection. And we shall also see that, as with respect to commercial advertising, the Court has formulated a middle position that provides an intermediate level of constitutional protection for still other categories of speech.

This chapter reviews the major categories of speech other than subversive advocacy for which the Court has developed special principles, with one conspicuous exception. Defamation is not considered here because it is discussed in the volume on freedom of the press in the *Reference Guides to the United States Constitution* series of which this book is a part.[1] Because First Amendment defamation cases typically involve the press, that speech category is more appropriately covered in that volume.

PROVOCATIVE SPEECH

In Brandenburg's speech, discussed in Chapter 3, the Ku Klux Klan leader relied on racial and anti-Semitic epithets to warn of a rising tide of white supremacist feeling that might culminate in "some revengeance" being taken against those who "continue[d] to suppress the white, Caucasian race." He also called for the removal of African Americans to Africa and of Jews to Israel. Brandenburg's speech took place on a farm before about a dozen true believers, and his urgings produced no action on their part. But what if Brandenburg had given that same speech, surrounded by his hooded followers, on a street corner in a crowded urban center, before a large, racially diverse audience that included many people who were deeply offended by his rhetoric and who were violently opposed to his ideology?

In such a setting, Brandenburg's speech would have presented a "provocative speech" problem, which is the mirror image of subversive advocacy. Although provocative speech, like subversive advocacy, threatens disruption of public order, it does so for a different reason. With respect to subversive advocacy, the fear is that the speech might persuade an audience to act illegally, as described by the following causal chain:

speech → persuasion → action → harm.

By contrast, the concern over provocative speech is that it might arouse such hostility among audience members that they respond violently against the speaker, or more generally into riot, or at the least, that such speech might offend the sensibilities of some listeners. The causal chain for provocative speech is thus revised:

speech → rejection → reaction → harm.

Not only is the government's assessment of the sources of potential disorder reversed for subversive advocacy and provocative speech, but also the free speech concerns are flipped in the two problems. Advocates of free expression worry that official efforts to silence subversive advocacy invariably end up stifling legitimate communications between speakers and their audiences. When government officials control speech because of its provocative nature, the First Amendment threat is that they are enforcing a "heckler's veto" over speakers with unpopular messages, that is, that they are allowing audience disagreement with a message to silence the messenger.

Notwithstanding these differences, the free speech problems presented by subversive advocacy and provocative speech have much in common. First, in both settings the central challenge facing reviewing courts is deciding when speakers should be liable for the actions of their audiences. Second, the speech that government officials regard as subversive or provocative typically is delivered by dissidents whose views sharply challenge the dominant sentiments of their communities. Finally, in both situations it is all too easy for government officials to conflate their legitimate interest in protecting public safety and order during truly dangerous emergencies with the impulse to protect the community from the "threat" of "dangerous ideas." Majoritarian censorship is thus a hovering presence in both subversive speech and provocative speech problems.

Hostile Audiences

The Supreme Court first took up the provocative speech issue in the early 1940s, not long after the justices had accepted the Holmes/Brandeis brief for strongly protecting freedom of speech as a fundamental, constitutional right. Jesse Cantwell, a Jehovah's Witness, was convicted of "inciting others to breach of the peace" as a result of his proselytizing on a public sidewalk in a "thickly populated," predominantly Catholic neighborhood in New Haven, Connecticut (Cantwell v. Connecticut, 1940). Cantwell stopped two men, who were Roman Catholics, and received their permission to play a phonograph record for them. The record, entitled "Enemies," attacked the Catholic Church and its pope in robust terms. According to the Court's recitation of the facts, the two men "were incensed by the contents of the record and were tempted to strike Cantwell unless he went away." There was no violence, however. When the two men told Cantwell to leave, he did.

The Court reversed Cantwell's conviction. The justices began by establishing their default position on provocative speech, that speakers enjoy "a right peacefully to impart [their] views to others." The government can trump that right, the Court held, only by proving a "clear and present danger of riot, disorder, interference with traffic upon the public streets, or other immediate threat to public safety, peace, or order." The First Amendment protected Cantwell because he had spoken "peacefully": He had not assaulted, threatened, or abused his audience. He was guilty only of trying "to persuade a willing listener to buy a book or to contribute money in the interest of what Cantwell, however misguided others may think him, conceived to be true religion." It was the content of Cantwell's speech that "naturally" had offended the two men. Cantwell had intended no offense, and the offense his speech had caused was itself insufficient to establish any "clear and present menace to public peace and order." The Court explained:

> In the realm of religious faith, and in that of political belief, sharp differences arise. In both fields the tenets of one man may seem the rankest error to his neighbor. To persuade others to his own point of view, the pleader, as we know, at times, resorts to exaggeration, to vilification of men who have been, or are, prominent in church or state, and even to false statement. But the people of this nation have ordained in the light of history, that, in spite of the probability of excesses and abuses, these liberties are, in the long view, essential to enlightened opinion and right conduct on the part of the citizens of a democracy.

The Court's adoption of the clear and present danger test in *Cantwell* provided strong constitutional protection for provocative speech, essentially limiting the government to silencing speakers whose remarks trigger a hostile audience reaction only as a last resort to maintain public order.

The justices elaborated and reinforced their acceptance of provocative expression within freedom of speech later in the 1940s when they set aside a conviction of an anti-Semitic, fascist speaker for violating a state law which prohibited speech that "stirs the public to anger, invites dispute, brings about a condition of unrest, or creates a disturbance" (Terminiello v. City of Chicago, 1949). In language that is often quoted, the Court explained, ironically, that the statute described protected rather than unprotected speech. The Court in *Terminiello* wrote:

> [A] function of free speech under our system of government is to invite dispute. It may indeed best serve its high purpose when it induces a condition of unrest, creates dissatisfaction with conditions as they are, or even stirs people to anger. Speech is often provocative and challenging. It may strike at prejudices and preconceptions and have profound unsettling effects as it presses for acceptance of an idea. That is why freedom of speech, though not absolute, . . . is nevertheless protected against censorship or punishment, unless shown likely to produce a clear and present danger of a serious substantive evil that rises far above public inconvenience, annoyance, or unrest. . . . There is no room under our Constitution for a more restrictive view. For the alternative would lead to standardization of ideas either by legislatures, courts, or dominant political or community groups.

After *Cantwell* and *Terminiello*, there seemed little doubt of the Court's commitment to protecting provocative speech under the clear and present danger rubric.

The Court's acceptance, even celebration, of provocative speech in these original cases is all the more striking when compared with the justices' initial, almost instinctual rejection of free speech claims in the original subversive advocacy cases that arose during World War I. But in truth, the facts of *Cantwell* and the state law in *Terminiello* made these cases easy marks for the clear and present danger test. Cantwell's speech was delivered to an audience of two, hardly the makings of a riot. And even though Cantwell's listeners apparently considered registering their offense over Cantwell's choice of records violently, Cantwell defused the situation by quietly acquiescing to their demand that he depart. In *Terminiello*, the Court never even assessed the factual context of the speech, which was far more explosive than that of *Cantwell*. The justices believed that the state law was so overbroad that no speaker could be convicted constitutionally under its terms, regardless of the facts. (The "overbreadth" doctrine is discussed in the following chapter.) Thus the potential difficulty of applying the clear and present danger test to speech that many members of a community believe to be highly threatening, a difficulty that would split the Court wide open in *Dennis*, lay dormant in these early, easy cases.

But not for long. Just over two years after deciding *Terminiello*, the Court upheld the disorderly conduct conviction of a "Young Progressive" for his soapbox oratory one Friday evening on a street corner in Syracuse, where such Friday addresses had become customary (Feiner v. New York, 1951). Feiner's speech included what the Court described as "derogatory remarks" about President Harry S. Truman (a "bum"), the Mayor of Syracuse ("a champagne-sipping bum"), and the American Legion ("a Nazi Gestapo"). This was not all. The Court reported that Feiner, who spoke in a "loud, high-pitched voice" before a racially mixed crowd of about 75 to 80 people, "gave the impression that he was endeavoring to arouse the Negro people against the whites, urging that they rise up in arms and fight for equal rights. The statements before such a mixed audience 'stirred up a little excitement.'" At least one member of the audience threatened violence if the police officers on hand did not put an end to Feiner's speech, and soon thereafter, the police dispersed the crowd. They arrested Feiner after he had ignored several demands to stop his speech.

The Court in *Feiner* followed the doctrine of *Cantwell* and *Terminiello*, but not the spirit of those two decisions. The justices accepted, almost summarily, a trial court finding that the police had silenced Feiner because "a clear danger of disorder was threatened," and not because of an intention to suppress his point of view. Chief Justice Vinson, writing for the Court, explained, "[Feiner] was neither arrested nor convicted for the making or the content of his speech. Rather, it was the reaction which it actually engendered." But as Justice Douglas noted in dissent, those two considerations cannot be so easily disentangled, for as in *Cantwell* it was the content of Feiner's speech that had triggered the audience reaction that led to his arrest. "[I]f the police throw their weight on the side of those who would break up meetings," Douglas argued, "the police become the new censors of speech." Indeed, Justice Black in his dissent asserted outright that Feiner had been convicted "for his unpopular views," and that by legitimating the conviction, the Court had sanctioned "a simple and readily available technique by which cities and states can with impunity subject all speeches . . . to the supervision and censorship of the local police."

Vinson responded to Black and Douglas by arguing that Feiner had not engaged in the kind of peaceful advocacy that had characterized *Cantwell*. To Vinson, Feiner left his constitutional protections behind when he "passe[d] the bounds of argument or persuasion and under[took] incitement to riot." The Court in *Cantwell* had hinted that a speaker intent on provoking a hostile reaction from the audience might be open to prosecution for any resulting disturbance of the peace, and Vinson suggested that Feiner's name-calling and the pitch of his voice pointed to such an intent. Such evidence provides an unconvincing basis upon which to deny a speaker First Amendment protection, however. As Justice Douglas, the author of the Court's opinion in *Terminiello*, reminded, it was "not unusual" for a speaker to resort to "exaggeration, to vilification of ideas and men, to the making of false charges." Such was an unavoidable byproduct of free speech. Moreover, it would betray rather than follow *Cantwell* to infer provocative intent from the controversial nature of a speaker's remarks or from an audience's hostile reaction to those remarks. As Justice Black, also evoking *Terminiello*, observed, violent disagreement often results from public discussion on "controversial topics." And finally, although *Cantwell* and *Terminiello* had left open the possibility of halting provocative speech when there was a clear and present danger of serious disorder, Black was surely correct in concluding, "It seems farfetched to suggest that [there had been] any imminent threat of riot or public disorder in *Feiner*."

Chief Justice Vinson wrote the majority opinion in *Feiner* less than six months before his plurality opinion in *Dennis* eviscerated the clear and present danger test. The two Vinson opinions shared a structural similarity: They proclaimed freedom of speech in the abstract, but in application they accorded decisive weight to official judgments that threatening expressive activity be limited in the interest of preserving public order. In both opinions, Vinson set the clear and present danger bar so low that it imposed no real barrier to law-enforcement officials intent on safeguarding the public from the perils they ascribed to dissident speech. In both instances, the bar was sufficiently low to allow considerable governmental censorship as well. Justice Black in his *Feiner* dissent showed the distance between a strong clear and present danger test and Vinson's flimsier version when he argued that even in a "critical situation," police officers were under a First Amendment obligation to make "all reasonable efforts" to protect the speaker's right of free speech. The First Amendment norm reflected by the clear and present danger test—that freedom of speech can be overcome only as a last resort to preserve public order—was lost in *Feiner* on the eve of *Dennis*.

The Court decided *Feiner* at the height of the Second Red Scare, a time in which the balance between individual freedom and state power had lurched decidedly in the direction of the latter. The pendulum swung back when the Red Scare receded and the nation took up the struggle for civil rights for African Americans. Feiner's speech had foreshadowed that struggle, but the wave of civil rights demonstrations in the 1960s, and official reaction to it, cast *Feiner* in a new light. Public officials in the segregated South certainly could claim that experience had proven the potential for violent public reaction against civil rights demonstrators. If anything, the threat of violence was far more ominous in southern streets and squares of the 1960s than it had been on Feiner's street corner. At the same time, nowhere was the censorial potential of *Feiner* more manifest than in the massive resistance by southern officials to civil rights demonstrations in their communities. Rarely, if ever, has the United States experienced such a formidable "heckler's veto" of dissident speech.

The pivotal, post-*Feiner* moment occurred in 1963, when the Court decided Edwards v. South Carolina. In *Edwards*, the Court reversed 187 convictions for breach of the peace lodged against African American students who had participated in coordinated protests on the grounds of the South Carolina State House. The protestors marched in small groups and carried signs decrying the state's official policy of racial segregation. Gradually, a crowd of between 200 and 300 onlookers gathered, but neither they nor the protestors threatened any violence. The police on the scene nevertheless demanded that the protestors disperse. The protesters responded by singing patriotic and religious songs, and they were promptly arrested. The Court described the peacefulness of the *Edwards* protest as "a far cry from the situation in *Feiner*." That peremptory description has had the effect of marginalizing *Feiner*, restricting its reach to cases involving speakers who had actually intended to "provoke[] a given group to a hostile reaction" (Cohen v. California, 1971). The Court in *Edwards*, by contrast, linked the South Carolina protestors to *Cantwell*: They had done nothing other than exercise "basic" First Amendment rights "in their most pristine form." Vindicating the dissenting opinions of Justices Black and Douglas in *Feiner*, the Court in *Edwards* concluded that the demonstrators had been convicted simply because "the opinion" they expressed was "sufficiently opposed to the views of the majority of the community to attract a crowd and necessitate police protection." Freedom of speech, the justices declared, "does not permit a State to make criminal the peaceful expression of unpopular views." The justices had revived the spirit of *Cantwell*.

The boldness of the *Edwards* declaration that speakers are immune from liability arising from hostile audience responses to the content of their message, was tested throughout the civil rights era. Significantly, the Court consistently overturned disorderly conduct convictions of civil rights demonstrators who contributed to crowd-control situations that were a "far cry" from that in *Edwards*. The most revealing example of the new judicial solicitousness toward provocative speakers occurred in the late 1960s, when a peaceful civil rights march in Chicago drew an expanding crowd of "unruly" onlookers. The police officers on the scene, who were accompanied by a city attorney, ordered the demonstrators to disperse in order to prevent what they believed, in apparent good faith, to be "an impending public disorder." The protestors were arrested after they refused to comply with that order. The Court acknowledged that the actions of the police were "reasonable" and that their motives were "laudable," and this being the case, it would appear that they had attempted to stop the demonstration because they believed there was clear and present danger of a riot. Even so, the justices overturned the conviction on the basis of the *Edwards* principle. It was the crowd, not the demonstrators, who had been disorderly (Gregory v. City of Chicago, 1969).

The justices brought hostile audiences doctrine up to date in Texas v. Johnson (1989), when they reversed the conviction of a demonstrator who had burned a flag of the United States as an act of public protest against the policies and actions of the Reagan administration. Johnson was convicted under a Texas law that prohibited "flag desecration," which the law defined as "defac[ing], damag[ing], or otherwise physically mistreat[ing]. . . [a flag] in a way that the actor knows will seriously offend one or more persons likely to observe or discover his action." Texas defended the law, in part, by invoking its interest in preventing breaches of the peace. But the only evidence the state could muster of any hostile reaction was the testimony of several observers who had been seriously offended by Johnson's burning of the flag. The Court in *Johnson* buried *Feiner* deeper by holding that such a scant showing would not do. The justices refused to indulge the presumption that "an audience that takes serious offense at particular expression is necessarily likely to disturb the peace and that the expression may be prohibited on this basis."

The Court in *Johnson* updated the *Edwards* revival of *Cantwell* by incorporating the *Brandenburg* revision of the clear and present danger test into hostile audiences doctrine. The Court wrote, "[W]e have not permitted the government to assume that every expression of a provocative idea will incite a riot, but have instead required careful consideration of the actual circumstances surrounding such expression, asking whether the expression 'is directed to inciting or producing imminent lawless action and is likely to incite or produce such action.'" The Court's application of the *Brandenburg* test in *Johnson* suggests that, as with subversive advocacy, it will be very difficult for government prosecutors to convince the courts that provocative speech is "likely" to produce harm in the absence of proof that such harm has actually occurred (see NAACP v. Claiborne Hardware Co., 1982).

Fighting Words

There is one exception to the Court's otherwise strong protection of provocative speech. The justices allow the prohibition of so-called "fighting words" (Chaplinsky v. New Hampshire, 1942). A fighting word is an insult that a speaker addresses to another, "face-to-face," which has "a direct tendency" to cause a violent response by one who has been so insulted (Gooding v. Wilson, 1972). Such personal insults are excluded from First Amendment protection because the justices regard them as essentially devoid of speech value. Fighting words typically constitute "no essential part of any exposition of ideas" (Chaplinsky); nor are they "in any proper sense communication of information or opinion safeguarded by the Constitution" (Cantwell v. Connecticut, 1940). Given the nearly total absence of free speech value, the threat that fighting words pose to "public order" clearly outweighs their "social value as a step to truth" (Chaplinsky).

It might seem surprising, but this limited exclusion of "personal abuse" (Cantwell) from the First Amendment protection otherwise afforded provocative speech has generated considerable controversy over the years. The source of the controversy is the tension that exists between the fighting words exception and the general sweep of provocative speech precedent. This tension is highlighted by the Supreme Court's decision in Cohen v. California (1971). *Cohen* is not a fighting words case. It involved the conviction of a young man for wearing a jacket with the inscription, "Fuck the Draft," during the height of the controversy over America's participation in the Vietnam War. Because Cohen's statement was a comment on the draft directed generally to anyone who might read it, and was not an insult directed personally at any individual, the expression fell into the broader category of speech that provokes a hostile audience. Nevertheless, the Court's rationale for invalidating Cohen's conviction undermined the justification for subjecting all fighting words to governmental prohibition.[2]

The state had argued that the inscription on Cohen's jacket was "inherently likely to cause violent reaction." This concern was hardly implausible. Because of the passions often aroused by antiwar advocacy during the Vietnam War, one might well anticipate that one or more of the many viewers of Cohen's jacket would so deeply resent such a vivid statement of protest that they would react violently against Cohen. But the Court held, in line with the hostile audiences precedent, that simple fear of violent reaction could not justify the state in prohibiting speech. The justices explained that the state's regulatory justification "amount[ed] to little more than the self-defeating proposition that to avoid physical censorship of one who has not sought to provoke such a response by a hypothetical coterie of the violent and lawless, the States may more appropriately effectuate that censorship themselves." *Cohen* thus reiterated the position of Justices Black and Douglas in their dissenting opinions in *Feiner*, which the Court has followed in hostile audience cases since *Edwards*.

Cohen thus suggests the following question: If the state cannot generally presume provocative speech to be "inherently" likely to cause violent reaction, why can it make such a presumption with respect to fighting words? If anything, the governmental interest in preventing group violence and possible riot should weigh more heavily than the one-on-one confrontation threatened by fighting words. The best response to this disparity in treatment is to be found on the speech side of the balance. The First Amendment premise in a hostile audience problem is that a *public* speaker is exercising the core free speech right of attempting to persuade an audience to a point of view, albeit an unpopular one. That core right, the argument goes, is not implicated when a speaker personally insults another. Not only are such insults typically for private rather than for public consumption, but also they are not "essential" (Chaplinsky) to the communication of a point of view. Paradoxically, then, the government's regulatory interest in preserving public order justifies the prohibition of fighting words not because that interest is especially strong, but because the speaker's free speech claim is especially weak.

It is the presumed weakness of the speech value of fighting words that *Cohen* questions most sharply, however. In *Cohen*, the state claimed authority to punish use of the word "fuck" as an unnecessary and unseemly way to express a point of view. The justices reminded, however, that the First Amendment generally left rhetorical strategy to the speaker, not to the state. Moreover, the Court recognized that language often serves a "dual communicative function," conveying speaker emotion as well as cognitive content. The statements "Stop the Draft" and "Fuck the Draft" each deliver an antidraft message. But who would claim that the impact—and meaning—of those statements are identical? Cohen's resort to the familiar expletive conveyed the depth of his revulsion against the war effort, a communication that might have been impossible with language that was more culturally acceptable. The very crudity and offensiveness of Cohen's use of profanity, in this sense, was essential to his message.

While personal insults undoubtedly at times are gratuitous, as are many public uses of profanity, is Chaplinsky's assumption that fighting words are *never* essential to communication, in the *Cohen* sense, correct? The factors that caused the Court to reject Cohen's conviction were present in *Chaplinsky*, the very decision that launched the fighting words exception. Chaplinsky, like Cantwell before him, was a Jehovah's Witness whose sidewalk proselytizing stirred his audience to anger. After a disturbance erupted, a police officer dispersed the crowd and led Chaplinsky toward the station house. En route, they happened upon the city marshal. Words were exchanged, during which Chaplinsky called the marshal "a God damned racketeer" and "a damned Fascist." The latter insult, leveled as it was near the beginning of World War II, surely must have stung, but did the insult's harm "clearly outweigh" its value as speech? Certainly, Chaplinsky's use of "Fascist" carried more First Amendment value than the usual insult. When leveled at the government official whom he considered responsible for violating his freedom of speech, Chaplinsky's use of "Fascist" had the undeniable ring of political protest, in much the way that Cohen's use of the expletive "fuck" drove home his strong opposition to the draft. Moreover, the risk of violent reaction seemed especially unlikely—or at least, untenable—in *Chaplinsky.* After all, Chaplinsky, while he was in police custody, insulted a government official. For the city marshal to attack Chaplinsky under such circumstances would have amounted to official misconduct. Thus, even if the *Chaplinsky* Court was correct that fighting words often, or even usually, do not merit First Amendment protection, that assumption would not seem to hold in Chaplinsky's case.

These arguments for First Amendment protection were unavailing in *Chaplinsky*, however, because the Court did not consider the particular speech context in which Chaplinsky had insulted the marshal. Having excluded the category of fighting words from First Amendment protection, the justices simply determined, as an abstract matter, that the insult "damned Fascist," delivered face-to-face, so qualified. They did not pause to calibrate the free speech, cost-benefit balance in Chaplinsky's case itself. And in the years since *Chaplinsky,* the Court has never developed a satisfactory, principled method for separating the "fighting words" that should merit constitutional protection from those that should not. At least, the justices have not done so formally.

Although the Court continues to declare that laws which generally prohibit fighting words are consistent with the First Amendment, *Chaplinsky* marks the one and only occasion on which the justices have upheld a fighting words conviction. The most revealing episode occurred in 1972, when the Court managed to overturn convictions in four fighting words cases without explicitly challenging the doctrinal integrity of *Chaplinsky*. Each of the 1972 quartet involved a speech context in which the speaker's resort to epithets and insults at least arguably served a communicative function similar to that recognized in *Cohen*, which the Court had decided the preceding year. Two of the four directly replicated *Chaplinsky*, involving angry citizens who had cursed an arresting officer (Gooding v. Wilson, 1972; Lewis v. New Orleans, 1972). These speakers, as had Chaplinsky and Cohen, used profanity to protest official action that they believed violated their individual rights. The two other cases tracked *Cohen*, but not *Chaplinsky*. They involved speakers who had used profanity in comments they had made at a public meeting (Brown v. Oklahoma, 1972; Rosenfeld v. New Jersey, 1972).

The best reading of the 1972 quartet might be that the Court has limited the meaning of fighting words, in practice if not in doctrine, to the utterance of face-to-face insults in speech contexts which make clear that the insult carries no First Amendment value. Such a limitation of the fighting words exception would be appropriate, but ironic. It would be appropriate, in light of *Cohen*, to trim *Chaplinsky* by limiting the fighting words exception to instances in which a speaker's insults truly had been private, gratuitous, and therefore valueless in the First Amendment sense. If the 1972 quartet means that the category of fighting words is so limited, the ironic result is that *Chaplinsky* no longer holds in the factual context of that case, namely, when individuals insult government officials as criticism of their official conduct.

Hate Speech

Hate speech is an old problem that has generated First Amendment controversy and confusion in recent years. There is disagreement even over the precise contours of "hate speech" as a speech category, but a useful working definition includes speech that is insulting or threatening to members of groups that have suffered a history of discrimination in American society. It is a sobering fact of American history that there are a number of such groups, including ethnic minorities, women, gays and lesbians, Jews, and other religious minorities. Race, however, has marked the principal fault line in hate speech jurisprudence, as it has more generally in American society.

The Supreme Court took up the problem of hate speech for the first time shortly after deciding *Feiner* (Beauharnais v. Illinois, 1952). Beauharnais was president of a group called the White Circle League. He had organized the distribution of leaflets that called on the elected leaders of Chicago to resist the "invasion" of the white race by blacks. Not surprisingly for this genre of protest, the leaflets were laced with derogatory characterizations of African Americans. For example, they described African Americans as a group that engages in "aggressions, rapes, [and] robberies," and that indulges in the use of marijuana. Beauharnais was prosecuted under a state law that made it illegal to publicly distribute any material that "portrays depravity, criminality, unchastity, or lack of virtue of a class of citizens of any race, color, creed or religion," and that either "exposes the citizens of any race, color, creed or religion to contempt, derision or obloquy," or "is productive of breach of the peace or riots."

The Court in *Beauharnais* read the state statue as a criminal prohibition of "group libel" and regarded the derogatory statements in the leaflets as libelous of African Americans as a group. Because libel of an individual traditionally had not been regarded as within the freedom of speech, Justice Felix Frankfurter, writing for the majority, reasoned that libel of a group should not be protected either. He buttressed this conclusion by referencing the "tragic" history which demonstrated that "willful purveyors of falsehood concerning racial and religious groups promote strife and tend powerfully to obstruct the manifold adjustments required for free, ordered life in a metropolitan, polyglot community." It would "deny experience," Frankfurter wrote, to provide a First Amendment license for "extreme racial and religious propaganda" designed to produce a "powerful impact" on its audience. To do so, Frankfurter charged, would fashion the Constitution into a tool for the incitement of racial and religious violence that denied members of targeted groups "their equal right to the exercise of their liberties."

Justice Frankfurter's eloquent majority opinion triggered a strong response from Justice Black, one of four dissenters in *Beauharnais*. Black began by noting that Beauharnais's leafleting was "a genuine effort to petition [his] elected representatives." The freedom to so petition, he reminded, has a long history in Anglo-American constitutionalism, and is itself explicitly protected by the First Amendment. For Black, "Every expansion of the law of criminal libel . . . to punish discussions of matters of public concern means a corresponding invasion of the area dedicated to free expression by the First Amendment." *Beauharnais* was not *Chaplinsky*, he argued. The leaflets, unlike personal, face-to-face insults, constituted "arguments on questions of wide public interest and importance." In Black's view, Beauharnais had been convicted "for publicly expressing strong views in favor of segregation." He thus found the majority guilty of "sugar-coating . . . [a] system of state censorship."

The analyses of Justices Frankfurter and Black in *Beauharnais* anticipated the basic positions for and against the constitutional legitimacy of hate speech regulation in contemporary free speech commentary. The five-four split on the Court in *Beauharnais* foreshadowed as well, the deep fissure the controversy over hate speech has opened among First Amendment scholars. But the *Beauharnais* decision itself, although never overruled, almost certainly has not stood the test of time. The Court itself has undermined the central position of *Beauharnais*—that group libel is unprotected because individual libel is unprotected—by deciding that defamatory speech is generally entitled to at least some measure of First Amendment protection (Gertz v. Robert Welch, Inc., 1974; New York Times v. Sullivan, 1964). The Court also has held outright that the First Amendment disallows defamation claims arising from statements that, like group libel, do not identify individuals (New York Times).

With the erosion of *Beauharnais*'s grounding on defamation law, the exclusion of hate speech from freedom of speech must be justified by its own categorical balancing analysis. It certainly is possible, citing the history to which Justice Frankfurter referred in *Beauharnais*, to make the *Chaplinsky* case that the harm associated with hate speech clearly outweighs its communicative value. The alignment with *Chaplinsky* is especially powerful when hate speech, like a fighting word, is directed personally and face-to-face to the member of a group that historically has suffered such verbal abuse. But when hate speech is employed by a public speaker in an effort to persuade an audience to a point of view, the more fitting analogy is the hostile audiences precedent. That doctrine, as we have seen, grants strong First Amendment protection to speakers who provoke or offend their audience by the content of their ideas or the language of their expression.

The difficulty of outlawing hate speech outside the fighting words context was highlighted in the best-known judicial encounter with this phenomenon. In 1970, the National Socialist Party of America, better known as the American Nazi Party, announced plans for a demonstration in Skokie, Illinois, a small, suburban village just north of Chicago. Skokie has a significant Jewish community, and many of its residents at the time were Holocaust survivors. The Skokie demonstration was to be one of a series that the Party had planned for various Jewish communities.

All of the makings for an explosive confrontation were present in Skokie. Party members planned to wear uniforms that mimicked those of the Nazi storm troopers of the Third Reich. Many residents of Skokie objected strongly to their city being selected as a site for a Nazi demonstration, and plans for a potent counter-demonstration quickly took shape. Meanwhile, at Skokie's request, a state court issued an injunction that prohibited anyone, while within the village, from, among other things, "parading" in Nazi uniforms and "displaying the swastika." The Illinois Supreme Court, however, quickly overturned the injunction as a violation of the First Amendment (Village of Skokie v. National Socialist Party of America, 1978). The deeply offensive nature of these Nazi symbols for many Skokie residents, the court ruled, could not justify their banishment. Such symbols "spoke," and even though what they expressed was anathema to almost everyone in and out of Skokie, the First Amendment protected this expression to the same degree it protects those who speak out against Fascism and anti-Semitism. ("Symbolic expression" is discussed in the final section of this chapter.)

While the injunction suit was pending, Skokie enacted several ordinances in a fallback effort to block the Nazi march. One of those ordinances, naturally enough, tracked the Illinois group libel law that the Supreme Court had upheld in *Beauharnais*. It outlawed the dissemination of material that intentionally "promotes and incites hatred against persons by reason of their race, national origin, or religion." The leader of the American Nazi Party successfully challenged the new Skokie ordinances in federal court (Collin v. Smith, 1978). Consistently with both subversive advocacy and hostile audiences precedent, the federal court of appeals ruled that the mere tendency of a speech act to produce violence was not sufficient to justify governmental suppression. Neither the unacceptability of Nazi ideology nor the torment their demonstration surely would cause many Skokie residents, particularly Holocaust survivors, justified the village's efforts to block the demonstration. In the process of upholding the First Amendment right of the Nazis to march in Skokie, the court of appeals made clear its belief that *Beauharnais* had long since been overwhelmed by contemporary free speech jurisprudence. The Supreme Court, for its part, remained mum by declining to review the case (Smith v. Collin, 1978). In an ironic (some would say, perverse) dénouement of this controversy, the American Nazi Party, having won the right to march in Skokie to the anguish of many, abruptly cancelled the demonstration. About twenty-five Party members instead held a rally in a Chicago park, without serious incident.

The *Skokie* litigation has become a symbol of First Amendment jurisprudence, for those who celebrate as well as for those who question the strength of the American commitment to free speech. Indeed, one constitutional scholar has based a general theory of justification for freedom of speech on the Skokie experience.[3] The importance of the *Skokie* litigation for the problem of hate speech, lies in what did not happen: neither the state court nor the federal court revised conventional free speech jurisprudence in order to allow Skokie to outlaw the expressive activity of a hate group. Instead, the courts held true to the central principle that all ideas have equal status under the First Amendment, and that the most hateful messages are to be protected with the same vigor as the most enlightened discourse. As Justice William J. Brennan, Jr., writing for the Court in the equally controversial decision that protected flag-burning as a First Amendment right (Texas v. Johnson, 1989), proclaimed:

> If there is a bedrock principle underlying the First Amendment, it is that the government may not prohibit the expression of an idea simply because society finds the idea itself offensive or disagreeable. . . . The First Amendment does not guarantee that . . . concepts virtually sacred to our Nation as a whole—such as the principle that discrimination on the basis of race is odious and destructive—will go unquestioned in the marketplace of ideas.

Skokie was the dog that did not bark.

The *Skokie* courts' treatment of hate speech as simply an example of provocative speech contrasts sharply with the more recent decision of the Supreme Court in R.A.V. v. City of St. Paul (1992), which seemed to especially protect hate speech from governmental restriction. *R.A.V.* involved another symbol that spoke—a cross-burning on the residential property of an African American family. The perpetrators were convicted of violating a city ordinance that prohibited the use of symbols that one should know "arouses anger, alarm, or resentment in others on the basis of race, color, creed religion or gender." The ordinance explicitly mentioned "a burning cross" as an example of such a prohibited symbol. The state supreme court proved itself willing to do what the *Skokie* courts had not done: It bent free speech doctrine in order to accommodate the ordinance and to validate the conviction. The state high court ruled that the ordinance was limited to hate speech that also qualified as fighting words, which as we have seen, the government is free to prohibit. That ruling was a stretch, though, because the ordinance, by its own terms, was not limited to speech that was delivered as a face-to-face insult.

The Court was unanimous in its decision that St. Pauls's hate speech ordinance violated the First Amendment, but they split five-four on the rationale. Four of the justices tracked the approach of the *Skokie* courts by applying conventional provocative speech doctrine. To these four, the state supreme court had stretched too far. They found the ordinance to be invalid precisely because it was not limited to hate speech uttered as fighting words. The five-justice majority, however, accepted the state court's interpretation, but held that the ordinance, even as limited to fighting words, violated the First Amendment. This was because the ordinance, according to the majority, targeted hate speech for special restriction because city officials disapproved of the message of hatred that it conveyed.

Although they reached opposite conclusions, the state supreme court's opinion justifying the ordinance and Justice Antonin Scalia's majority opinion invalidating the ordinance mirrored each other. While the state supreme court stretched the fighting words category in order to uphold the hate speech ordinance, the Supreme Court majority undermined the logic of categorization in an apparent effort to inhibit governments from targeting hate speech for any special restriction. As we have seen, the Court developed the categorization principle in order to allow the state to prohibit certain types of speech, such as fighting words, on the ground that their harm overwhelmed their First Amendment value. The justices had never before invalidated a governmental prohibition of expression that it had found to be within an otherwise unprotected category of speech. The *R.A.V.* majority decided, however, that the selective regulation of hate speech within the otherwise unprotected category of fighting words constituted a message-based restriction that was inherently censorial, and for that reason, unconstitutional.

The Court's conclusion in *R.A.V.* that a hate speech prohibition which is limited to fighting words constitutes government censorship is highly doubtful, however. Justice Scalia acknowledged in his majority opinion that there was "no significant danger" of official censorship when a selective, content-based restriction of speech that otherwise is unprotected was based "entirely [on] the very reason the entire class of speech . . . is proscribable." As the four justices who disassociated themselves from the majority opinion in *R.A.V.* emphasized, Scalia's acknowledgment fit a hate speech restriction that was limited to fighting words. Surely, a government might conclude that personal insults based on the race, religion, gender, or sexual orientation of the recipient are more harmful and are more likely to trigger violence, and thus are more appropriate for official prohibition, than are other types of insults that a recipient is more likely to brush off.

In recent decisions, the justices have retreated from the implication in *R.A.V.* that hate speech enjoys some special immunity from selective governmental restrictions within otherwise unprotected expression or activity. Just one year after deciding *R.A.V.*, in fact, the Court upheld a typical hate crime statute against a First Amendment challenge (Wisconsin v. Mitchell, 1993). A Wisconsin law authorized increasing the prison terms of perpetrators who had selected their victims "because of [their] race, religion, color, disability, sexual orientation, national origin or ancestry." A broad reading of *R.A.V.* would have made such sentence enhancements vulnerable to the claim that they turned on the viewpoint or ideology of the perpetrator, rather than on the severity of the criminal action per se. If a racial fighting word was not more harmful than a nonracial fighting word, as *R.A.V.* seemed to have held, could it be said that a racially motivated attack on a victim was more harmful than one that was not so motivated? The answer in *Mitchell*, surprisingly, was, "yes." Even more surprising was the Court's explanation, which adopted the reasoning of the four justices who had disagreed with the *R.A.V.* majority opinion. The Court wrote in *Mitchell*, "[T]he Wisconsin statute singles out for enhancement bias-inspired conduct because this conduct is thought to inflict greater individual and societal harm. For example, . . . bias-motivated crimes are more likely to provoke retaliatory crimes, inflict distinct emotional harms on their victims, and incite community unrest. . . . The State's desire to redress these perceived harms provides an adequate explanation for its penalty-enhancement provision over and above mere disagreement with offenders' beliefs or biases."

If this explanation was adequate to justify the hate crime law in *Mitchell*, why was it insufficient to support the hate speech law in *R.A.V.*? The Court answered this awkward question by invoking the speech-conduct distinction. *R.A.V.*, the *Mitchell* Court explained, applied only to governmental restrictions on *speech*, and not to "*conduct* unprotected by the First Amendment" (emphasis added). A sentence-enhancement provision keyed to the racial motivation of the perpetrator was not different, the Court reasoned, from the many federal and state laws that prohibit harmful actions, such as the denial of employment or housing, when they are taken with a discriminatory purpose. Indeed, a perpetrator's motivation for committing a criminal offence, the Court observed, is a common factor in sentencing.

Although the justices in *Mitchell* provided a convincing account of why sentence enhancement for hate crimes did not violate the First Amendment, they were less successful in distinguishing *R.A.V.* The speech-conduct distinction is of limited utility when the speech (fighting words), like the underlying conduct in *Mitchell*, is generally subject to prohibition without violating the First Amendment. It therefore is no surprise that the facile *R.A.V./Mitchell* distinction did not hold when the justices returned to the problem of cross burning in Virginia v. Black (2003). On the surface, *Black* might seem consistent with *R.A.V.* The justices in *Black invalidated* a Virginia law prohibiting cross-burning undertaken with "intent to intimidate a person or group of persons." But the Court's justification for its ruling undercut the *R.A.V.* rationale.

The Court in *Black* began by confirming what had been suggested in a couple of earlier cases (see, e.g., Watts v. United States, 1969), that "true threats," like fighting words, constitute a category of expression that states may outlaw without violating the First Amendment. The Court thus announced itself willing to uphold a law that was limited to prohibiting cross-burning as a true threat, that is, with the intent "to communicate a serious expression of an intent to commit an act of unlawful violence to a particular individual or group of individuals." The problem with the Virginia law was that it was not so limited because it permitted a jury to find the requisite intent from the mere fact of cross-burning. In order to qualify as a true threat, the Court held, the state had to prove, rather than presume, that the cross-burner intended to communicate a threat to a particular person or to a distinct group of persons.

This was precisely the line of reasoning advanced by the four justices who had disassociated themselves from the majority opinion in *R.A.V.* Those justices had voted to invalidate the hate speech ordinance not because it targeted for prohibition only those fighting words that constituted hate speech (as had the majority), but because the prohibition was not limited to speech that fell within the unprotected category of fighting words. They had insisted as well that a law limited to prohibiting hate speech within an otherwise unprotected category of speech should be constitutional. That position became the majority view in *Black.* The Court in *Black* explained, "The First Amendment permits [the government] to outlaw cross burnings done with the intent to intimidate because burning a cross is a particularly virulent form of intimidation. Instead of prohibiting all intimidating messages, [the government] may choose to regulate this subset of intimidating messages in light of cross burning's long and pernicious history of impending violence."

Although the Court has not had the opportunity to reconsider whether governments may outlaw hate speech more generally within otherwise unprotected speech categories (such as fighting words), it is quite possible that the majority opinion in *R.A.V.* has not withstood the Court's second and third looks at the hate speech problem in *Mitchell* and in *Black*. In a brief, separate opinion in *R.A.V.*, Justice Harry A. Blackmun had suggested the possibility that the *R.A.V* majority opinion would not "significantly alter First Amendment jurisprudence but, instead, [would] be regarded as an aberration—a case where the Court manipulated doctrine to strike down an ordinance whose premise it opposed, namely, that racial threats and verbal assaults are of greater harm than other fighting words." It was also possible, and "even more regrettable," Justice Blackmun believed, that "the Court ha[d] been distracted from its proper mission by the temptation to decide the issue over 'politically correct speech' and 'cultural diversity.'" If Blackmun's surmise was correct, it might be that the facts of *Mitchell* and *Black* had convinced enough of the *R.A.V.* majority that the individual and social harms caused by hate speech and hate crimes are real, and that governmental efforts to target such activity are not necessarily censorship, at least when those efforts are confined to speech and conduct that is not generally afforded First Amendment protection.

On this reading, hate speech remains simply a type of provocative speech. It is thus subject to neither more nor less First Amendment protection, or governmental restriction, than are other forms of provocative speech.

SEXUAL EXPRESSION

Although the Supreme Court's struggle with the problem of subversive advocacy for most of the twentieth century is the central narrative of the protection of freedom of speech in the United States, it is oddly revealing of American culture that efforts at government control over sexual expression run a respectable second place. But perhaps the American preoccupation with sexual expression is not so strange. As Justice William J. Brennan observed, sex is "a great and mysterious motive force in human life" that has "indisputably been a subject of absorbing interest to mankind through the ages" (Roth v. United States, 1957). Justice Brennan's observation provides not only the rationale for First Amendment protection of much sexual expression, but also, paradoxically, the motivation that has driven government officials over the years to target sexual expression for special restriction. Sexual expression, no less than political speech or other forms of social commentary, at times provides a powerful means for individuals to explore, as well as to challenge, the central cultural commitments and values of their society. And sexual expression, no less than other forms of speech that we value highly, can be deeply subversive of those values and thus offer a tempting target for official censorship.

Although government restrictions on sexual expression have taken a variety of forms, anti-obscenity laws have the longest pedigree. Today, the states generally, together with the United States, outlaw the production, distribution, and exhibition of "obscenity," which often is described as "hard core pornography." In recent years, the regulatory focus on sexual expression has broadened to include laws against child pornography, special zoning restrictions on the venues for sexual expression, and laws that shield children from exposure to sexual expression. Regardless of the nature of the restriction, the Court has found itself in the difficult position of balancing its general commitment to free speech, including sexual expression, with its belief that states should possess greater power to restrict sexual expression than other types of speech. The jurisprudence that has resulted from the Court's balancing act has been at least as controversial as any other area of free speech.

Obscenity

Although obscenity[4] has been prevalent since the dawn of western civilization—obscenity was commonplace, for example, in ancient Greece—it was not a great source of official concern in antebellum America. Only four states had anti-obscenity laws at the beginning of the Civil War. Although a number of states at the time regarded obscenity as an offense at common law, there were no serious governmental efforts to suppress obscenity. As recounted in our consideration of the history of free speech in the United States in Chapter 1, that official complaisance changed abruptly with the emergence of Anthony Comstock's crusade against the "monstrous evil"[5] of obscenity in the last quarter of the nineteenth century. Because the Comstock campaign had pretty much played out by the beginning of World War I, it was the subversive advocacy cases that arose from that war, rather than obscenity convictions, that ushered in modern free speech jurisprudence. But while the sense of urgency faded, public concern over obscenity never disappeared. Ever since the Comstock era, the issue of obscenity has ebbed and flowed in the national consciousness.

It is surprising, in the light of this history, that the Supreme Court did not resolve the question whether obscenity was within the freedom of speech protected by the First Amendment until 1957 (Roth v. United States). In the prior century, the justices had brushed off a First Amendment challenge to the Comstock Act, but as we have seen, this was before the Court had activated freedom of speech as a fundamental right (Ex Parte Jackson, 1878). The modern Court in Chaplinsky v. New Hampshire (1942) also assumed that obscenity was among the speech categories that "have never been thought to raise any Constitutional problem," but that assumption was not tested until the Court was petitioned to set aside an obscenity conviction arising from the publication of Edmund Wilson's *Memoirs of Hecate County* (Doubleday & Co. v. New York, 1948). The Court affirmed the conviction, but only by default because the justices divided equally on the question.

The Court in *Roth* finally made official the exclusion of obscenity from First Amendment protection. The anti-obscenity statute at issue placed the justices in a position that had become familiar from their experience in subversive advocacy and provocative speech cases. Congress and state legislatures outlawed obscenity on the same general reasoning that had prompted statutes prohibiting subversive advocacy and provocative speech: Legislators believed that such expression produced a social harm that was their responsibility to prevent. The difference lay in the elusiveness of the claim of harm for obscenity. The challengers in *Roth* focused their attack on that vulnerability, arguing that anti-obscenity laws were incompatible with the First Amendment because the government had failed to prove that obscene materials created a "clear and present danger of antisocial conduct." There is no indication in Justice Brennan's majority opinion in *Roth* that the government had shouldered that burden. Brennan finessed that shortcoming by categorizing obscenity out of First Amendment protection. Because the First Amendment does not protect obscenity, Brennan reasoned, the government had a free hand in outlawing expression that fell within that category, even without proof of harm. This stance seemed inconsistent with the categorization method the Court had outlined in *Chaplinsky*, which provided for the exclusion of a particular speech category from First Amendment protection only if the justices were satisfied that the harms associated with that speech greatly exceeded its communicate value. Instead of undertaking such a cost-benefit balancing, Justice Brennan justified the exclusion of obscenity from First Amendment protection essentially by invoking "the universal judgment that obscenity should be restrained." That judgment was manifested to the Court's satisfaction by historical assumptions and by contemporary anti-obscenity laws enacted by Congress and by all of the states. To the justices, the "universal" outlawing of obscenity in the United States registered an authoritative cultural judgment that obscenity was "utterly without redeeming social importance," and for that reason alone, was outside the conventional American understanding of the freedom of speech.

Unlike the Court's initial encounter with subversive advocacy, the justices in *Roth* were mindful of the constitutional risks of excluding obscenity from First Amendment protection. They tried to minimize those risks by defining obscenity in a way which would ensure that sexual expression generally would remain protected, subject only to a narrow exception for depictions of sex that went beyond the pale. To the *Roth* Court, the distinctive characteristic of obscenity was its appeal to the "prurient interest" of its audience, which, incorporating a statement from the American Law Institute, the justices defined as "a shameful or morbid interest" in sexuality. Sexual expression untainted by the dominance of such an appeal, the Court emphasized, remained protected. "[S]ex and obscenity," Justice Brennan advised in his majority opinion, "are not synonymous," and the mere "portrayal of sex . . . is not itself sufficient reason to deny material the constitutional protection of freedom of speech and press." In *Roth*, then, the Court attempted to define a First Amendment position that would allow an "unfettered interchange of ideas" exploring human sexuality, regardless how "unorthodox" or "controversial," while preventing what, in the *Roth* view, amounted to an abuse of that freedom, namely, sexual expression intended simply to "excite lustful thoughts."

The Court's decision in *Roth* proved to be less a settlement of the obscenity issue than the beginning of a long, contentious argument. The Court's commitment to free sexual expression was tested almost immediately after the *Roth* decision (Kingsley Int'l Pictures Corp. v. Regents of the University of the State of New York, 1959). In *Kingsley*, the justices overturned a state's refusal to license the showing of a film version of *Lady Chatterley's Lover*. Although the film was not obscene under the *Roth* definition, the state nevertheless had banned it because "the whole theme" of the film was "immoral." According to the state, the film depicted "adultery as a desirable, acceptable and proper pattern of behavior." The Court ruled that the state's conception of "thematic obscenity" was no substitute for the *Roth* definition of obscenity, and accordingly, that it did not provide a basis for prohibiting sexual expression. By shifting emphasis from "the manner of [the] portrayal" of a sexual relationship to the *idea* communicated by the portrayal, the Court in *Kingsley* held, the state had struck "at the very heart" of the freedom of speech. Thematic obscenity constituted official censorship, pure and simple. It was no answer that the idea advocated by the film defended activity—adultery—that itself violated state law, for as the Court reminded, subversive advocacy doctrine protected the mere advocacy of unlawful action absent a clear and present danger that the film would immediately incite the action. *Kingsley* thus delivered on *Roth*'s promise that obscenity doctrine would function as a relatively narrow exception to an otherwise robust freedom of individuals to express "[a]ll ideas" on sexual subjects that have "even the slightest redeeming social importance," regardless how "unorthodox" or "controversial."

Ironically, even as the justices united to prevent states from using such dodges as thematic obscenity to bypass the restrictions *Roth* had placed on the scope of obscenity regulation, their allegiance to the *Roth* definition itself unraveled. This should have come as no great surprise. Only five justices—the slimmest of majorities—had signed onto the *Roth* definition in the first place. When, nearly a decade later, Justice Brennan tweaked that definition, only two other justices joined him (Memoirs v. Massachusetts, 1966). The justices went their separate ways, agreeing to disagree on the obscenity issue. The Brennan group used the *Memoirs* variation of the *Roth* definition, while others invented their own definitions of obscenity. Another group of justices was disdainful of the entire definitional enterprise because they opposed the constitutionality of all anti-obscenity laws. The sense of exasperation that arose from the post-*Roth* doctrinal disarray was forever captured by Justice Potter Stewart when he wrote, "[P]erhaps I could never succeed in intelligibly [defining obscenity]. But I know it when I see it." (Jacobellis v. Ohio, 1964).

In 1967, one year after Justice Brennan's failed attempt in *Memoirs* to reconstruct a consensus on the Court by reassembling a constitutional definition of obscenity, the justices institutionalized their disagreement on the definitional question by launching the process of "redrupping" obscenity convictions (Redrup v. New York, 1967). In this process, each justice reviewed the expression at issue and determined, according to his own definitional understanding, whether or not it constituted obscenity. If five or more justices found the expression to be obscene, the Court affirmed the conviction without opinion. If five or more justices found the material not to be obscene, the Court reversed the conviction, again without opinion. As the Court later confessed, "The *Redrup* procedure . . . cast us in the role of an unreviewable board of censorship for the 50 states, subjectively judging each piece of material brought before us" (Miller v. California, 1973). Redrupping was the antithesis of principled constitutional adjudication, and it powerfully symbolized the breakdown of obscenity doctrine in the wake of *Roth*.

During the redrupping era, the justices, naturally enough, experimented with an alternative approach to categorization in their continuing effort to solve the obscenity problem. Labeled "variable obscenity," this approach drew on Chief Justice Earl Warren's concurring opinion in *Roth*, in which he insisted that the "conduct of the defendant" should be "the central issue" in obscenity cases, not the content of the defendant's expression. "It is not the book that is on trial," Warren observed, "it is the person." Eschewing the strict categorization approach of *Roth*, Warren would have had the Court examine the defendant's expression "in context."

It therefore would be appropriate, he argued, for the Court to reach different judgments regarding the same speech content in "different setting[s]."

The Court developed Chief Justice Warren's concept of variable obscenity in the years following *Roth* as a contextual counterpoint to the otherwise dominant approach of categorization. In this line of cases, two variables seemed especially important to defining the context for evaluating allegedly obscene materials. The first variable was whether the defendant could be said to have engaged in "pandering." The concern with pandering came directly from Warren's concurring opinion in *Roth*, where the Chief Justice had suggested that obscenity prosecutions were best targeted against those who had engaged in "conduct" that amounted to "the commercial exploitation of the morbid and shameful craving for materials with prurient effect." In Ginzburg v. United States (1966), the Court followed Warren's suggestion, holding that "the commercial exploitation of erotica solely for the sake of their prurient appeal" could support an obscenity conviction even if the content of the expression, standing alone, did not satisfy the *Roth* definition. *Ginzburg* supplemented, but did not supplant, *Roth* categorization. The pandering variable broadened anti-obscenity laws to reach defendants who were engaged in otherwise protected sexual expression, but it did not limit the application of those statutes to panderers.

The other prominent variable that affected the Court's review of obscenity convictions during the redrupping era was the presence of children in the audience. In Butler v. Michigan (1957), which the Court decided the same year as *Roth*, the justices invalidated a statute that prohibited the general distribution of sexual expression that, among other things, "manifestly tend[ed] to the corruption of the morals of youth." The Court cautioned legislators that they could not "reduce the adult population . . . to reading only what is fit for children." *Butler*, like *Kingsley*, reinforced the definitional approach of *Roth* by preventing states from expanding the field of illegal sexual expression beyond the bounds of the newly created category of obscenity. But just one year after *Redrup*, in Ginsberg v. New York (1968), the Court allowed states to outlaw the sale of non-obscene, sexual expression to minors. As with pandering, the child-audience variable allowed the states to expand the reach of anti-obscenity statutes to sexual expression that did not fit the constitutional definition of obscenity.

The subversive potential of variable obscenity for the *Roth* regime became apparent soon after the *Ginzburg* and *Ginsberg* decisions. In Stanley v. Georgia (1969), the Court for the first time drew on the contextual orientation of variable obscenity to reduce, rather than to expand, the constitutional range of anti-obscenity laws. Stanley had been convicted for possessing obscenity in his home. The "mere categorization" of material as obscene, the Court ruled, was "insufficient justification" for such an "unwarranted governmental intrusions into one's privacy." Context was all. Following Chief Justice Warren's alternative method of evaluating obscenity regulation, the Court distinguished *Stanley* from *Roth* because of the conduct of the defendants, not the content of their expression. While Roth had engaged in the "public distribution" of obscenity, Stanley had simply possessed such materials at home.

The subversiveness of *Stanley* was not limited to its protection of the private possession of unprotected expression. The Court's First Amendment rationale in *Stanley* undercut the constitutional grounding of *Roth*, and indeed, the legitimacy of the entire anti-obscenity project. Writing for the Court, Justice Thurgood Marshall directly challenged the *Roth* premise that obscenity could be pushed outside the freedom of speech because it lacked social value. He wrote, the "right to receive information and ideas, *regardless of their social worth*, . . . is fundamental to our free society" (emphasis added). Marshall rejected as well the paternalistic assumptions behind anti-obscenity laws in general as irreconcilable with free speech values. Marshall again: "If the First Amendment means anything, it means that a State has no business telling a man, sitting alone in his own house, what books he may read or what films he may watch. Our whole constitutional heritage rebels at the thought of giving government the power to control men's minds." Finally, Justice Marshall's opinion for the Court in *Stanley* dismissed Georgia's effort to justify its prohibition of the possession of obscenity as a hedge against "deviant sexual behavior or crimes of sexual violence." Marshall noted the insufficiency of empirical support for any such showing, observing, "Given the present state of knowledge, the State may no more prohibit mere possession of obscene matter on the ground that it may lead to antisocial conduct than it may prohibit possession of chemistry books on the ground that they may lead to the manufacture of homemade spirits." Marshall reminded that the First Amendment generally limits states to punishing individuals for what they do, not for what they read or view.

Although the Court in *Stanley* was careful to limit its holding to the constitutional protection of the "mere private possession of obscene material," Justice Marshall's withering rejection of the conventional justifications for anti-obscenity laws in general provided a platform for a reconsideration, and possible overruling, of *Roth* itself. Surely state efforts at "controlling a person's private thoughts" were just as chilling outside the home. Similarly, the empirical support for the legislatively presumed linkage between obscenity and sexual misconduct was no more compelling when the reader or viewer of the material was outside the home. The Court nevertheless quickly drew back from the broadest implications of its opinion in *Stanley*, insisting that it "neither overruled nor disturbed the holding in *Roth*" (United States v. Reidel, 1971). But having answered the *Stanley* challenge, the Court once again found itself in an awkward doctrinal position, having held, essentially, that states may criminalize the sale of materials that individuals have a constitutional right to possess.

The doctrinal uncertainty introduced by variable obscenity in general, and by *Stanley* in particular, coupled with the erosion of judicial integrity that attended the Court's redrupping of obscenity cases, undermined the coherency of the *Roth* regime. The status quo was unsustainable, and in 1973, the justices announced a new settlement of the obscenity issue (Paris Adult Theatre I v. Slaton (1973); Miller

v. California (1973)). *Paris* and *Miller* were companion cases that interrelated tantalizingly to hint that the Court might abandon *Roth* categorization entirely for the more contextual variable obscenity method. *Paris* concerned the application of an anti-obscenity law to a so-called "adult" movie theater that exhibited motion pictures to consenting adults only, while *Miller* involved the mailing of unsolicited advertisements containing obscene materials to unsuspecting recipients. One might distinguish the two cases on variable obscenity grounds as mirror images of each other. The method of distribution in *Miller* created a significant danger of offending the sensibilities of unwilling recipients and of exposure to children, two factors that the Court had recognized as significant variables when reviewing obscenity convictions. By contrast, the exhibitor in *Paris* avoided such judicial sensitivities by taking precautions to avoid exposure of obscene films to either unwilling adults or to children. And indeed, several justices, led by Justice Brennan, the author of *Roth*, used *Paris* to urge that states no longer should be permitted to prohibit obscene expression entirely, but rather should be restricted to regulating such expression to protect children or unwilling adults from exposure. A bare five-justice majority of the Court, however, pointedly ignored the factual differences between *Paris* and *Miller* and used the pair of cases to reaffirm their commitment to *Roth*.

The Court used *Paris*, the more difficult of the two cases, to reaffirm *Roth*'s exclusion of obscenity from First Amendment protection. Given all that had transpired since *Roth*, it is not surprising that the majority's justification extended beyond the earlier decision's simple reliance on the history and uniformity of anti-obscenity laws in the United States. The Court now emphasized "the interest of the public in the quality of life and the total community environment" as a legitimate and sufficient basis upon which states might outlaw obscenity. The *Paris* majority analogized the spread of obscenity outside the privacy of the home to the emission of pollutants into the atmosphere. The result of this moral toxicity, according to the Court, was the corrosion of community standards. The justices recognized that the existence of moral pollution, unlike environmental pollution, could neither be proved nor measured. But they nevertheless insisted that local communities possessed a right "to maintain a decent society," and that communities could "reasonably determine" that anti-obscenity laws served that purpose. The *Paris* Court's identification of a community harm caused by obscenity responded to *Stanley*'s challenge to the conventional justifications of obscenity regulation, even as it supported the limitation of *Stanley* to protecting the private possession of obscene materials.

In *Miller*, the Court drew on the community interest in preserving a moral environment identified in *Paris* to revise, or rather to augment, the *Roth* definition of obscenity. In their refinement of *Roth*, the justices attempted to make anti-obscenity laws usable by communities, while limiting the reach of those laws to "hard core pornography." The *Miller* definition of obscenity incorporated the *Roth* limitation to material that is dominated by an appeal to the "prurient interest," and added two additional requirements. To be obscene, the material also must depict or describe "specifically defined sexual conduct" in "a patently offensive way," as well as lack "serious literary, artistic, political, or scientific value." The *Miller* Court regarded its limitation of obscenity to depictions or descriptions of "hard core" sexual conduct "specifically defined" by statute as an important tightening of the *Roth* definition, in the interest of furthering freedom of speech. A loosening, however, complemented that constriction. While the Court in *Roth* expressed its commitment to protect "[a]ll ideas having even the slightest redeeming social importance," the *Miller* definition upped the ante for sexual expression that otherwise qualified as obscenity by requiring that it possess "serious" value in order to escape that designation. The Court believed this loosening of the definition to be a significant improvement of *Roth* as well, in the interest of enabling state prosecutors to enforce anti-obscenity laws.

Perhaps the most important innovation of *Miller* was the stipulation that jurors, acting as a collective "average person" applying the standards of their community, would determine each element of the new definition of obscenity, with the exception of the serious value criterion (see Pope v. Illinois, 1987). The justices thought it "an exercise in futility" to devise a national community standard for obscenity, explaining, "our Nation is simply too big and too diverse for this Court to reasonably expect that such standards [as "prurient interest" and "patently offensive"] could be articulated for all 50 States in a single formulation." The Court continued, "It is neither realistic nor constitutionally sound to read the First Amendment as requiring that the people of Maine or Mississippi accept public depictions of conduct found tolerable in Las Vegas, or New York City." Yet, given the demands of national marketing, the effect of allowing local communities to apply the *Miller* requirements through the lens of their own standards risked denying the people of Las Vegas and New York City access to sexual expression that is unacceptable in Maine or Mississippi. In resolving this dilemma, the Court had a choice to make, and the justices in *Miller*, as they had in *Paris*, chose to err on the side of empowering local communities to block the entry of obscene sexual expression.

The Court has made clear that each jury supplies the content of the *Miller* standards on an ad hoc basis, drawing on its "own understanding of the tolerance of the average person in their communit[ies]" (Smith v. United States, 1977). The depth of *Miller*'s commitment to the primacy of jury determinations in obscenity cases was strikingly apparent when the Court prohibited state legislatures from defining the content of the community standards to be applied by the juries of their respective states (Smith v. United States, 1977). In deciding obscenity cases, jurors uniquely represent, because they re-present, the community.

The community-standards overlay of the *Miller* criteria was as important institutionally as it was substantively. *Miller* operates as an inverse *Redrup*: it prescribes that juries, rather than the justices, shoulder the primary responsibility of distinguishing protected sexual expression from unprotected obscenity. It is no accident that the Court's docket of obscenity cases has reduced markedly since *Miller*. Indeed, shortly after deciding *Paris/Miller*, the Court ruled, again five-four, that even prosecutions for violation of national anti-obscenity laws would be determined by juries applying the local standards of the communities from which they were drawn (Hamling v. United States, 1974).

The jury-administered, community-standards orientation of the *Miller* definition of obscenity fits the *Paris* community-morality justification for anti-obscenity laws. If such laws protect the level of decency and moral tone of life in a community, as *Paris* would have it, there is a symmetry in allowing randomly selected representatives of each community to determine for themselves which material crosses the line separating legitimate expression and unprotected obscenity. But because *Miller*'s reliance on jurors as community filters of sexual expression enables majoritarian control over freedom of speech, such a system is in severe tension with conventional First Amendment practice. A core function of the First Amendment, after all, is to protect expression that challenges majoritarian sentiment. Indeed, one might say that modern free speech jurisprudence began with Holmes's recognition that the impulse to censor is a natural, human reaction to expression that challenges deeply held community values. The typical First Amendment concern over the possibility of majoritarian censorship, moreover, is especially acute with respect to obscenity because criteria such as "patently offensive" and "prurient interest" are freighted with subjectivity. *Miller*, thus, threatened to "solve" the redrupping problem by substituting local juries for the Supreme Court as boards of censorship.

Yet, the experience of the last quarter century has shown that juries generally have handled their *Miller* responsibilities remarkably well. There has been no upsurge in obscenity convictions in the thirty years following the *Paris/Miller* resettlement. Perhaps this development has not been so remarkable after all. Jurors, no less than judges and other Americans, have internalized the cultural commitment to freedom of expression, and they have oriented their decision making accordingly. Their administration of *Paris/Miller* thus reflects a notable convergence of legal and social norms governing sexual expression. In addition, obscenity doctrine creates a web of constraints on juries that provides judges the authority to rectify the inevitable instances of majoritarian overreaching. The justices emphasized that juries would not enjoy carte blanche in obscenity cases when, just one year after *Paris/Miller*, they overturned a verdict by a Georgia jury finding the mainstream film *Carnal Knowledge* to be obscene (Jenkins v. Georgia, 1974). Just as the Court had emphasized in *Roth* that sex could not be equated with obscenity, the justices in *Jenkins* reemphasized that nudity alone, without "patently offensive" depictions of "hard core sexual conduct for its own sake," could not rob sexual expression of First Amendment protection. *Jenkins* thus provided a reassuring, doctrinal counterpoint analogous to that of *Kingsley*'s protection of so-called thematic obscenity in the wake of *Roth*, namely, that the Court, in the language of *Miller*, would invoke its "ultimate power" to safeguard the Constitution by not allowing juries to roam beyond the "carefully limited" boundaries of obscenity in order to censor sexual expression more generally.

The Court's opinions in *Paris/Miller* brought a measure of peace to the longstanding constitutional controversy over obscenity. At the least, the justices, by their reliance on juror applications of community standards to decide obscenity cases, managed largely to extricate themselves from these conflicts. In a larger sense, however, the promise of a more general settlement with respect to sexual expression that *Roth/Paris/Miller* had promised has not materialized. The original *Roth* settlement, which held that the First Amendment generally protects sexual expression, with the exception of material that falls within a narrowly confined category of obscenity, has been challenged by two developments. The most fundamental challenges have come from attempts to add additional categories of unprotected sexual expression to the traditional exception for obscenity. The most prominent example of this challenge has been the Court's addition of child pornography to the unprotected list. A second, subtler challenge has come from the efforts of government officials to impose restrictions on sexual expression short of outright prohibitions. These developments are briefly discussed, in turn.

Child Pornography and the Border Security of Protected Sexual Expression

Just as the Court has described "hard core pornography" as the "obscenity" that is unprotected by the First Amendment, it may be said that obscenity itself is the core of unprotected sexual expression. Sexual expression need not be obscene, however, in order to be denied First Amendment protection. This became apparent when the Court accepted the constitutionality of child pornography laws in New York v. Ferber (1982). Ferber had been charged with violating New York's laws prohibiting obscenity and child pornography for his role in selling films depicting young boys masturbating. The jury acquitted Ferber on the obscenity count, but convicted him of promoting child pornography. Based on the definitional approach to obscenity begun in *Roth* and cemented in *Paris/Miller*, one might have thought that because the films were not obscene, the First Amendment disallowed outright prohibition of them because of their sexual content. The *Ferber* jury, by operation of *Miller*, must have found that the films were *not* dominated by an appeal to the prurient interest, or that the films did *not* depict sexual conduct in a patently offensive manner, or that the films possessed serious value. At least one such finding had saved the films from the unprotected category of obscenity.

The justices, however, used *Ferber* to revise, once again, their settlement over sexual expression. While *Roth/Paris/Miller* had found obscenity to be an unprotected subcategory of the larger category of sexual expression, the Court now held, those decisions did not foreclose the creation of additional unprotected subcategories. In *Ferber*, the Court held that child pornography lacked First Amendment protection as well. Moreover, the *Ferber* Court made clear that states would have "greater leeway" in restricting child pornography than *Roth/Paris/Miller* allows them with respect to obscenity.

The Court justified the broader prohibitive power of the government to address child pornography by invoking *Chaplinsky's* cost/benefit assessment. The societal costs of child pornography, which center on the harm suffered by the child subjects of such depictions, are indeed profound. As the Court in *Ferber* explained, "[t]he prevention of sexual exploitation and abuse of children constitutes a governmental objective of surpassing importance." By contrast, the moral-environmental harms the *Paris* Court associated with obscenity seem attenuated and speculative. The Court's conclusion in *Ferber* was irresistible: the governmental interest underlying child pornography laws is both more "particular" and more "compelling" than that which justifies anti-obscenity laws.

The focus of child pornography statutes on the protection of child subjects not only accounted for the heightened social interest at stake, but also for a diminished judicial concern over the free speech values potentially threatened by such laws. Although the Court in *Ferber* acknowledged that child pornography laws, like anti-obscenity laws, run "the risk of suppressing protected expression," those risks seemed less pressing. The Court explained:

> The value of permitting live performances and photographic reproductions of children engaged in lewd conduct is exceedingly modest, if not *de minimis*. We consider it unlikely that visual depictions of children performing sexual acts or lewdly exhibiting their genitals would often constitute an important and necessary part of a literary performance or scientific or educational work. . . . The First Amendment interest is limited to that of rendering the portrayal somewhat more "realistic" by utilizing or photographing children.

Free expression of ideas or practices concerning juvenile sexuality can be accommodated readily by the use of older performers or models able to pass for children, subject of course, to anti-obscenity constraints. Accordingly, the Court noted, child pornography laws do not "censor[] a particular literary theme or portrayal of sexual activity." They simply prohibit the use of child subjects.

To the justices, *Ferber*'s cost/benefit analysis revealed the inadequacy of the *Miller* test in addressing child pornography. While obscenity and child pornography are each subcategories of sexual expression, their defining characteristics fundamentally differ. The key signifier of obscenity is a work's appeal to the prurient interest of the audience. By contrast, the distinctive quality of the prohibition of child pornography is its focus on the harm experienced by the child subjects. According to the *Ferber* Court, the presence or absence of an appeal to the prurient interest of the audience "bears no connection to the issue of whether a child has been physically or psychologically harmed in the production of the work." That observation applies to another *Miller* criterion—the offensiveness of the depiction. Moreover, community standards, the framework within which juries evaluate "prurient interest" and "patent offensiveness" for obscenity determinations, likewise are out of place in child pornography cases.

As to the serious value of the work, the *Ferber* Court suggested, somewhat startlingly to those accustomed to the presence of this First Amendment safety valve of obscenity jurisprudence, that "a work which, taken on the whole, contains serious literary, artistic, political, or scientific value may nevertheless embody the hardest core of child pornography." But the Court hedged that seeming disavowal of the value element of *Miller* with regard to child pornography. When the *Ferber* Court described how the *Miller* test would be "adjusted" to fit child pornography, the justices explicitly deleted only *Miller*'s "prurient interest" element and its requirement that depictions of sexual conduct be "patently offensive." While the justices also decided that "the material at issue need not be considered as a whole," they did not address the relevancy of the value of the depiction itself.

The Court in *Ferber* ultimately finessed the issue of whether socially valuable material that otherwise fits the definition of child pornography might retain First Amendment protection. The justices had in mind two possibilities—photographs appearing in a medical text or in *National Geographic*. They believed, however, that such cases would be rare and decided to save them for another day. A child pornography law, the *Ferber* Court concluded, is "the paradigmatic case of a state statute whose legitimate reach dwarfs its arguably impermissible applications." While the Court has not yet definitively resolved whether the value of material that otherwise fits the definition of child pornography would redeem the expression sufficiently to bring it within the protective embrace of the First Amendment, the strong suggestion throughout the cases is that it does not.

The Court's reluctance in *Ferber* to endorse explicitly even the serious value criterion of *Miller* highlights the expansive potential of the child pornography exception to First Amendment protection. As in *Roth*, though, the justices in *Ferber* acknowledged their responsibility to limit the category of child pornography in order to accommodate free speech values. Early in its opinion, the *Ferber* Court described child pornography laws as legislation "directed at or limited to depictions of sexual activity involving children." The Court's essential statement on the First Amendment limits of such laws required that "the state offense" be tied to "the nature of the harm," and thus be "limited to works that *visually* depict sexual conduct by children below a specified age." (Emphasis in original.) The *Ferber* Court emphasized that non-obscene material which does not involve "live performance or photographic or other visual reproduction of live performances" of children remained protected by the First Amendment. As to the appropriate statutory definition of "children," the Court in *Ferber* appeared to embrace state laws that included those under the age of eighteen.

The *Ferber* opinion reflects clearly that the Court saw, and approached, child pornography as a different and far more ominous social evil than obscenity. While the justices have been consistent in their exclusion of obscenity from First Amendment protection, they have always understood anti-obscenity laws as a troubling constitutional project. In *Ferber*, the justices revealed no trace of the ambivalence so prevalent in their obscenity decisions. Paradoxically, the convincing constitutional support for child pornography laws may pose more of a threat to the cultural and constitutional values of free expression than that presented by anti-obscenity laws. It is revealing that the *Ferber* Court, certain of the cultural and constitutional grounding of governmental efforts to eradicate child pornography, emphasized the reach, not the limits, of that regulatory project.

The wholehearted endorsement of child pornography laws in *Ferber* laid the groundwork for extending governmental prohibitions significantly beyond that approved in the *Ferber* decision itself, not to mention that envisioned in *Roth/Paris/Miller*. Such an outward push of the doctrine legitimating state restrictions on child pornography stood in marked contrast to the post-*Roth* and post-*Paris/Miller* experiences. Recall that the Court quickly followed *Roth* with a decision disallowing states from prohibiting so-called thematic obscenity, ensuring that the expression of ideas challenging conventional sexual mores would continue without the threat of government prosecution. Recall as well that soon after *Paris/Miller*, the Court set aside a jury verdict finding the film *Carnal Knowledge* obscene, ensuring that overly sensitive juries would not expand obscenity beyond "hard core pornography" to include simple nudity. In child pornography jurisprudence, by contrast, the Court's early moves after *Ferber* projected in the opposite direction.

For example, the justices exhibited no hesitation in affirming an expansive reading of *Ferber* that allowed states to prohibit not only depictions of children engaged in sexual conduct, but also depictions of nude children, at least where there is a "lewd exhibition" of or a "graphic focus" on genitalia (Osborne v. Ohio, 1990). The movement from sexual conduct to nudity, of course, is precisely what the Court had rejected in obscenity regulation after *Paris/Miller*. In addition, because of "the importance of the State's interest in protecting the victims of child pornography," the Court allowed prosecutions for the simple possession of child pornography in the privacy of the home, another extension the justices have prohibited regarding obscenity (Osborne v. Ohio, 1990).

The Court finally identified a firm boundary limiting future extensions of *Ferber* in Ashcroft v. The Free Speech Coalition (2002). *Aschcroft* involved the longest, most suggestive legislative stretch of *Ferber*. In the Child Pornography Prevention Act of 1996,[6] Congress outlawed so-called "virtual child pornography," that is, visual images that *appeared* to be depictions of children engaging in sexual conduct. Such apparent depictions included computer generations, which were the primary target of the law, as well as images of adult models portraying minors. The prohibition of virtual child pornography reached beyond the explicit limits of *Ferber*, which because of its focus on the harm suffered by the child subjects exploited in the production of child pornography, had limited the unprotected category of child pornography to depictions of actual, not simulated, children. In order to uphold the new Act, the *Ashcroft* Court believed, it would have been "necessary" to make "virtual child pornography . . . an additional category of unprotected speech," and this the justices declined to do. The very concept of virtual child pornography troubled the justices. Such a category, unlike *Ferber* child pornography, would have been "much more" than a "supplement" to the obscenity exception of free speech protection for sexual expression. Rather, in the Court's assessment, the ban of virtual child pornography was an example of the kind of thematic obscenity that the Court protected almost fifty years earlier in *Kingsley*. The Court in *Ashcroft* wrote, "The statute proscribes the visual depiction of an idea—that of teenagers engaging in sexual activity—that is a fact of modern society and has been a theme in art and literature throughout the ages."

In resisting the congressional effort to ban virtual child pornography, the Court in *Ashcroft* suggested that *Ferber* might be the only exception to the "general rule" that sexual expression "can be banned only if obscene" within the meaning of *Miller*. This suggestion helps to explain the judicial rejection of anti-pornography laws put forward by some (but by no means all) feminists as an alternative to *Miller* obscenity. In this alternative, pornography is considered harmful not because it appeals to the prurient interest of its audience, but because it discriminates against women. This is so, supporters of such laws claim, because pornography engenders in men a distorted view of women as subordinate sexual objects rather than as equal and fully human, a view that encourages discrimination and violence toward women. As described by Andrea Dworkin, one of the pioneers of this alternative understanding of the harmful potential of sexual expression, "Pornography, unlike obscenity, is a discrete, identifiable system of sexual exploitation that hurts women as a class by creating inequality and abuse."[7] Following that diagnosis, the essence of unlawful pornography is expression that depicts "the graphic sexually explicit subordination of women." The social, literary, or artistic value of any depiction that qualifies as pornography, in this approach, is trumped by the harm it caused, and thus, as is probably true of *Ferber* child pornography, any such value cannot save the depiction from governmental prohibition.

This alternative approach to *Miller* obscenity was halted in its tracks when the Supreme Court summarily affirmed (that is, upheld without opinion) a decision by a federal court of appeals which invalided a city ordinance that embodied the anti-pornography approach to sexual expression (American Booksellers Association v. Hudnut, 1985). The court of appeals in *Booksellers* found the definition of pornography in this approach to be fatally infected by viewpoint discrimination. As the court explained, "Speech treating women in the approved way—in sexual encounters 'premised on equality' . . .—is lawful no matter how sexually explicit. Speech treating women in the disapproved way—as submissive in matters sexual or as enjoying humiliation—is unlawful no matter how significant the literary, artistic, or political qualities of the work taken as a whole. The state may not ordain preferred viewpoints in this way."

The court of appeals's rejection of anti-pornography laws in *Booksellers* anticipated the *Ashcroft* rationale for invalidating virtual child pornography. In both instances, legislatures had stepped beyond the boundaries marked by *Miller* and *Ferber* for the prohibition of sexual expression. While *Miller* had allowed communities to enforce their standards of moral decency concerning the explicitness of sexual expression and *Ferber* had allowed communities to protect children from the abuse caused by their use as subjects in the portrayal of sexual activity, upholding the anti-pornography and virtual child pornography laws would have given legislators a free hand to outlaw ideas and themes of sexuality with which they disapproved. This amounted to censorship in its purest form. From the perspective of what might have been, obscenity, as supplemented by child pornography, represent limited exceptions to the general right under the First Amendment to engage in sexual expression.

With that said, any careful reading of the court of appeals's dismissal of anti-pornography laws in *Booksellers* (as well as *Ashcroft*'s protection of virtual child pornography) calls into question the constitutional case for permitting anti-obscenity laws as well. Just as the two kinds of anti-pornography laws are constitutionally suspect because they seek to enforce a government-preferred view of sexual ideas and themes, anti-obscenity laws should be equally suspect for their effort to enforce a majoritarian view of sexual morality. Each legislative effort is paternalistic, and in the stark expression of the court of appeals in *Booksellers*, each on some level constitutes "thought control." Each law is grounded on the legislative worry that sexual expression of a particular kind will generate a mental predisposition in the audience to act in an antisocial manner. Indeed, if anything, the basis for legislative concern with respect to antisocial conduct is probably more supportable with respect to virtual child pornography and pornography than it is with respect to obscenity. The Court flashed recognition of this fundamental conflict between anti-obscenity laws and free speech principles in *Stanley*, but as we have seen, the justices almost immediately backed away from the implications of that insight. It is only the prohibition of *Ferber* child pornography that "does not rely on a paternalistic interest in regulating [the recipient's] mind" (Osborne v. Ohio, 1990), and thus it is only the exclusion of that category from protected sexual expression that squares with the First Amendment.

Ultimately, the First Amendment exception for obscenity might best be explained not as a reasoned elaboration of free speech principles, but rather as a strategic judgment by the Court reflecting the difficulty of challenging anti-obscenity laws that many local communities believe are necessary to preserve their moral integrity. Perhaps that is the meaning of the *Roth* Court's otherwise tautological emphasis of the "universal" outlawing of obscenity by the states as a justification for denying such expression First Amendment protection.

Channeling Non-obscene Sexual Expression

After *Ashcroft*, legislatures will be hard-pressed to justify banning sexual expression that does not fall within the *Miller* definition of obscenity or the *Ferber* definition of child pornography. But the Court has allowed government officials considerably more leeway in restricting sexual expression, short of outright prohibition, than it has with respect to other forms of protected speech. The justices have not offered a satisfactory account of why this is so. The constitutional clearance for greater regulatory control over sexual expression might be explained by a judicial reluctance to accord such expression the same degree of First Amendment protection provided other types of speech. Or perhaps the justices believe that governments have especially powerful regulatory justifications for restricting the times and places of sexual expression. Most likely, the answer lies in some combination of those two explanations.

The initial position of the Court following *Paris/Miller* suggested that the First Amendment prevented government officials from targeting non-obscene sexual expression for special restrictions. Just a couple of years after upholding anti-obscenity laws in *Paris* and in *Miller*, the Court invalidated a local ordinance that prohibited drive-in theaters from showing films that included nudity on screens that were visible to the public outside the theater (Erznoznik v. City of Jacksonville, 1975). The ordinance reflected a legislative judgment that nude scenes would be "especially offensive to passersby." But nudity alone, the Court had held just the prior year, does not render a film obscene (Jenkins v. Georgia, 1974). The Court in *Erznoznik* thus put the Jacksonville ordinance through the constitutional wringer of strict scrutiny reserved for "censorship of otherwise protected speech on the basis of its content." The ordinance was doomed. As the Court explained, "when the government, acting as censor, undertakes selectively to shield the public from some kinds of speech on the ground that they are more offensive than others, the First Amendment strictly limits its power." The Court in *Erznoznik* thus reinforced the understanding, traceable to *Roth* and consistent with *Ferber*, that sexual expression, which was neither obscene nor otherwise proscribable remained fully protected. The First Amendment denied government officials carte blanche to inhibit sexual expression because they or some community members found it offensive.

Chief Justice Warren E. Burger, the author of the majority opinions in *Miller* and *Paris*, dissented in *Erznoznik*. He was joined by the future Chief Justice, William H. Rehnquist. Burger accused the majority of engaging in a "rigidly simplistic" application of the categorization and content distinction principles. He discounted the free speech interests affected by the Jacksonville ordinance because, as he put it, the nude scenes possessed only a "slight to nonexistent" communicative value to passersby. Burger ignored, however, the expressive value of such scenes for those who viewed the film in the theater. Burger, on the other hand, assessed the community's regulatory interest as quite high, owing to the uniquely "eye-catching" nature of drive-in movie screens. Because his cost/benefit balance decisively favored the nudity restriction, the Chief Justice criticized the majority for slavishly following conventional free speech doctrine to invalidate the Jacksonville ordinance.

The very next year, the justices began to experiment along the lines advocated by Chief Justice Burger in his *Erznoznik* dissent (Young v. American Mini Theatres, Inc., 1976). *Young* involved a city zoning ordinance that placed special restrictions on the location of movie theaters that specialized in sexually explicit, but non-obscene films, restrictions that did not apply to theaters that limited themselves to more mainstream fare. By targeting so-called "adult" movie theaters, the *Young* ordinance would seem to fit the *Erznoznik* description of "censorship of otherwise protected speech on the basis of its content," and thus, to face the same fate of the Jacksonville ordinance. But a bare majority of the justices voted to uphold the *Young* zoning restriction, although they were unable to agree on a justification for doing so. All five justices who endorsed the constitutional legitimacy of the *Young* ordinance agreed on one proposition, however, that "there is surely a less vital interest in the uninhibited exhibition of material that is on the borderline between pornography and artistic expression than in the free dissemination of ideas of social and political significance."

In an opinion for the Court that in the critical section only gathered a four-justice plurality, Justice John Paul Stevens built on that premise to suggest a modification of the categorization principle to accommodate government regulation of sexual expression on the "borderline" of First Amendment protection. Following the lead of Chief Justice Burger's dissenting opinion in *Erznoznik*, Justice Stevens claimed that the erotic films targeted by the zoning law in *Young*, while not obscene, nevertheless did not merit full First Amendment protection. Rejecting the all-or-nothing, protected-or-unprotected dichotomy of categorization analysis, Stevens envisioned as an alternative, a sliding scale allowing the justices to calibrate a distinct level of First Amendment protection for particular categories of protected speech, with each adjusted according to its level of service to free speech values. Stevens, writing for the *Young* plurality, argued for a low level of constitutional protection for "erotic materials" because their First Amendment value was "of a wholly different, and lesser magnitude than the interest in untrammeled political debate that inspired Voltaire's immortal comment." The Voltaire quotation to which Justice Stevens referred was, "I disapprove of what you say, but I will defend to the death your right to say it." In *Young*, Stevens famously added, "few of us would march our sons and daughters off to war to preserve the citizen's right to see [sexually explicit films] exhibited in the theaters of our choice." Having reduced the level of protection for erotic materials, and perhaps for sexual expression generally, Stevens was careful not to eliminate First Amendment protection entirely. The *Young* plurality made clear that it would not condone "the total suppression" of such fare. But the plurality justices were willing to assess regulations of erotic materials short of a total ban permissively, against the background understanding that the speech at stake resided at the periphery, rather than at the center, of constitutional concern.

Justice Stevens's devaluing of sexually explicit films marked a departure from *Erznoznik*, which had treated films containing nudity no differently than other types of protected speech. Indeed, that was precisely Chief Justice Burger's objection to the *Erznoznik* decision. There was another departure from *Erznoznik* in the *Young* plurality opinion. Whereas the *Erznoznik* Court had labeled the targeting of a disfavored subject matter (nudity) as censorship, the *Young* plurality was unfazed by the government's use of the sexual content of a film as the basis for special restrictions. The Stevens plurality limited its censorship concern to laws directed at the "social, political, or philosophical message" communicated by a film.

Young's rejection of strict scrutiny for laws imposing special restrictions on protected expression based on its sexual content hardly went unchallenged. Justice Potter Stewart, writing for the four dissenting justices in *Young*, criticized the plurality's revisionism in strong terms, charging the plurality with "rid[ing] roughshod over cardinal principles of First Amendment law." To the dissenters, Stevens had "[stood] 'Voltaire's immortal comment' on its head." Stewart explained, "For if the guarantees of the First Amendment were reserved for expression that more than a 'few of us' would take up arms to defend, then the right of free expression would be defined and circumscribed by current popular opinion. The guarantees of the Bill of Rights were designed to protect against precisely such majoritarian limitations upon individual liberty."

There is considerable power in Justice Stewart's objection to Stevens' challenge to conventional free speech doctrine. But there is an undeniable commonsense appeal to Justice Stevens's sliding scale of First Amendment protection as well. It seems obvious that the myriad varieties of protected speech do not equally serve free speech values. Yet categorization divides all expression into two basic groups, protected and unprotected. Such an approach provides a blunt instrument indeed, at least for some kinds of speech. A sliding scale of First Amendment protection, as opposed to the bipolar model of protected-or-unprotected speech, is alluring because it would allow courts to calibrate more carefully the nature and level of protection appropriate for the various types of expression that merit at least some First Amendment protection.

There are nevertheless hazards associated with Stevens's proposed undertaking. Especially for those who are attracted by negative free speech theory—that is, those who are skeptical, even cynical, concerning the competence and integrity of government officials to regulate expression—the prospect of fine-tuning free speech doctrine to provide for less-than-fully-protected speech would be an ominous development. As the experience with obscenity and child pornography shows, it can be perilously difficult for judges to define a satisfactory boundary between the broad categories of protected and unprotected speech. The difficulty is compounded by proliferating subcategories of lesser-protected speech. Along with the increased difficulty, there would be greater danger of official censorship was well. The sliding scale approach provides government officials, including judges, broader discretion to register both their own and their sense of the community's approval or disapproval of particular kinds of expression. It is easier, and for that reason tempting, to reduce First Amendment protection for disfavored forms of speech than it is to justify denying such protection altogether. The Stevens plurality in *Young*, as the Stewart-led dissenters charged, may have been guilty of this very failing when they removed erotic materials to the borderline of First Amendment protection.

The hazards associated with the kind of wholesale sliding scale approach that Justice Stevens advocated in *Young* were exacerbated by his relaxation of the content distinction principle. Although the *Young* plurality opinion encouraged judges to vigorously review restrictions placed on sexual expression because of any particular message it conveys, it permitted them to lower their guard when evaluating restrictions on the basis of the sexual content of the expression. While viewpoint discrimination is the paradigmatic instance of censorship, and message-based restrictions are therefore highly suspect, it hardly follows that subject-matter discrimination is constitutionally trouble-free. Although a governmental focus on subject matter rather than on viewpoint makes it plausible that a restriction may have been grounded on legitimate regulatory concerns and not simply on official or majoritarian disapproval of the restricted speech, any such assumption is treacherous when the subject matter is sexual expression. The Court ordinarily invokes strict scrutiny to evaluate subject-matter distinctions because it is prudent to presume the worst and to obligate judges to review regulatory justifications closely and skeptically to ensure that they are not pretexts for censorship. The lesser scrutiny of *Young*, by contrast, lulled the Court into accepting at face value the city's proffer of conventional zoning justifications for its targeting of adult theaters for special restrictions, while a closer, more skeptical look may well have uncovered a censorial motive.

Justice Stevens was never quite able to garner majority support for his revised approach to sexual expression. While the Court has retained its permissiveness toward zoning laws that impose special restrictions on adult entertainment venues, the justices have subtly shifted their rationale for doing so. In an important later decision that, like *Young*, upheld a city zoning restriction that targeted adult movie theaters, the Court virtually ignored the centerpieces of the *Young* plurality's analysis—the supposed lesser-protected status of erotic materials and the assumed benign quality of subject-matter restrictions—and relied instead on the content distinction principle (City of Renton v. Playtime Theatres, Inc., 1986). But just as the *Young* plurality found it necessary to adjust conventional free speech doctrine in order to accommodate such a zoning restriction, the Court in *Renton* had to tweak the content distinction principle to achieve that result. The justices evaded strict scrutiny in *Renton* by finding the zoning law to be content neutral, even though it, like the law in *Young*, had explicitly imposed special zoning restrictions on theaters that specialized in erotic films. The Court reached this conclusion in the spirit of *Young*, by looking beyond the content-specific text of the law to the legislative purpose behind limiting the location of adult movie theaters. According to the Court, strict scrutiny of the restriction would have been appropriate had the "predominate concerns" of the legislature concerned the "primary effect " of the adult films, that is, the effect of the films on its viewers. The Court found, however, that the legislators had focused on the "secondary effects" associated with adult movie theaters, such as increases in crime and decreases in property values in neighboring areas. Because such secondary effects were not caused by the audience response to the content of the films those theaters exhibited, the Court considered them to be content-neutral justifications for the zoning restriction. In the *Renton* revision of the content distinction principle, then, the government's use of speech content as a basis for restriction is not itself a sufficient warning of official censorship to warrant strict judicial scrutiny. Unless it also can be proven that the law was "enacted for the purpose of restraining speech on the basis of its content," the more forgiving, but still heightened, level of intermediate scrutiny suffices.

This revised understanding of the content distinction principle allowed the Court to distinguish the zoning laws that it upheld in *Young* and *Renton* from the regulation of drive-in theaters that it invalidated in *Erznoznik*, even though in each case the community had restricted the exhibition of certain films explicitly on the basis of the content of those films. The key difference was that the zoning laws involved in *Young* and *Renton*, unlike the law in *Erznoznik*, were not *justified* by reference to the primary effect of the films on those who viewed them. The restriction invalidated in *Erznoznik* reflected a legislative desire to protect passersby from the offense they might experience upon viewing nudity on a drive-in movie screen. But the restrictions in *Young* and *Renton*, the Court found, were predominately motivated not by a legislative design to suppress the erotic content of adult *films*, but by the more benign agenda of controlling the secondary effects of adult movie *theaters* on their neighborhoods. In the *Renton* framework, while a community cannot *ban* completely sexually explicit, non-obscene expression, it has considerable leeway in *channeling* such expression to times and places that minimize their secondary effects (City of Los Angeles v. Alameda Books, Inc., 2002).

The effort in *Renton* to settle the controversy created by the doctrinal innovations of the *Young* plurality was itself controversial. The Court's acceptance of a content-neutral justification to lessen the scrutiny of a content-based law created a concern that lawmakers would seize on such justifications as a pretext to cover up censorship. This concern was exacerbated by the *Renton* Court's disinclination to require that legislators be motivated *exclusively* by concerns over the secondary effects of regulated speech before considering a content-based law to be neutral. It is highly questionable whether a judicial finding that legitimate regulatory concerns predominated over an illegitimate censorial agenda in the legislature should justify lessening the usual strict scrutiny that attends content-based speech restrictions. The legislature's use of a content distinction principle in a speech restriction itself signals a strong possibility of a censorial agenda and should not be set aside lightly. It is often difficult, to say the least, for courts to determine with any sense of confidence whether one legislative intent predominated over another in the enactment of a statute. Moreover, a statute that regulates the right of expression on the basis of speech content has the same censorial effect regardless of whether a censorial or a noncensorial intent predominated in the legislature. The effect of the restrictions in *Young* and *Renton* was that theaters that exhibited erotic films, and the audiences for those films, were denied venues that were open to theaters that exhibited films that were not sexually explicit.

Nevertheless, the *Renton* focus on governmental purpose as keying the content distinction fit conventional free speech jurisprudence better than had the innovations Justice Stevens had suggested in *Young*. And perhaps for that reason, the effect of the *Renton* revision of the content distinction principle has been far more limited than that which would have followed the Court's adoption of the *Young* plurality position. The cases involving the selective zoning of adult businesses remain the only instances in which the justices have allowed textually content-based statutes to escape strict scrutiny through a governmental showing of a secondary effects motivation. Indeed, Justice Anthony M. Kennedy, while endorsing the outcomes in *Young* and *Renton*, recently labeled the *Renton* rationale a "fiction" (see City of Los Angeles v. Alameda Books, Inc., 2002, concurring in the judgment).

Moreover, the Court's refusal in *Renton* to endorse the *Young* plurality's finding of a lesser-protected position for sexual expression importantly suggested that the justices were prepared to presume the unconstitutionality of governmental restrictions enacted for the purpose of addressing the "primary effects" of such expression, most commonly, the offense experienced by some unintended audience members. And indeed, the Court has since made clear that *Young* and *Renton* have "no application to content-based regulations targeting the primary effects of protected speech" (see United States v. Playboy Entertainment Group, Inc., 2000). Such laws, like the law invalidated in *Erznoznik*, receive strict scrutiny if they target protected, sexually explicit expression because it offends "the sensibilities of listeners [or viewers]."

But to hold such laws to strict scrutiny does not mean that they are necessarily invalid. The Court has continued to enforce the line of variable obscenity precedent allowing prohibitions on the distribution of non-obscene sexual expression to minors. The justices in *Playboy*, for example, recognized the authority of the government to restrict the free flow of sexual programming, via broadcast media, cable television, or the Internet, "unwanted into homes where children might see or hear it against parental wishes or consent." Because of strict scrutiny, however, the Court accepts this justification only if the regulation is the least restrictive option for prohibiting access by children. In the years since *Renton*, the justices have tended to inquire whether available technology allows parents to block the access of their children to the sexual expression from which they wish to shield them. If so, the Court has not allowed governmental restrictions (see, e.g., Ashcroft v. American Civil Liberties Union, 2004; Playboy; Sable Communications of California, Inc., v. FCC, 1989). If not, the Court has accepted restrictions of protected sexual expression that are appropriately tailored to the overriding and long-recognized societal interest in preventing the harmful effects of exposing children to erotic materials (see Ashcroft v. American Civil Liberties Union, 2002).

COMMERCIAL SPEECH

In the formative years of free speech jurisprudence, the Supreme Court attempted the same kind of categorical exclusion of commercial speech that it later would try with obscenity. The justices believed that government restrictions on commercial speech, which they defined as "purely commercial advertising," did not implicate the First Amendment because such restrictions did not threaten "the freedom of communicating information and disseminating opinion" (Valentine v. Chrestensen,

1942). *Valentine* provides an amusing illustration of this early treatment. Chrestensen had attempted to distribute leaflets advertising the availability of submarine tours for a stated fee. Local law prohibited the distribution of commercial leaflets, and the authorities advised Chrestensen to desist. Chrestensen then revised his leaflet, adding a second side that protested the locality's refusal to provide certain services for his submarine. The Court held that the newly added protest did not transform Chrestensen's commercial advertising into protected advocacy, for "[i]f that evasion were successful, every merchant who desires to broadcast advertising leaflets in the streets need only append a civic appeal, or a moral platitude, to achieve immunity from the law's command."

There is commonsense appeal to the Court's refusal in *Valentine* to protect commercial speech. At first it seems readily apparent that "purely commercial advertising" does not merit inclusion in the freedom of speech. To paraphrase Justice Stevens, few of us would march our children off to war to defend the right of business firms to hawk their products. But Justice Stevens's rhetorical flourish provides a self-defeating approach to defining First Amendment boundaries because it subordinates free speech to majoritarian tastes. On inspection, what is it about commercial speech that justifies its exclusion from First Amendment protection? Does not commercial advertising typically involve the communication of "information" and "opinion," which the *Valentine* Court described as defining characteristics of protected speech? The traditional answer conceded the point, but distinguished the business nature of the information and opinion communicated by commercial advertising from the social and political commentary that lay at the heart of the First Amendment. Commercial speech was conceptualized as a business practice rather than as individual expression, and government restrictions on advertising were regarded as unproblematic instances of economic and business regulation, not censorship.

The categorical exclusion of commercial speech, like the similar exclusion of obscenity, relied heavily on the ability of judges to distinguish commercial speech from noncommercial speech. And as with obscenity, this enterprise proved to be exceedingly difficult. What was it precisely that marked an advertisement as "purely commercial," and thus outside the freedom of speech? It was not simply that the speech took the form of an advertisement. In New York Times Co. v. Sullivan (1964), the Supreme Court strongly protected the newspaper against a defamation claim for running an advertisement soliciting contributions for the civil rights movement in the South. Even though the *Times* is a business and was compensated for running the ad, the Court rejected the argument that the advertisement was unprotected commercial speech within the meaning of *Valentine*. The Court distinguished *Times* from *Valentine* based on the content of the advertisements in the two cases. While Chrestensen's ad promoted tours on his submarine, the ad in the *Times* "communicated information, expressed opinion, recited grievances, protested claimed abuses, and sought financial support on behalf of a movement whose existence and objectives are matters of the highest public interest and concern." The Court described the *Times* ad as an "editorial advertisement," which was protected under the First Amendment because it provided "an important outlet for the promulgation of information and ideas by persons who do not themselves have access to publishing facilities." Simply put, the *Times* ad promoted a cause, not a product.

The *Times* distinction between commercial and editorial advertising followed *Valentine*'s separation of commercial speech from protected speech. The Court's refusal to allow a commercial motive (that is, the desire to make money) on the part of the *speaker* to determine its categorization of the nature of the *speech* was shrewd. Had the justices not so held, they would have pulled the constitutional rug out from under professional authors and their publishers. But the *Times* focus on advertising content was hardly foolproof. The Court's decision in Bigelow v. Virginia (1975) is a striking illustration of the difficulty inherent to the commercial/noncommercial distinction. Bigelow had been convicted of violating a Virginia statute that made it unlawful to distribute a publication that encouraged or facilitated abortions. His newspaper, which was distributed in Virginia at a time when abortions were illegal there, carried an advertisement offering counseling and placement services for lawful abortions in New York. (The ad ran before the Court had decided Roe v. Wade (1973), which recognized a constitutional right for women to have an abortion.) Was Bigelow's advertisement commercial speech? Like the ad in *Valentine*, his ad promoted a service-for-fee arrangement, but like the ad in *Times*, it also promoted a cause, abortion access. Bigelow's advertisement, in other words, shared the qualities of both commercial and editorial advertising, without fully fitting in either category. Yet, however one described Bigelow's ad, one thing seemed clear: it was not "purely commercial advertising," which was how the Court in *Valentine* had defined the unprotected category of commercial speech. Bigelow's advertisement included, the Court found, "factual material of clear 'public interest.'" Moreover, the Virginia law banning publications that encouraged or facilitated abortions followed the blueprint for official censorship rather than economic regulation. It reflected a transparent legislative effort to stifle advocacy of, and to deny information concerning, abortion access, which, then as now, was a highly charged political and social issue.

The Court in *Bigelow* could have used the free-speech soundings of the abortion-services advertisement to conclude, as it had in *Times*, that the ad was not "purely commercial advertising" and thus was not excludable from the First Amendment under *Valentine*. The justices instead used *Bigelow* far more provocatively to challenge *Valentine* head on, declaring for the first time, "commercial advertising enjoys a degree of First Amendment protection." The Court declared, "The relationship of speech to the marketplace of products or of services does not make it valueless in the marketplace of ideas." The suggestion in *Bigelow* that commercial speech would be afforded "a degree of First Amendment protection," however, suggested less than a full-fledged, judicial embrace of such speech within the freedom of speech. And while the Court was prepared to provide some constitutional protection, it was not ready to define the nature and extent of that protection. The justices settled for the observations that the abortion-services advertisement was neither "deceptive nor fraudulent," that the advertised activity (abortion) was lawful in the state in which it would take place (New York), and that Virginia lacked any substantial interest in shielding its residents from information concerning the availability of lawful abortion services. The Court overturned Bigelow's conviction as a violation of the First Amendment.

The Court expanded the *Bigelow* opening for the constitutional protection of commercial speech the following year in the breakthrough decision, Virginia State Board of Pharmacy v. Virginia Citizens Consumer Council (1976). At issue was another Virginia law. This one prohibited licensed pharmacists from advertising the prices of prescription drugs. Because Virginia permitted only licensed pharmacists to dispense such medications, the effect of the law was to impose a complete ban on price advertising of prescription drugs in the state. Unlike the ads of *Times* and *Bigelow*, the advertising Virginia targeted in *Virginia Pharmacy* was purely, indeed paradigmatically, commercial in nature. The Court observed, "Our pharmacist does not wish to editorialize on any subject, cultural, philosophical, or political. He does not wish to report any particularly newsworthy fact, or to make generalized observations even about commercial matters. The 'idea' he wishes to communicate is simply this: 'I will sell you the X prescription drug at Y price.'" The justices seemed to relish the opportunity to return to *Valentine*.

If *Times* and *Bigelow* had taught how elusive the distinction between commercial and traditionally protected speech can be, *Virginia Pharmacy* revealed to the justices a public interest cognizable by the First Amendment even in what the *Valentine* Court had written off as "purely commercial advertising." Notably, the First Amendment challenge to the Virginia statute had been brought not by pharmacists who wished to promote their products, but by a group that represented consumers who required price and product information in order to purchase necessary medications at affordable prices. The trial record in *Virginia Pharmacy* demonstrated that the prices charged by pharmacies for prescription drugs differed markedly within the same locality, but that the Virginia ban on price advertising kept consumers in the dark about those price differences. Reflecting on the effect of Virginia's ban, the justices became convinced that an individual's interest in "the free flow of commercial information . . . may be as keen, if not keener by far, than his interest in the day's most urgent political debate." They also recognized that commercial advertising served a crucial societal function as well. The Court explained:

> Advertising, however tasteless and excessive it sometimes may seem, is nonetheless dissemination of information as to who is producing and selling what product, for what reason, and at what price. So long as we preserve a predominantly free enterprise economy, the allocation of our resources in large measure will be made through numerous private economic decisions. It is a matter of public interest that those decisions, in the aggregate, be intelligent and well informed. To this end, the free flow of commercial information is indispensable.

The indispensable role of commercial advertising in pumping price and product information through the market system, the Court decided in *Virginia Pharmacy*, justified constitutional protection. In addition, the justices expanded *Bigelow*'s anti-paternalism theme, suggesting that the First Amendment was offended whenever states manipulate consumer choice by denying the information consumers need to make their own purchasing decisions.

Notwithstanding the boldness of its rhetoric, the Court in *Virginia Pharmacy* retained the purposeful ambiguity of *Bigelow* on the place of commercial speech within the freedom of speech. As in *Bigelow*, the Court carefully circumscribed the holding in *Virginia Pharmacy*, asserting just that commercial speech would not be denied *all* First Amendment protection. Because of what the justices regarded as "commonsense differences" between commercial speech and other types of protected speech, they explicitly stopped short of providing commercial advertising the same protection they afforded to speech on political or social issues. The Court made clear the limits of *Virginia Pharmacy* at the conclusion of its opinion, when the justices cleared government officials to continue restricting commercial advertising that is "false or misleading." Outside the commercial speech area, the Court steadfastly has refused to make truth a prerequisite for First Amendment protection (see New York Times Co. v. Sullivan, 1964). The Court in *Virginia Pharmacy* also stipulated that advertising which promoted unlawful activity would be denied protection as well, even though as we have seen, *Brandenberg* generally protects advocacy of law violation except in cases of incitement. In the end, the Court in *Virginia Pharmacy*, as it had in *Bigelow*, left commercial speech in the ambiguous middle position of being neither fully protected nor completely neglected by the First Amendment. *Virginia Pharmacy* produced the muddled effect of freeing commercial advertising from the otherwise pervasive power of governments to regulate economic activity, while subjecting such advertising to forms of government control that otherwise were anathema in conventional free speech jurisprudence.

Within a couple of years the Court made explicit what *Bigelow* and *Virginia Pharmacy* had implied: commercial speech does not warrant full constitutional protection (Ohralik v. Ohio State Bar Ass'n, 1978). This consignment of commercial speech to a lesser-protected status was roughly contemporaneous with Justice Stevens's effort to reduce the protection of erotic but non-obscene films to a similar middling position (Young v. American Mini Theatres, Inc., 1976; see also FCC v. Pacifica Foundation, 1978). The rationale for less-than-full First Amendment protection was similar in both instances. Listening to the Court in *Ohralik* one hears Stevens in *Young*: "[W]e . . . have afforded commercial speech a limited measure of protection, commensurate with its subordinate position in the scale of First Amendment values, while allowing modes of regulation that might be impermissible in the realm of noncommercial expression."

Not long after the *Ohralik* pronouncement, the justices institutionalized the "subordinate position" of commercial speech by adopting a multi-factored test for evaluating government restrictions on commercial advertising (Central Hudson Gas &

Electric Corp. v. Public Service Comm'n of New York, 1980). At the outset, the so-called *Central Hudson* test, following *Bigelow* and *Virginia Pharmacy*, completely denied constitutional protection to commercial advertising that promotes an unlawful activity or that is false or misleading. For advertising that crosses that threshold, the *Central Hudson* test is essentially an adaptation of the intermediate level of judicial scrutiny that courts use when reviewing content-neutral restrictions of speech: The government must justify a restriction of protected commercial speech as being narrowly tailored to serve a substantial public interest. Notwithstanding the relaxation of constitutional protection for commercial speech, the Court served warning in *Central Hudson* that, as in *Bigelow* and *Virginia Pharmacy*, governments would be hard-pressed to justify a total ban of protected advertising.

The intermediate scrutiny prescribed by *Central Hudson* no doubt appealed to the Court because it finessed the hard choice between strict scrutiny and no scrutiny of content-based commercial speech restrictions. Those all-or-nothing alternatives apparently struck the justices as inappropriate. Moreover, intermediate scrutiny enabled the Court to evaluate commercial speech restrictions on an ad hoc basis and within a flexible, moderate framework. But that very flexibility produced an indeterminacy that has plagued commercial speech jurisprudence. The *Central Hudson* test, for example, provides no guidance for determining how "substantial" a government interest must be in order to justify an advertising restriction. Nor does it specify how neatly the restriction must fit that interest in order to be "narrowly tailored." To make matters worse, the Court's application of the *Central Hudson* test has exacerbated rather than ameliorated its inherent indeterminacy. In some cases, the Court has applied the test permissively to allow substantial restrictions on advertising content (e.g., Posadas de P.R. Assocs. v. Tourism Co., 1986). In others, the Court has strictly applied the same criteria to invalidate similar restrictions (e.g., Rubin v. Coors Brewing Co., 1995). Having compromised the decision whether or not to strongly protect commercial speech, the justices were left without a normative anchor to secure commercial speech jurisprudence.

In recent years, however, the Court seems to have addressed the problem of indeterminacy by embracing the norm of anti-paternalism to guide its commercial speech jurisprudence. That norm has encouraged the justices to review closely and skeptically commercial speech restrictions that "seek to keep people in the dark for what the government perceives to be their own good" (44 Liquormart, Inc. v. Rhode Island, 1996, Justice Stevens, prevailing opinion). Such paternalism often drives content-based restrictions on truthful advertising. Indeed, government paternalism accounts as well for many content-based restrictions outside the commercial speech area and in general is a strong indicator of official censorship. The anti-paternalism norm thus has firm grounding in the free speech tradition. It also was a prominent theme both in *Bigelow* and in *Virginia Pharmacy*.

The anti-paternalism norm blurs the difference in First Amendment status between fully protected speech and commercial advertising. If the First Amendment generally disfavors speech restrictions that are infected by government paternalism, the nature of the speech restricted in a particular instance seems less important. It is the nature of the speech restriction, rather than the nature of the speech restricted, that is of paramount constitutional concern. It is not surprising, then, that the Court in recent years has applied the *Central Hudson* test with considerable vigor and has consistently invalidated paternalistic restrictions on commercial advertising (e.g., 44 Liquormart; Greater New Orleans Broadcasting Ass'n v. United States, 1999). Indeed, the Court's application of the *Central Hudson* test has been so vigorous that its commercial speech decisions of late are more in tune with the strict scrutiny visited upon content-based restrictions of fully protected speech than with the middling judicial concern normally associated with intermediate scrutiny. While the Court has shown no inclination to open up First Amendment protection for commercial advertising that is false, misleading, or a promotion of illegal activity, the justices have closely reviewed restrictions on the content of commercial speech that do not fall within one of those unprotected categories. Notwithstanding its "subordinate position" in the First Amendment pantheon, commercial speech receives considerable constitutional protection by the contemporary Court.

SYMBOLIC EXPRESSION

The final category of speech we shall consider differs from the others. The speech categories we have surveyed thus far are defined by the subject-matter content of the expression. Symbolic expression, by contrast, is marked by its nonverbal mode of expression. The symbolic "speaker" communicates a message by conduct, rather than by the spoken or written word. We saw such speech-by-conduct in the *Skokie* litigation, where the silent march by American Nazi Party members, clad in uniforms that evoked those of the storm troopers of the Third Reich, would have spoken volumes had it occurred as planned. Symbolic expression also raises a different categorization question than we have seen. In fact, the doctrine of symbolic expression is a mirror image of the categorization principle. Instead of examining whether a particular category of speech forfeits First Amendment protection because its social costs overwhelm its communicative value, symbolic expression cases require judges to determine whether a particular action merits constitutional protection because of its expressive quality. Thus, while the categorization principle excludes some types of literal speech from the freedom of speech, the doctrine of symbolic expression opens the First Amendment to at least some forms of non-literal speech.

Although it might seem linguistically counterintuitive to treat some forms of conduct as speech, one suspects that this reading of the First Amendment would have neither surprised nor disappointed the founding generation. Surely they appreciated that the Boston Tea Party of December 16, 1773 communicated the emerging revolutionary resistance to British rule in America at least as forcefully as the best colonial pamphlets, and it did so more succinctly.[8] We know from our everyday experience that individuals sometimes intend for their actions to communicate a message, as when one nods in agreement to a point made, winks or blows a kiss to a loved one, or waves goodbye to a companion. We also know, as the saying goes, that "actions speak louder than words," so that on occasion, symbolic conduct may provide a far more powerful medium of communication than oral or written speech. To speak against the Vietnam War was one thing; for a veteran of that war to return his or her medals in protest to the government was quite another. For free speech jurisprudence to deny First Amendment protection outright to such symbolic expression would be to deny the reality and richness of human communication. Yet, to bring all conduct that speaks within the protective umbrella of the First Amendment would be equally unrealistic. What of terrorists who destroy lives and property in order to send a message of intimidation? Or the assassin who advocates regime change by killing a political leader? Those actions also speak clearly, but few would protect them as free speech.

Symbolic expression creates a constitutional dilemma. It intertwines an element of speech, which as a default matter is protected by the First Amendment, with an element of conduct, which typically is subject to government control without First Amendment constraints. Symbolic expression thus collapses the traditional distinction between speech and conduct, which has had a formative influence on free speech jurisprudence. The interplay between speech and conduct, with the resultant cross-pulls toward protection and non-protection, were evident in United States v. O'Brien (1968), the Court's initial effort to solve the symbolic expression puzzle. O'Brien had been convicted of burning his draft card on the steps of the South Boston Courthouse. He testified that his purpose was to persuade those who witnessed the event to reevaluate their position on the Vietnam War. The justices had no difficulty recognizing the expressive quality of O'Brien's act of protest, and they assumed, without discussion, "the alleged communicative element in O'Brien's conduct [was] sufficient to bring into play the First Amendment." But they coupled that assumption with the advisory, "We cannot accept the view that an apparently limitless variety of conduct can be labeled 'speech' whenever the person engaging in the conduct intends thereby to express an idea." The Court's advisory became a warning when the justices ultimately denied O'Brien's free speech claim because of what they regarded as an overriding governmental interest "in assuring the continued availability of issued Selective Service certificates."

The Court's initial ambivalence over protecting symbolic expression gradually evolved into a two-part analysis that attempts to steer *O'Brien*'s middle course, protecting some, but not all, conduct with an "alleged communicative element." In this approach, courts first decide whether the conduct at issue qualifies as "speech." To so qualify, the conduct, in context, must be sufficiently communicative to warrant First Amendment protection. More specifically, courts decide whether the individual engaged in the conduct at issue with the "intent to convey a particularized message," which "in the surrounding circumstances," was likely to be understood by those who saw it (Spence v. Washington, 1974). If so, the individual's conduct communicated a message to an audience, and therefore, it was the functional equivalent of speech.

The Court has not been particularly demanding when enforcing the requirement that a symbolic message be "particularized" in order to qualify for First Amendment protection. O'Brien's burning of his draft card, delivered during the heat of controversy over Vietnam, unmistakingly conveyed a message of opposition to the draft, as well as to the war, that would have satisfied any definition of "particularized." But the justices have not pressed this requirement when assessing conduct that spoke with less particularity. The Court has protected flag-burning, for example, even though the act often expresses only the most general message of anti-Americanism (Texas v. Johnson, 1989; United States v. Eichman, 1990). In a further stretch, the justices also assumed that demonstrators, by sleeping at a protest site in a downtown park, symbolically expressed the plight of the homeless (Clark v. Community for Creative Non-Violence, 1984). The requirement that an actor's conduct convey a "particularized" message has not imposed much of a barrier to the First Amendment's protection of symbolic expression.

The important limitation has arisen from the second part of the Court's analytic framework. When courts find that an individual's conduct was sufficiently communicative to qualify as speech, they then apply the content distinction principle to the governmental restriction at issue. This move from the nature of the individual's expressive act to the nature of the government's restriction finds its genesis in the *O'Brien* decision itself. The Court signaled in *O'Brien* that the symbolic speaker's First Amendment claim would be far stronger in cases "where the alleged government interest in regulating conduct arises in some measure because the communication allegedly integral to the conduct is itself thought to be harmful." But when the government's regulatory interest is "limited to the noncommunicative aspect" of a symbolic speaker's conduct, as the Court held was the case in *O'Brien*, the justices were prepared to accept more readily restrictions on the individual's conduct. The content distinction principle provides the contemporary method of enforcing the *O'Brien* distinction between the restrictions of symbolic expression that are constitutionally suspect and those that are not.

The content distinction principle addresses the symbolic expression dilemma posed by the fusion of speech and conduct by disentangling those elements. If an act of symbolic expression violates a law that targeted the "expressive element" of a symbolic speaker's conduct, courts treat the law as a content-based restriction of speech (Texas v. Johnson, 1989). Because such a law is activated by what the symbolic conduct "said," it is no different from any other attempt by the government to silence a speaker because officials believe that the content of the speech is itself harmful to the public interest. So long as the speech content does not fall within a category of unprotected speech, such a law is presumptively censorial and will survive only if it withstands strict judicial scrutiny, which is a rare event indeed. If on the other hand, the law at issue targets the conduct element of symbolic expression, courts reduce their scrutiny to the intermediate level appropriate for content-neutral speech restrictions (see Clark v. Community for Creative Non-Violence, 1984). This relaxation of the standard of review is justified because the conduct itself is harmful, regardless whether it happens to be expressive, and the First Amendment typically does not limit the state in prohibiting harmful conduct. Perhaps for this reason, the Supreme Court has suggested that governments have more leeway in addressing the "noncommunicative impact" (O'Brien) of expressive conduct than they possess when imposing content-neutral restrictions on pure speech (Texas v. Johnson, 1989).

The content distinction principle thus provides that the intertwining of speech and conduct in symbolic expression neither authorizes government censorship of valuable speech nor immunizes harmful conduct from governmental control. While the justices have never upheld a restriction on symbolic expression that they have understood to be a regulation of speech content, they have accepted almost uncritically every restriction that they have understood to be concerned solely with harmful conduct by a symbolic speaker.

NOTES

* Frederick Schauer, "Codifying the First Amendment: New York v. Ferber," *The Supreme Court Review* (1982): 285–317, pp. 287–88.

1. Lyrissa Lidsky and George Wright, *Freedom of the Press: A Reference Guide to the United States Constitution* (New York: Praeger Press, 2004).

2. See Mark C. Rutzick, "Offensive Language and the Evolution of First Amendment Protection," *Harvard Civil Rights-Civil Liberties Law Review* 9 (1974): 1–28.

3. See Lee Bollinger, *The Tolerant Society: Freedom of Speech and Extremist Speech in America* (New York: Oxford University Press, 1986).

4. The discussion of obscenity and child pornography in this section borrows from my essay: Keith Werhan, "The Tie that Binds: Constitutional Law and Culture, Obscenity and Child Pornography," *South Atlantic Quarterly* 100 (2001): 897–917.

5. The description is that of Anthony Comstock, quoted in David M. Rabban, *Free Speech in its Forgotten Years* (Cambridge: Cambridge University Press, 1997): p. 29.

6. 18 U.S.C. §§ 2256–2260.

7. Andrea Dworkin, "Against the Male Flood: Censorship, Pornography, and Equality," 8 *Harvard Women's Law Journal* (1985): 1–29, pp. 8–9.

8. See Louis Henkin, "On Drawing Lines," *Harvard Law Review* 82 (1968): 63–92, p. 79.

6

The Procedural First Amendment

"'The history of American freedom,' Mr. Justice Frankfurter once observed, 'is, in no small measure, the history of procedure.'... Responding to this realization, courts have ... construct[ed] a body of procedural law which defines the manner in which they and other bodies must evaluate and resolve ... first amendment 'due process'."

Henry P. Monaghan*

The Supreme Court has codified First Amendment jurisprudence not only by developing special rules for particular categories of speech content, but also by categorizing free speech doctrine according to the varying nature of the restrictions that governments impose on speech. The justices have recognized that particular types of speech regulation, like certain categories of speech, raise distinctive First Amendment issues. They also have recognized that different methods of speech regulation, like different types of speech content, create differing degrees of First Amendment concern, thus warranting distinct levels of judicial scrutiny. But there is a difference between categorizing speech content and speech regulation: When assessing speech content, the Court begins from a baseline of full First Amendment protection and inquires whether a particular category of speech dictates a retreat from that norm. When the Court examines the nature of a speech restriction, the justices may heighten as well as lower the level of constitutional protection generally afforded free speech.

We have already seen the Court's most important doctrine categorizing governmental restrictions on speech—the content distinction principle. That doctrine is grounded on the judicial sense that restrictions predicated on the government's desire to limit or to eradicate a specific speech content are more likely censorial than are restrictions that the government imposes without regard to the content of speech. Thus content-based distinctions are presumptively unconstitutional and are typically subjected to strict judicial scrutiny, whereas content-neutral restrictions face only an intermediate level of review. Within that basic two-level structure, however, the Court has integrated several additional doctrines that further calibrate judicial scrutiny according to the nature of government speech restrictions. This chapter takes a brief look at these complementary, restriction-based doctrines.

The public forum doctrine, which is discussed first, applies to government regulations of expressive activity on public property. The doctrine directs reviewing courts to adjust First Amendment scrutiny according to the nature of the public property that a speaker wishes to use as a forum for speech. The other restriction-based doctrines considered in this chapter—the doctrines of prior restraint, overbreadth, and vagueness—serve only to ratchet up judicial scrutiny. These latter three doctrines address speech restrictions that are so invidious or threatening to First Amendment values that the courts at times prohibit their use against otherwise unprotected expressive activity.

THE PUBLIC FORUM DOCTRINE

The public forum doctrine provides individuals a First Amendment right to engage in expressive activity on public property. The doctrine got off to a false start in the final years of the nineteenth century, however (Davis v. Massachusetts, 1897). Davis was convicted of delivering a sermon on Boston Common without having obtained the necessary city permit. He defended by challenging the constitutionality of the permit requirement. As recounted in the Court's opinion, Davis argued, "Boston Common is the property of the inhabitants of the city of Boston, and dedicated to the use of the people of that city and the public in many ways; and the preaching of the gospel there has been, from time immemorial to a recent period, one of these ways." It should not be surprising that Davis's argument resonated more with property law than with freedom of speech. The case arose during the "dark age" of First Amendment jurisprudence, before the development of truly protective free speech doctrine (see Chapter 1). The justices responded to Davis's constitutional claim in kind, ruling that as holder of legal title to Boston Common, the city could control public use of the park. The Court essentially rubber-stamped the opinion that Justice Oliver Wendell Holmes, Jr., then a member of the Supreme Judicial Court of Massachusetts, had written when *Davis* was before that court. According to Holmes, "For the Legislature absolutely or conditionally to forbid public speaking in a highway or public park is no more an infringement of the rights of a member of the public than for the owner of a private house to forbid it in his house" (Commonwealth v. Davis, 1895). The Court's decision in *Davis*, as well as Holmes's opinion for the state high court, was emblematic of pre-modern First Amendment jurisprudence in its failure to appreciate freedom of speech as a fundamental right deserving of strong constitutional protection.

The justices reversed their position on the public forum near the end of the 1930s, when, not coincidentally, the Court finally came to accept the fundamental nature of the free speech guarantee. The turning point came in Hague v. Committee for Industrial Organization (1939), which invalidated a city ordinance that local officials had used systematically to prevent labor organizations and their advocates from holding assemblies on public property. Justice Owen J. Roberts, writing only for a plurality of three justices, accepted Davis's original argument for speaker access to public property. In language that has been quoted frequently, Roberts wrote, "Wherever the title of streets and parks may rest, they have immemorially been held in trust for the use of the public and, time out of mind, have been used for purposes of assembly, communicating thoughts between citizens, and discussing public questions. Such use of the streets and public places has, from ancient times, been a part of the privileges, immunities, rights, and liberties of citizens." Justice Roberts thus turned Holmes's position in *Davis* on its head. A democratic government does not stand in the shoes of a private property owner, as Holmes would have it, but rather it controls public places merely as trustee for the benefit of a sovereign people. Justice Roberts conceded that public use of public property for expressive purposes could not be absolute, however. Expressive activity is hardly the only public use of "streets and public places." According to Roberts, the government, in its role as property custodian, may *regulate* speaker access to public property in order to accommodate competing uses of the property. But it may not "abridge[] or den[y]" speaker access to public places "in the guise of regulation."

Justice Roberts's use of the rhetoric of property rights met *Davis* on its own terms, but his conception of public places as public fora was informed by a vision of free speech that was wholly absent from the prior decision. In Roberts's plurality opinion in *Hague*, the public forum is nothing less than a physical manifestation of the marketplace of ideas, an American *agora*. Streets, sidewalks, and parks comprise the central nervous system of local communities. They are the places where residents come into contact with each other on a daily basis. The public forum doctrine requires the government to recognize that social reality by opening these common areas to those who seek expressive encounters with their fellow citizens.

The public's expressive use of public places is necessary for freedom of free speech because these places frequently offer the only venues available to advocates who lack the financial heft to reach an audience through the media. The expressive uses for which speakers might commandeer public property are many and varied. Groups can take to the streets to stage public demonstrations in support of their causes. Individuals can use public sidewalks to facilitate such one-on-one encounters as leafleting, soliciting financial support, or engaging in conversation. Or they might convene a meeting in a public auditorium in order to discuss issues of the day, or to hold a rally in a public park. The public forum doctrine serves as a First Amendment equalizer, providing access not so much to a piece of property, but to potential audiences that many speakers could not otherwise hope to reach.

The protective potential of *Hague*'s conceptualization of a community's common areas as public fora matured in a series of cases involving municipal efforts to prevent proselytizing by Jehovah's Witnesses. Members of that group often spread their word and distributed their literature by house-to-house canvassing and by engaging passersby on sidewalks. Many people found these encounters annoying. And because Jehovah's Witnesses at times caustically criticized other religions, especially Catholicism, these activities often proved to be provocative as well. Municipal officials in a number of communities responded to residents' complaints about Jehovah's Witnesses by generally restricting various kinds of expressive activity on public property, rather than by targeting the group explicitly. The Jehovah's Witnesses often registered their rejection of these restrictions by simply ignoring them, and they were duly prosecuted in a number of localities. The result of the Jehovah's Witnesses controversies was a series of First Amendment decisions involving "petty offenses that raised constitutional questions of the most serious magnitude" (Watchtower Bible and Tract Society of New York v. Village of Stratton, 2002).

The Court's Jehovah's Witnesses decisions enforced and elaborated the nascent public forum doctrine of *Hague*. The central theme of the decisions was that the First Amendment required municipal officials to open public property even to expressive activity that imposed real costs on the cities and its residents. The leading decision sounding this theme was Schneider v. State (1939), which the Court decided the same year as *Hague*. *Schneider* involved First Amendment challenges to four municipal ordinances that restricted leafleting in public places. Following the Roberts plurality opinion in *Hague*, the Court emphasized the duty of municipal officers, as "trustees for the public," to ensure that public streets and sidewalks provide a place where individuals can exercise their "fundamental personal rights" to free expression. Streets and sidewalks, the Court explained, were "natural and proper places for the dissemination of information and opinion," and keeping those places available for that purpose was "vital to the maintenance of democratic institutions." The cities had expressed a concern that leafleting led to littering, but the municipal duty to maintain the cleanliness of public property, the Court held, was insufficient to trump the powerful free speech values sacrificed by the ordinances.

Schneider thus gathered the majority support for Justice Roberts's public forum doctrine that was absent in *Hague*. The decision also tweaked the doctrine by requiring that any cost/benefit balancing regarding speaker access to the public forum be calibrated, in Harry Kalven's famous description, with a judicial "thumb . . . on the speech side of the scales."[1] As the Court put it in a later decision, "The right to use a public place for expressive activity may be restricted only for weighty reasons" (Grayned v. City of Rockford, 1972). In assessing the weight of the government's reasons for restricting expressive activity in the public forum, the Court in *Grayned* focused on the "nature of [the] place" together with "the pattern of its normal activities." In *Grayned*, the Court identified the "crucial question" in public forum analysis as "whether the manner of expression is basically compatible with the normal activity of a particular place at a particular time." This so-called "compatibility test" focused public forum doctrine on one simple, functional inquiry: whether the expressive activity would materially interfere with an overriding governmental interest regarding the property at issue. If not, *Grayned* required the government to accommodate speaker access.

The vitality of the public forum doctrine elaborated in *Hague*, *Schneider*, and *Grayned* has been diluted in recent years by two developments. The first of these developments is the content distinction principle. That doctrine began its firm hold on free speech jurisprudence with the Court's opinion in Police Department of City of Chicago v. Mosley (1972), which, ironically, the justices decided on the same day as *Grayned*. Justice Thurgood Marshall, writing for the Court in *Mosley*, integrated the presumption against content-based restrictions on speech with the public forum doctrine in rhetoric which rivaled that of Justice Roberts's opinion in *Hague*. Justice Marshall wrote:

> [G]overnment may not grant the use of a forum to people whose views it finds acceptable, but deny use to those wishing to express less favored or more controversial views. And it may not select which issues are worth discussing or debating in public facilities. There is an 'equality of status in the field of ideas,' and government must afford all points of view an equal opportunity to be heard. Once a forum is opened up to assembly or speaking by some groups, government may not prohibit others from assembling or speaking on the basis of what they intend to say. Selective exclusions from a public forum may not be based on content alone, and may not be justified by reference to content alone.

While *Mosley* made clear that the Court would not tolerate content-based exclusions of expressive activity from the public forum except, if at all, in the most extraordinary of circumstances, the negative implication of that declaration emerged only with the passage of time: the Court would be more accepting of content-neutral restrictions on speaker access to the public forum than *Schneider* and *Grayned* had suggested.

While the justices in *Grayned*, consistent with *Schneider*, had limited governmental authority to restrict expressive activity in the public forum on a content-neutral basis "only for weighty reasons," the contemporary Court has not consistently held itself to that standard. The Court, for example, has allowed content-neutral restrictions on speaker access to the public forum in the interest of facilitating the orderly movement of patrons on state fairgrounds (Heffron v. International Society for Krishna Consciousness, 1981), of maintaining the aesthetic appearance of a city (Members of City Council v. Taxpayers for Vincent, 1984; Metromedia, Inc. v. San Diego, 1981), and of maintaining the attractiveness of public parks (Clark v. Community for Creative Non-Violence, 1984). Justice Marshall, the author of the Court's opinions in both *Mosley* and *Grayned*, decried the tendency of the justices to allow themselves to be lulled by the content neutrality of public forum restrictions into ignoring the weight of the rationale that supported the restrictions. Because the Court "dramatically lowered its scrutiny" of content-neutral restrictions on speaker access, Justice Marshall observed, the justices have "transformed the ban against content distinctions from a floor that offers all persons at least equal liberty under the First Amendment into a ceiling that restricts persons to the protection of First

Amendment equality—but nothing more." The Court on occasion has invalidated overly broad, content-neutral restrictions on speaker access to the public forum, as when a restriction manifestly failed to serve the government's stated interests (see United States v. Grace, 1983), or when a restriction almost completely banned a medium of communication (see City of Ladue v. Gilleo, 1994). But such decisions are decidedly the exception to what has become an otherwise permissive judicial approach to content-neutral restrictions on speaker access to the public forum.

The second limitation on the speech protectiveness of the public forum doctrine finds its roots in the originator of the doctrine, *Hague* itself. Justice Roberts, recall, ushered in the right of speaker access by emphasizing that "streets and public places" had been used as fora for expression, "time out of mind." But what of the many kinds of government property that have not traditionally been so used? Was the mere fact of government ownership sufficient to open property to speakers? Or did the absence of a free speech tradition for a particular type of property justify the government in making it off limits to expressive activity?

The Court's decision in *Grayned*, by focusing on the compatibility of expressive activity with the non-speech uses of the public property in question, had deemphasized the importance of the historical use of property as a forum for speech. But the Court abruptly shifted direction in Greer v. Spock (1976). In *Greer*, the Court upheld the refusal by the commanding officer of Fort Dix to allow several minor party candidates for president onto the base to hold a campaign rally, distribute literature, and discuss issues with soldiers. The *Greer* logic, in its simplicity, was devastating to the candidates' public forum claim. Unlike the streets, sidewalks, and parks embraced in *Hague* as public properties that "time out of mind" had provided a forum for free expression, the purpose of military bases, as the Court succinctly put it, was "to train soldiers." Because the government's purpose in maintaining the bases did not include providing a forum for expression, the Court held, they were not public fora. And because the bases were not public fora, the Court further held, individuals had "no generalized constitutional right" to enter the base in order to engage in expressive activity. The Court in *Greer* did not concern itself with the question of whether the government could have accommodated the expressive activity without compromising the security of the base or its training mission. Nor did it matter that the speakers had sought access only to areas within the base that generally were open to the public. The key for the Court was whether the property qualified as a public forum, and the crucial determinant of that designation was the government's purpose in holding and maintaining the property.

The Court cemented the *Greer* transformation of the public forum doctrine in Perry Education Ass'n v. Perry Local Educators' Ass'n (1983), declaring, "[t]he existence of a right of access to public property and the standard by which limitations upon such a right must be evaluated differ depending on the character of the property at issue." In *Perry*, the Court constructed a three-level hierarchy of public property. *Hague*'s "traditional public forum" resided at the pinnacle. These are public places that, in the language of *Perry*, "by long tradition . . . have been devoted to assembly and debate." The Court since *Perry* essentially has limited the category of traditional public fora to streets, sidewalks, and parks. The usual rules of free speech jurisprudence apply when individuals seek to engage in expressive activity in a traditional public forum: content-based restrictions are subjected to strict judicial scrutiny, while content-neutral restrictions receive intermediate scrutiny. Although the rhetoric of the Court's opinions at times suggest that government restrictions on speaker access to the traditional public forum trigger an especially critical look by the justices, the Court's actual decision-making seldom evidences any such heightened judicial concern. There is one distinctive feature of a property's designation as a traditional public forum, however. The Court in *Perry* retained the *Hague* injunction that governments cannot completely close traditional public fora to expressive activity.

At the bottom of the *Perry* hierarchy was "non-forum property," which includes all public property, like the military base in *Greer,* that governments maintain for purposes other than to provide a forum for expression. In a disconcerting nod to *Davis*, the *Perry* Court compared the government's control over non-forum property with that of a private property owner. When the state restricts the expressive use of non-forum property, it acts as a "proprietor, managing its internal operations, rather than . . . as [a] lawmaker," regulating individuals' right of free expression (International Society for Krishna Consciousness v. Lee, 1992). In the *Perry* scheme, the First Amendment provides no right of speaker access to non-forum property. The government, as property custodian, is free to deny such access so long as the denial is reasonable and viewpoint-neutral.

Residing in a variable middle position between the traditional public forum and non-forum property was the "designated public forum." This category includes public property that governments have voluntarily "opened for use by the public as a place for expressive activity" (Perry). In a designated public forum, the scope of a speaker's right of access is determined by the extent to which the government has opened the property for expressive use. If the government has opened property generally to expressive activity, the broad free speech rights of the traditional public forum apply, although the government may close a designated forum to all expressive activity whenever it wishes (Perry). But the government may also choose to limit free speech rights when it designates a public forum. In that event, officials can restrict expressive activity in such fora consistently with the limitations the government has imposed, so long as the restrictions are reasonable and viewpoint-neutral.

The Court has allowed the government to limit use of a designated forum to certain speakers and to speech on specified subjects. For example, a public university may limit access to its facilities to students enrolled at the university (see Widmar v. Vincent, 1981), or the governmental sponsors of a pre-election debate may reserve the podium for candidates who have satisfied reasonable criteria of electability (see Arkansas Educational Television Comm'n v. Forbes, 1998). In addition to such speaker-based restrictions, the Court has permitted the state to designate fora for particular subject matter. For example, a school board may limit public comments at its meetings to items on the agenda (see City of Madison Joint School District v. Wisconsin Public Employment Relations Comm'n, 1976). The government, however, is bound by the rules governing speaker access that it has created, at least until it closes or re-designates the forum. Thus, in the examples mentioned above, the university could not deny access to its facilities to a student group whose message it opposed; the debate sponsors could not reject a qualifying candidate whom they did not wish to see elected; and the school board could not rule out of order those who intended to speak in opposition to an agenda item its members supported. As these examples illustrate, whenever the government denies speaker access in violation of the rules it has established for use of a designated public forum, official censorship looms as the likely explanation.

Because the Court has essentially closed the category of the traditional public forum to all public places except for streets, sidewalks, and parks, the dynamic of much contemporary public forum litigation involves a struggle over whether to categorize the public property at issue as a designated public forum or as a non-forum. The Court has been strict in these disputes, insisting that in order for property to qualify as a designated public forum, the government must have "intentionally open[ed]" the property to "public discourse" (NAACP Legal Defense and Educational Fund v. Cornelius, 1985). True to *Greer*, the government's purpose for maintaining the property is key. And as *Greer* illustrates, the Court has not been persuaded by a showing that the property in question was generally open to the public or that the property was capable of accommodating expressive activity. Nor has it been sufficient to prove that the property on occasion has provided a venue for expression. In order to find the requisite designation, the Court expects to see a government policy or a manifest practice establishing that the purpose of the property in question is to serve as a public forum (Cornelius; Perry).

The Court's categorization of public property into three discrete levels of forum status resembles the justices' categorization of speech into three levels of First Amendment protection. Both efforts flow from the justices' perceived need to establish limits to strong free speech protection. They also reflect the commonsense judgment that the nature and degree of free speech protections should vary for different types of speech and different kinds of public property. Both approaches create similar problems as well. Neither public property nor speech arranges itself into neat categories. Just as lesser protected or unprotected categories of speech at times implicate free speech values, non-forum property often can accommodate expressive activity. Allowing the government free rein to restrict expression in these instances often undermines freedom of speech.

In one important sense, the *Perry* approach to categorizing public property is more troubling than the Court's traditional categorization of speech. In categorizing speech, the Court begins with a default position that expression is fully protected by the First Amendment, and places the burden on the government to persuade the justices that lessening or rejecting such protection is appropriate. Under *Perry*, however, the default position is that all public property other than streets, sidewalks and parks are non-forum property, and thus are largely immune from free speech obligations unless the government has consciously adopted a policy or practice to open the property to expressive activity. Because it is the government's purpose that largely dictates public forum status, it is government officials, not the courts, who make the crucial judgments in defining free speech rights on public property. Whereas *Hague* created the public forum doctrine to loosen the control of government custodians over expressive activity on public property, the contemporary doctrine has largely returned that control.

With these criticisms in mind, Justice Anthony M. Kennedy recently proposed a revision of the public forum doctrine that would reorient the doctrine in a speech-protective direction (International Society for Krishna Consciousness v. Lee, 1992, concurring in the judgment). Rather than relying on the government's purpose for maintaining a public place to define public forum status, Justice Kennedy, in the spirit of *Grayned*, would look more functionally at the "actual, physical characteristics and uses of the property." Kennedy would provide public forum status not only to streets, sidewalks, and parks, but also more generally to all public property where "the objective physical characteristics . . . and the actual public access and uses which have been permitted by the government indicate that expressive activity would be appropriate and compatible with those uses." Justice Kennedy's reform, which came within one vote of a majority, would return the focus of the public forum doctrine to where it began in *Hague*, *Schneider*, and *Grayned*. Were the Court to adopt Kennedy's proposed reformation of the public forum doctrine, government officials once again would be required to accommodate expressive activity in public places unless the activity would be incompatible with other overriding uses for the property.

THE PRIOR RESTRAINT DOCTRINE

The irreconcilability of a program of government censorship with a system of free expression, as well as the identification of prior restraints on expression as the essence of censorship, was ingrained in Anglo-American constitutionalism long before the founding of the United States. As recounted in our consideration of the history of free speech in Chapter 1, England responded to the invention of the printing press by creating a licensing system that required printers to receive the permission of royal officials before publishing a text. In free speech theory, such a licensing system constitutes a paradigmatic "prior restraint" on expression, because it requires governmental permission *before* a speaker is legally entitled to disseminate ideas and information to the public. The incompatability of the prior restraint of the English licensing system and free expression inspired John Milton in 1644 to write *Areopagitica*, which presented a defense of freedom of speech that became a milestone in Anglo-American constitutional history. England interred its licensing system in 1695, and, by the time of the American Revolution, it had enshrined a common law principle that defined "liberty of the press," and by extension, freedom of speech, as a freedom from "*previous* restraints on publication." (Emphasis in original.) William Blackstone, the authoritative expositor of English common law in the eighteenth century, justified that principle by equating prior restraints with government censorship, a system that "subject[s] all freedom of sentiment to the prejudices of one man, and make[s] him the arbitrary and infallible judge of all controversial points in learning, religion, and government." At common law, according to Blackstone, "[e]very freeman has an undoubted right to lay what sentiments he pleases before the public: to forbid this, is to destroy the freedom of the press."[2]

Blackstone's focus on prior restraints as the essence of censorship, and thus as the antithesis of free expression, strongly influenced American constitutional thought. In their early nineteenth century legal commentaries, James Kent and Joseph Story both followed Blackstone by equating freedom of the press, and again by extension, free speech, to the freedom from prior restraint.[3] Moreover, the Supreme Court emphasized early on that "the main purpose" of the First Amendment was to provide a bulwark against prior restraints (Patterson v. Colorado, 1907; Schenck v. United States, 1919). Such judicial rhetoric has been a staple of free speech jurisprudence ever since. For example, the modern Court characterized "prior restraints on speech and publication [as] the most serious and the least tolerable infringement on First Amendment rights" (Nebraska Press Ass'n v. Stuart, 1976). Accordingly, the Court has frequently emphasized that "[a]ny system of prior restraints of expression [bears] a heavy presumption against its constitutional validity" (Bantam Books, Inc. v. Sullivan, 1963).

Because of the historic linkage between prior restraints on expression and official censorship, it is easy to understand the deep antipathy to prior restraints that is such a prominent feature of contemporary First Amendment jurisprudence. Determining the doctrinal content of the special judicial hostility to prior restraints remains somewhat elusive, however. After all, content-based restrictions on speech generally are considered presumptively unconstitutional and rarely survive the strict judicial scrutiny they face. What greater protection, then, is afforded against prior restraints? The Court has never absolutely prohibited prior restraints, but it has cautioned that the "exceptional nature" of prior restraints requires that they be reserved for "exceptional cases" (Near v. Minnesota, 1931). The implication is that prior restraint systems trigger a kind of hyper-scrutiny. And such has been the case. The justices have subjected content-based prior restraints to a super-strict scrutiny, and they have given content-neutral prior restraints a more careful look than often is the case at intermediate scrutiny. Indeed, the Court's antipathy toward prior restraints runs so deep that the justices have invalidated such restrictions on unprotected categories of speech (see Near v. Minnesota, 1931). That is, even in cases where the First Amendment permits the imposition of civil or criminal liability on a speaker, the government often is unable to prevent that speaker from engaging in the expressive activity in the first place. As Blackstone observed, such a speaker is free "to lay what sentiments he pleases before the public," but he must be prepared to "take the consequences of his own temerity" if his expressive activity is unprotected.

The most celebrated instance of the prior restraint doctrine in action is the *Pentagon Papers* case (New York Times Co. v. United States, 1971). The *Pentagon Papers* was a top-secret Pentagon study entitled, "History of U.S. Decision-Making Process on Viet Nam Policy." The study analyzed U.S. involvement in Southeast Asia from 1945 until 1968. The Johnson administration had undertaken the *Pentagon Papers* project in its waning years as part of a major reassessment of Vietnam policy. President Richard M. Nixon apparently had not even known that the *Pentagon Papers* existed until *The New York Times* began publishing portions of the study in the summer of 1971. *The Washington Post* began publishing its own installments of the *Papers* several days later.

The Nixon administration quickly filed suit asking federal courts in New York City and in Washington, D.C., to enjoin further publication of the *Pentagon Papers* by the two newspapers in order to avoid what the government claimed to be grave and irreparable harm to the national interest. These suits marked the first occasion on which the United States had sought a prior restraint of expression on national security grounds. There were still over 140,000 troops stationed in Southeast Asia at the time, and national security agencies were united in the belief that public disclosure of the *Pentagon Papers*, in various ways, might prolong the war and jeopardize the lives of U.S. personnel. The National Security Agency feared that information in the study would help America's adversaries to break U.S. codes. The Central Intelligence Agency worried about exposing sources and methods of U.S. intelligence gathering. The Defense Department was concerned over disclosing military plans, strategy, and tactics to the enemy. And the State Department noted that publication of the *Pentagon Papers* might compromise the delicate peace talks with North Vietnam because such a massive leak of highly classified information suggested that the United States could not be trusted to keep a secret.[4]

Both district courts ordered a temporary halt to publication. Because of the constitutional sensitivity surrounding prior restraints, the cases flew to the Supreme Court with only the briefest of stops in the courts of appeals. Only sixteen days separated the government's commencement of the suits in the district courts and the Supreme Court's final decision overturning the lower court injunctions. In the ordinary operation of the rules of federal civil procedure, a defendant has nearly twice that amount of time simply to answer a complaint. Justice John Marshall Harlan, writing for the three dissenters in *New York Times*, complained that the "frenzied" pace of the litigation, which had been undertaken "in the name of the presumption against prior restraints," left the judiciary with a "wholly inadequate" amount of time to "giv[e] these cases the kind of consideration they deserve." Justice Harlan surely had a point. The 47 monographs that constituted the *Pentagon Papers* included about 7,000 mimeographed pages, some 2.5 million words. No one who had helped to prepare the *Papers* remained in the government. And more to the point, no one involved in the litigation—including the lawyers, newspaper editors, national security agency officials, and judges—had been able to process the information contained in the study during the short life of the litigation.

Nevertheless, a six-justice majority of the Court concluded that a prior restraint on the publication of the *Pentagon Papers* was incompatible with the First Amendment. The majority joined together in a brief *per curiam* ("by the court") opinion, which simply stated that the government had not met its "heavy burden" in overcoming the strong presumption against the constitutionality of prior restraints on expression. Each of the justices in the majority wrote a concurring opinion, with no one opinion gaining the allegiance of more than two justices. Nevertheless, there is a common theme in the views of several justices which suggests that the government's failure to justify the injunctions lay in the speculative nature of the claims of harm to the national security. Certainty, not guesswork, was required. Justices William J. Brennan, Jr., and Potter Stewart, two of the concurring justices, seemed to use a hyper-*Brandenburg* standard in assessing the government's case. Justice Brennan described the standard for obtaining a prior restraint on national security grounds as obligating the government to prove that "publication must inevitably, directly, and immediately cause the occurrence of an event kindred to imperiling the safety of a transport already at sea." Justice Stewart, in an opinion joined by Justice Byron R. White, used similar language, requiring that "disclosure . . . will surely result in direct, immediate, and irreparable damage to our Nation or its people." And Justices Hugo L. Black and William O. Douglas, two other concurring justices, went even further, absolutely prohibiting any prior restraint on publication of information that the press had in its possession.

In operation, there may be scant difference between the hyper-*Brandenburg* standard of Justices Brennan and Stewart and the absolute prohibition advocated by Justices Black and Douglas, for surely it would be only the most extraordinary of cases where the government could actually prove that any publication was *certain* to cause immediate and grave harm. Prior restraints look to the future, not the past, at what will happen, and not at what has happened. Predicting the future with certainty is seldom, if ever, possible. The rigorous nature of the *New York Times* burden of proof for prior restraints on national security grounds came through most clearly with the acknowledgment by several concurring justices that publication of the *Pentagon Papers* would likely (although not *certainly*) cause at least some of the harms cited by the national security agencies. Indeed Justice White, joined by Justice Stewart, used his concurring opinion to make clear that the government's inability to justify the prior restraint on publication did not compromise its "constitutional entitlement to a conviction for criminal publication." Justice White, in fact, all but pleaded with the government to proceed criminally against the newspapers for publishing the leaked Pentagon study.

The special First Amendment hostility to systems of prior restraint so vividly on display in the *Pentagon Papers* case results from the lesson of history that such systems invariably operate as an "apparatus of censorship" (Freedman v. Maryland, 1965). The central First Amendment concern over prior restraint systems is that, like many other regulatory regimes, they suffer from a tendency to over-regulate the activity they are designed to control. This concern is especially acute when the regulated activity is expression. The natural tendency of government regulators is to err on the side of caution by preventing potentially harmful speech. The value of expression often seems abstract when compared with threats of concrete harms. This explains why the national security agencies in *New York Times* unanimously supported a prior restraint of the *Pentagon Papers* based on fears that, at least in retrospect, seem overdrawn. Erwin Griswold, who as Solicitor General of the United States argued the government's case in *New York Times*, later wrote, "I have never seen any trace of a threat to the national security from the publication. Indeed, I have never seen it even suggested that there was such an actual threat."[5] Leslie Gelb, who oversaw the compilation of the *Pentagon Papers*, has concurred in that view.[6] *New York Times* illustrates that decisions to issue a prior restraint are necessarily hampered by the speculative nature of the predicted consequences of speech that has not yet occurred. In cases where the harmful effects of speech are uncertain, the First Amendment counsels erring on the side of free expression, not suppression. Because government regulators cannot be expected to heed that counsel, courts have largely displaced their authority to issue prior restraints on expression.[7]

The strong presumption against prior restraints in First Amendment jurisprudence, however, is not simply a prescription for a diagnosis of regulatory failure. As Blackstone understood, prior restraints on expression are anathema in a constitutional order dedicated to freedom of speech. The distinction between the *deterrence* of legally questionable speech by subsequent punishment schemes and the *prevention* of such speech by prior restraint systems, while subtle, is nevertheless profound. As the Supreme Court observed, "A prior restraint, by contrast [to a subsequent punishment], has an immediate and irreversible sanction. If it can be said that a threat of criminal or civil sanctions after publication 'chills' speech, prior restraint 'freezes' it at least for the time" (Nebraska Press Ass'n v. Stuart, 1976). The chilling effect of criminal penalties for proscribed categories of speech, of course, is hardly trouble-free. Speakers are motivated to think carefully, and at times too cautiously, before sharing their ideas and information publicly. But as Blackstone argued, such speakers retain the freedom to speak out, and if need be, to defend their reasons for doing so. Prior restraints rob individuals of that freedom. They are anathema under the First Amendment precisely because they lodge the ultimate decision on whether to speak with government officials, rather than with speakers themselves.

* * *

In addition to instances where, as in the *Pentagon Papers* case, the government has asked judges to enjoin expressive activity, the Court also has deployed the strong presumption against prior restraints in its more traditional setting—government licensing systems for expressive activity. In the modern era, licensing systems have drawn the Court's attention primarily in two areas, and have elicited different responses from the justices. The Court has virtually disabled systems requiring governmental pre-clearance of motion pictures in order to prevent the exhibition of obscene films. But the Court generally allows governments to use licensing systems in order to control access to the public forum. These two lines of prior restraint precedent are discussed in turn.

Modern Licensing Systems: Obscenity

Beginning in the early 1950s, the Supreme Court began to take an interest in schemes for the licensing of motion pictures that a number of states created in an effort to prevent the exhibition of obscenity. Although the Court held to the position that states could impose criminal penalties for the exhibition of obscene films (see Roth v. United States, 1957), the justices greatly trimmed the constitutional contours of these licensing schemes because, as systems of prior restraint on expressive activity, they were "always fraught with danger and viewed with suspicion" (Freedman v. Maryland, 1965; see Joseph Burstyn, Inc. v. Wilson, 1952). The Court explained:

> The administration of a censorship system for motion pictures presents peculiar dangers to constitutionally protected speech. Unlike a prosecution for obscenity, a censorship proceeding puts the initial burden on the exhibitor or distributor. Because the censor's business is to censor, there inheres the danger that he may well be less responsive than a court—part of an independent branch of government—to the constitutionally protected interests in free expression. And if it is made unduly onerous, by reason of delay or otherwise, to seek judicial review, the censor's determination may in practice be final. (Freedman)

The Court in *Freedman* nevertheless did not invalidate motion picture licensing systems per se. Instead, the justices addressed the special First Amendment threats such systems created by demanding especially rigorous procedural requirements for their operation.

The Court in *Freedman* aligned motion picture licensing schemes with the usual First Amendment default rule that all expression is constitutionally protected. The *Freedman* procedures thus operate on a presumption that the First Amendment protects motion pictures that are subject to a licensing system. Licensing officials bear the burden of proving that a film is obscene. Moreover, the *Freedman* procedures deny licensing officials final authority to halt the distribution of films that they regard as obscene. They must ask a court to do so. "[B]ecause only a judicial determination in an adversary proceeding ensures the necessary sensitivity to freedom of expression," the *Freedman* Court explained, "only a procedure requiring a judicial determination suffices to impose a valid final restraint." In order to prevent licensing officials from blocking the exhibition of disfavored films simply by failing to act on a request for a license, the Court in *Freedman* required that the officials make their pre-clearance decisions "within a specified brief period." Finally, the *Freedman* Court required that motion picture licensing schemes ensure "a prompt final judicial decision" on any effort by the state to stop the exhibition of a film that officials consider obscene (see also City of Littleton v. Z.J. Gifts D-4, 2004). The requirement that a speaker proceed through the licensing process, of course, is itself a prior restraint on expression that infringes freedom of speech until the final decision is made. The Court's emphasis in *Freedman* on minimizing processing delays helps to explain the extraordinarily swift adjudication of the *Pentagon Papers* controversy.

It is worth emphasizing that *Freedman* imposed a procedural rather than a substantive barrier against motion picture licensing schemes. The decision operates on the premise that there is no First Amendment right to exhibit obscene films, and that states constitutionally may choose to prevent the exhibition of such films rather than, or in addition to, punishing their exhibition. *Freedman* is thus inconsistent with other Supreme Court decisions that have disallowed prior restraints on unprotected speech (see, e.g., Near v. Minnesota, 1931). But true to the traditional judicial hostility to prior restraints, *Freedman*'s strict procedural requirements reflect the justices' strong distrust of the competence and good faith of licensing officials to pre-clear expressive activity. The *Freedman* procedures minimize the role of licensing officials by forcing them to grant or deny licenses promptly, and in the event of a denial, by immediately transferring the final licensing decision to the courts. The *Freedman* procedures hem in the authority of licensing officials to such a degree that states have been discouraged from establishing such preclearance requirements.

Modern Licensing Systems: Access to the Public Forum

The Supreme Court has not applied the "extraordinary" procedural safeguards of *Freedman* to licensing systems that control access to the public forum (see Thomas v. Chicago Park District, 2002). The justices designed the *Freedman* procedures to fit an acute free speech problem. Motion picture licensing schemes pose an extreme risk of censorship because they authorize government officials to ban films because of their content. The *Freedman* procedures are especially stringent because they seek to minimize the risk that licensors will abuse their discretion by withholding approval of constitutionally protected films. These procedures would be overkill for licensing systems governing the use of public property. They are unnecessary because the public forum doctrine largely prohibits government officials from restricting access to public property because they disapprove of the legitimate content of a speaker's speech. The stringency of the *Freedman* procedures also would undermine the role of government officials as property custodian, a role that requires them to balance the public's expressive and non-expressive uses of public property. While one suspects that the Court was comfortable in discouraging the maintenance of motion picture licensing schemes, the justices have always recognized that some form of licensing system is useful, and perhaps necessary, for managing public fora (see Cox v. New Hampshire, 1941).

The Court has endeavored to reduce the risk of censorship in licensing schemes controlling access to the public forum by ensuring that the standards governing the license-granting authority not provide cover for content-based censorship. Consistent with the spirit of *Freedman*, the justices have been rigorous in demanding such assurance. They have insisted, in the first instance, that the standards governing the availability of a license be textually content-neutral (see Cox v. New Hampshire, 1941). More pointedly, the Court has required that the standards also be sufficiently "specific and objective" as to rob licensing officials of any discretion to make content-discriminatory decisions in allocating access to public fora (Thomas v. Chicago Park District, 2002; see Lakewood v. Plain Dealer Publishing Co., 1988; Lovell v. Griffin, 1938). These standards also provide a baseline for judicial review of licensing decisions, thereby enabling judges to assure themselves that the officials' application of content-neutral standards governing use of a public forum not serve as a pretext for discrimination.

In the end, the Court's approach to modern licensing schemes tracks the content distinction principle. The justices put a content-based scheme that smacked of governmental censorship (motion picture licensing) through a strict scrutiny wringer, but they allowed considerably more procedural flexibility for a system (public forum licensing) that ensured content neutrality.

THE OVERBREADTH DOCTRINE

The overbreadth doctrine establishes the unremarkable proposition that a law violates freedom of speech if its prohibitory sweep is so broad that it encompasses a substantial amount of expressive activity that is protected by the First Amendment (see Ashcroft v. The Free Speech Coalition, 2002). The origins of the doctrine trace to Thornhill v. Alabama (1940), where the Court declared that the mere "existence of [an overbroad] statute . . . results in a continuous and pervasive restraint on all freedom of discussion that might reasonably be regarded as within its purview." Overbroad statutes, the *Thornhill* Court also warned, invite discriminatory enforcement against officially disfavored speakers and points of view. The overbreadth doctrine therefore enforces a First Amendment requirement that legislatures "carefully" write statutes that restrict expressive activity in order to "punish only unprotected speech," without being "susceptible of application to protected expression" (Gooding v. Wilson, 1972).

The distinctive bite of the overbreadth doctrine lies in its availability to those whose activity stands outside First Amendment protection. An individual to whom a statute may be applied consistently with the First Amendment may nevertheless challenge the statute "on its face" (that is, as written) as unconstitutionally overbroad if the statute applies as well to activity that is protected by the First Amendment. This is a departure from the usual rules of constitutional adjudication, in which litigants generally are allowed to challenge the constitutionality of statutes only as applied to their particular circumstances. Litigants typically lack standing to make legal claims that belong to third parties who are not before the court. The Court made an exception to that customary limitation on litigant standing in free speech cases because of "the transcendent value to all society of constitutionally protected expression" (Gooding). An overbroad statute generates a "chilling effect" on protected speech because those to whom the statute applies, albeit unconstitutionally, are likely to forego their right to free expression rather than to risk prosecution (Gooding). In this view, a litigant, even one who has engaged in unprotected criminal activity, performs a public service by successfully challenging an overbroad statute.

In recent years, the Court has emphasized that the overbreadth doctrine is "strong medicine" that should be used only sparingly (Broadrick v. Oklahoma, 1973). Because the doctrine obligates the justices to assess the constitutionality of legislation based on hypothetical applications of the statute, there is risk that the free speech problems that the doctrine highlights might prove to be merely fanciful. Moreover, the overbreadth doctrine also forces outcomes that the Court sometimes finds distasteful. The litigant claiming statutory overbreadth at times has engaged in activity that clearly is beyond First Amendment protection and would be vulnerable to conviction under a properly limited statute, but because of the legislature's drafting error, that guilty party goes free.

While the justices remain committed to the overbreadth doctrine as an indispensable tool for the maintenance of the First Amendment system of free expression, the Court has trimmed its operation. The principal limit was devised in Broadrick v. Oklahoma (1973), where the Court held that in order to invalidate legislation as overbroad, the unconstitutional applications of the statute must be "substantial" in comparison with the statute's "plainly legitimate sweep." Dissenting in *Broadrick*, Justice Brennan chastised the majority for "mak[ing] no effort to define what it [meant] by 'substantial overbreadth.'" In the years since *Broadrick*, the justices have acknowledged their inability to provide "an exact definition" of the "substantial overbreadth" requirement (Members of City Council v. Taxpayers for Vincent, 1984). But the central meaning of the *Broadrick* test is clear: In order to mount an overbreadth attack, a litigant cannot simply hypothesize "some impermissible applications of a statute" (Vincent). To be successful, a litigant must convince the Court that there exists "a realistic danger that the statute itself will significantly compromise recognized First Amendment protections of parties not before the Court" (Vincent).

As modified by *Broadrick* and explained by *Vincent*, the overbreadth doctrine is a flexible tool that empowers judges to invalidate a statute when they believe it is necessary to do so in the interest of protecting free expression, but which does not require judges to invalidate a statute simply because there exists some minimal or merely theoretical possibility of future First Amendment violations. If the threat of unconstitutional application is not "substantial," the Court simply will allow the statute to stand and will monitor its constitutionality on a case-by-case basis, which after all, is the typical judicial method of protecting constitutional rights.

THE VAGUENESS DOCTRINE

The doctrine of vagueness resembles the prior restraint and overbreadth doctrines because it, too, is focused on the means by which governments limit or prohibit expressive activity. As with the doctrines of prior restraint and overbreath, the vagueness doctrine identifies the nature of the speech restriction itself as a cause of special free speech concern. There is this difference, however: unlike the doctrines of prior restraint and overbreadth, the constitutional prohibition against unduly vague statutes is not a product of the First Amendment.

The vagueness doctrine arises from the constitutional guarantee of "due process of law" in the Fifth and Fourteenth Amendments, which requires that the federal and state governments, respectively, provide individuals with fair and reasonable notice of the boundaries between lawful and unlawful conduct. (Connally v. General Construction Co., 1926). The doctrine "insist[s] that laws give the person of ordinary intelligence a reasonable opportunity to know what is prohibited, so that he may act accordingly" (Grayned v. City of Rockford, 1972). In addition to securing the due process value of fundamental fairness, the vagueness doctrine also serves a vital First Amendment function when speech is at issue. Vague statutes, like laws that are overbroad, create a constitutionally unacceptable risk of official censorship because they invite arbitrary and discriminatory enforcement (Smith v. Goguen, 1974).

Although the vagueness doctrine, as an element of due process, applies generally to all criminal legislation, the justices have recognized that the doctrine assumes a special urgency with respect to laws that prohibit expressive activity. Accordingly, the Court "demands a greater degree of specificity" when First Amendment rights are at risk (Smith). A vague law, like an overbroad statute, signals that the legislature has not carefully considered the free speech values it has jeopardized by its enactment. And because vague statutes leave the boundaries between lawful and unlawful conduct indeterminate, they, like overboard laws, instill caution in individuals, encouraging them to forego expressive activities that might conceivably be prohibited (Grayned v. City of Rockford, 1972). Vague statutes thus have a "chilling effect" on freedom of speech similar to that caused by overbroad laws.

Ironically, the test for determining whether a statute is unconstitutionally vague is itself vague. The Court applies the vagueness doctrine against a background understanding that statues typically do not "map out" individual behavior in advance (Smith). The justices therefore do not demand "mathematical certainty" from a statute (Grayned). The Court, moreover, often looks beyond the text of a law in an effort to supply the specificity that the legislature failed to provide. Vague statutory language can be clarified by judicial interpretations of the law, by analogous laws, and "perhaps to some degree," by the interpretation of the law by enforcement authorities (Grayned).

The Court's vagueness decisions illustrate the elusiveness of the doctrine. The justices, for example, rejected a vagueness challenge to a statute that prohibited the use of sound trucks that emit "loud and raucous noises" because the description "convey[ed] to any interested person a sufficiently accurate concept of what is forbidden" (Kovacs v. Cooper, 1949). The Court also rejected a vagueness challenge to a law that prohibited individuals, when near a school that was in session, from making "any noise or diversion which disturbs or tends to disturb the peace or good order of such school session or class thereof" (Grayned v. City of Rockford, 1972). Yet the Court invalidated a statute that prohibited treating the flag of the United States "contemptuously," because that description did not distinguish with reasonable clarity between treatments of the flag that were criminal and those that were not (Smith v. Goguen, 1974). The Court also invalidated a law that prohibited the assembly on any sidewalk of three or more persons who "conduct themselves in a manner annoying to persons passing by." The Court found the "annoying" standard to be no standard at all (Coates v. Cincinnati, 1971).

On close inspection, however, there is a discernable pattern in the Court's vagueness jurisprudence. For one thing, it is clear that "vagueness" means more than ambiguity. The key to understanding the Court's deployment of the vagueness doctrine in free speech cases is to view the doctrine less as imposing a formal requirement on legislative drafting than as providing a functional tool enabling judges to stifle the potential for governmental censorship against officially disfavored speakers or points of view. In this light, judges might take some comfort that a law enforcement official's determinations that the sound level of a truck's loudspeaker was unduly loud or that noise near a school disturbed classes would prove less prone to the subjective biases of enforcement officials, or perhaps more capable of judicial verification, than would decisions that an assembly of individuals might annoy passersby or that an individual had treated a U.S. flag with contempt. In this light, the Court's vagueness decisions in the free speech align with—indeed, they implement—the content distinction principle. If this understanding of the Court's use of the vagueness doctrine in free speech cases is accurate, the doctrine merits consideration as a distinctive First Amendment requirement.

NOTES

* Henry P. Monaghan, "First Amendment 'Due Process,'" *Harvard Law Review* 83 (1970): 518–51, p. 518.

1. Harry Kalvan, Jr., "The Concept of the Public Forum: Cox v. Louisiana," *The Supreme Court Review* (1965): 1–32, p. 28.

2. *Blackstone's Commentaries on the Laws of England*, Bk. IV, Ch. XI, Wayne Morrison, ed., (London: Cavendish Publishing Ltd., 2001): **151–52.

3. See James Kent, *Commentaries on American Law*, v. III, lecture XXIV, originally published, 1827 (New York: Da Capo Press, 1971): pp. 12–24; Joseph Story, *Commentaries on the Constitution of the United States*, v. III, ch. XLIV, §§1878–86, originally published, 1833 (New York: Da Capo Press, 1970).

4. My factual account of the *Pentagon Papers* case is drawn from David Rudenstine, "The Pentagon Papers Case: Recovering its Meaning Twenty Years Later," *Cardozo Law Review* 12 (1991): 1869–1913.

5. Erwin N. Griswold, "Secrets Not Worth Keeping," *The Washington Post National Weekly Edition*, Feb. 20–26, 1989, p. 28.

6. Leslie H. Gelb, "The 100 Questions," *The New York Times*, June 16, 1991, p. E17.

7. Thomas Emerson made the case for the distinction between prior restraints and subsequent punishment presented in the text. See Thomas I. Emerson, "The Doctrine of Prior Restraint," *Law and Contemporary Problems* 20 (1955): 648–71.

Afterword

THE FUTURE FIRST AMENDMENT

Freedom of speech is not only a bedrock principle of American constitutionalism; it is also a part of the American identity. Because of the centrality of this concept in American culture, I suspect that more than a few readers of this volume were surprised to learn that the United States Supreme Court did not begin to strongly protect freedom of speech until well into the 1930s. To a large degree, the evolution of free speech doctrine in the approximately seventy years of its existence has been a story of progress, that is, of an ever-expanding conception of the breadth and depth of First Amendment protection. However, there are enough examples of judicial retrenchment to caution against indulging the assumption that continued progress in the actualization of free speech values in the United States is inevitable. The experience of the Second Red Scare following World War II teaches that even such strongly protective (and canonical) doctrines as the clear and present danger test are just one Supreme Court decision away from evisceration, if the setting is right. Might the War on Terrorism provide such a setting? The more recent Supreme Court decisions regarding sexual expression and the public forum doctrine, to take just two examples, remind that the Court's decisionmaking often involves negotiation among justices who seldom are of one mind on how to draw the boundaries between government control and individual right in hard cases.

Any candid look at American history and constitutional jurisprudence reveals that freedom of speech, although revered as an abstract concept, is often contested in real world applications. Vexing questions concerning the application of freedom of speech are on the American agenda for the twenty-first century. Should free speech protections be scaled back, maintained, or strengthened, as the United States settles into what appears to be a global War on Terrorism? Should freedom of speech trump or accommodate aggressive legislative efforts to reform campaign finance practices? Finally, and perhaps most far-reaching of all, is conventional free speech jurisprudence salient in the rapidly advancing telecommunications era characterized by the Internet? As we enter the twenty-first century, we can see, but not yet resolve, these questions. And surely the new century will generate free speech problems that we cannot now identify.

It is best that we engage these new issues of free expression with the understanding that the development of freedom of speech in the United States was not inevitable. It was the result of courageous litigants, lawyers, and judges who were willing to challenge the majority sentiment of the moment during times of societal stress. There is no reason to believe that the continued development of free speech doctrine will be possible without such courage in the future.

Bibliographical Essay

CHAPTER 1: A HISTORY OF FREEDOM OF SPEECH IN THE UNITED STATES

The English Background

Fredrick Seaton Siebert's *Freedom of the Press in England, 1476–1776: The Rise and Decline of Government Control* (Urbana: University of Illinois Press, 1952) provides a detailed account of freedom of speech and freedom of the press in England before the American Revolution. The first chapter of Leonard Levy's *Emergence of a Free Press* (New York: Oxford University Press, 1985) provides a brief, yet authoritative discussion of the English understanding of free speech before the American Revolution, with an emphasis on the law of seditious libel. Philip Hamburger's "The Development of the Law of Seditious Libel and the Control of the Press," *Stanford Law Review* 37 (1985): 661–765, is a detailed examination of the English approach to the freedom of speech before the American Revolution, emphasizing the importance of the law of seditious libel in the eighteenth, rather than the seventeenth century. For a very good, brief summary of the English historical background to the freedom of speech, see William T. Mayton, "Seditious Libel and the Lost Guarantee of a Freedom of Expression," *Columbia Law Review* 84 (1984): 91–142, pp. 97–108.

The American Colonial Background

Zechariah Chafee, Jr., a leading First Amendment legal scholar, for many years led scholars generally to accept the view that American colonials, and thus the framers of the First Amendment, broadly embraced the right of individuals to criticize their government without fear of state punishment for that criticism. See his *Free Speech in the United States* (Cambridge, MA: Harvard University Press, 1967) (originally published, 1941). Chafee, however, did not provide convincing historical support for his thesis, and in 1960 Leonard Levy's *Legacy of Suppression* replaced Chafee's interpretation with a new orthodoxy that saw only the most constricted understanding of free speech in colonial America. Levy moderated his position somewhat in *Emergence of a Free Press* (New York: Oxford University Press, 1985), which remains the leading history on freedom of speech during the colonial era. It is a detailed, careful study that is passionately written and strongly argued. Levy's interpretation of the American colonial experience has its critics, however. For accounts that disagree with Levy and argue for the view that American colonials held a more embracing view of free speech than Levy would allow, and thus that the framers' intent of the First Amendment's protection of the freedom of speech should be understood more broadly as well, see Larry D. Eldridge, *A Distant Heritage: The Growth of Free Speech in Early America* (New York: New York University Press, 1993) (focusing on the seventeenth century); Willaim T. Mayton, "Seditious Libel and the Lost Guarantee of a Freedom of Expression," *Columbia Law Review* 84 (1984): 91–142; and David M. Rabban, "The Ahistorical Historian: Leonard Levy on Freedom of Expression in Early American History," *Stanford Law Review* 37 (1985): 795–856.

The First Amendment

Leonard Levy's *Emergence of a Free Press* (New York: Oxford University Press, 1985): pp. 220-281, contains an excellent discussion of the drafting history of the speech and press clauses of the First Amendment. Chapter 5 of Levy's more recent *Origins of the Bill of Rights* (New Haven: Yale University Press, 1999), covers this material as well. Chapter 2 of Neil H. Cogen, ed., *The Complete Bill of Rights: The Drafts, Debates, Sources, & Origins* (New York: Oxford University Press, 1997) collects the documentary record of the speech and press clauses of the First Amendment. Finally, David S. Bogen, "The Origins of Freedom of Speech and Press," *Maryland Law Review* 42 (1983): 429–65, offers a brief account of the strands of intellectual history that tie into the First Amendment's protection of free expression.

The "Dark Age" of Free Speech Jurisprudence: From the Early National Period to World War I

The Sedition Act of 1798

An important book-length history of the Sedition Act is James Morton Smith, *Freedom's Fetters: The Alien and Sedition Laws and American Civil Liberties* (Ithaca: Cornell University Press, 1956). More recent, excellent discussions of this episode can be found in Michael Kent Curtis, *Free Speech, "The People's Darling Privilege": Struggles for Freedom of Expression in American History* (Durham: Duke University Press, 2000): pp. 52–116; Stanley Elkins and Eric McKitrick, *The Age of Federalism* (New York: Oxford University Press, 1993): pp. 581–93, 694–13; and Leonard Levy, *Emergence of a Free Press* (New York: Oxford University Press, 1985): pp. 282–349.

From the Sedition Act to the Civil War

The leading works on free speech during this period is Michael Kent Curtis, *Free Speech, "The People's Darling Privilege": Struggles for Freedom of Expression in American History* (Durham: Duke University Press, 2000): pp. 117–299, and Russel B. Nye, *Fettered Freedom: Civil Liberties and the Slavery Controversy, 1830–1860* (East Lansing: Michigan State College Press, 1949). William Lee Miller, *Arguing About Slavery: The Great Battle in the United States Congress* (New York: Alfred A. Knopf, 1996), provides a richly detailed account of congressional deliberations on the slavery issue, focusing on the second quarter of the nineteenth century.

The Civil War

The leading study on Lincoln's handling of civil liberties issues during the Civil War is Mark E. Neely, Jr., *The Fate of Liberty: Abraham Lincoln and Civil Liberties* (New York: Oxford University Press, 1991). Michael Kent Curtis's *Free Speech, "The People's Darling Privilege": Struggles for Freedom of Expression in American History* (Durham: Duke University Press, 2000): pp. 300–56, focuses on Lincoln's policies regarding free speech.

From the Civil War to World War I

For a careful exploration of the history surrounding the drafting and adoption of the Fourteenth Amendment, as well as the early judicial interpretations of the Amendment, see William E. Nelson, *The Fourteenth Amendment: From Political Principle to Judicial Doctrine* (Cambridge, MA: Harvard University Press, 1988). For a look at that history with a special eye on freedom of speech, see Michael Kent Curtis, *Free Speech, "The People's Darling Privilege": Struggles for Freedom of Expression in American History* (Durham: Duke University Press, 2000): pp. 357–83.

The leading treatment of free speech issues from the Civil War to World War I is David M. Rabban, *Free Speech in Its Forgotten Years* (Cambridge: Cambridge University Press, 1997).

CHAPTER 2: WHAT MAKES FREEDOM OF SPEECH SPECIAL?

Thomas I. Emerson, "Toward a General Theory of the First Amendment," *Yale Law Journal* 72 (1963): 877–956, pp. 878–86, is a good starting place for an exploration of the theory that supports special constitutional protection for freedom of speech. His "general theory" incorporates each of the leading justifications for protecting freedom of speech, and his summary of those justifications is both succinct and accessible. Frederick Schauer, *Free Speech: A Philosophical Enquiry* (Cambridge: Cambridge University Press, 1982): pp.15–72, provides a dense, detailed, and rewarding philosophical critique of the commonly cited justifications for providing special protection to the freedom of speech. Finally, Kent Greenawalt, "Free Speech Justifications," *Columbia Law Review* 89 (1989): 119–55, is a thoughtful, measured assessment of the commonly advanced justifications of the freedom of speech.

Positive Justifications for the Freedom of Speech

Self-government

Alexander Meiklejohn, "Free Speech and its Relation to Self-government" (1948), as revised and reprinted in *Political Freedom: The Constitutional Powers of the People* (New York: Harper & Brothers, 1960): pp. 3–89, is the leading treatment of the relationship between freedom of speech and self-government. Meiklejohn further elaborated his theory in "The First Amendment is an Absolute," *The Supreme Court Review* (1961): 245–66. Other scholars who have followed Meiklejohn in emphasizing this political account of free speech include Lilian R. BeVier, "The First Amendment and Political Speech: An Inquiry into the Substance and Limits of Principle," *Stanford Law Review* 30 (1978): 299–358; Robert H. Bork, "Neutral Principles and Some First Amendment Problems," *Indiana Law Journal* 47 (1971): 1–35; and Cass R. Sunstein, *Democracy and the Problem of Free Speech* (New York: The Free Press, 1993). For particularly effective critiques of Meiklejohn's theory, see Zechariah Chaffee's review of Meiklejohn's *Free Speech and its Relation to Self-government* in the *Harvard Law Review* 62 (1948): 891–901, and the more recent Robert Post, "Meiklejohn's Mistake: Individual Autonomy and the Reform of Public Discourse," *University of Colorado Law Review* 64 (1993): 1109–37.

The Search for Truth

In addition to Chapter 2 of John Stuart Mill's *On Liberty*, cited in the text, Karl R. Popper, *The Open Society and its Enemies* (Princeton: Princeton University Press, 5th ed., rev., 1971), is an important statement of the role of free inquiry and free expression in exposing societal error, and thus in advancing the search for truth. For especially helpful critiques of the search-for-truth rationale, see Frederick Schauer, *Free Speech: A Philosophical Enquiry* (Cambridge: Cambridge University Press, 1982): pp. 15–34, and Kent Greenawalt, "Free Speech Justifications," *Columbia Law Review* 89 (1989): 119–55, pp. 130–41. Owen Fiss, "Why the State?," *Harvard Law Review* 100 (1987): 781–94, argues that in the contemporary United States, the operation of the actual marketplace of ideas constrains rather than frees speech.

Individual Autonomy

In addition to Emerson's account of the autonomy justification for freedom of speech, cited in the test, the leading statements along this line include C. Edwin Baker, *Human Liberty and Freedom of Speech* (New York: Oxford University Press, 1989); C. Edwin Baker, "Scope of the First Amendment Freedom of Speech," *UCLA Law Review* 25 (1978): 964–1040; Martin H. Redish, "The Value of Free Speech," *University of Pennsylvania Law Review* 130 (1982): 591–645; and David A.J. Richards, "Free Speech and Obscenity Law: Toward a Moral Theory of the First Amendment," *University of Pennsylvania Law Review* 123 (1974): 45–91.

Negative Justification for the Freedom of Speech

Frederick Schauer is the leading proponent of a negative justification for the special protection afforded freedom of speech. See his *Free Speech: A Philosophical Enquiry* (Cambridge: Cambridge University Press, 1982): 80–86, and his "The Second-Best First Amendment," *William and Mary Law Review* 31 (1989): pp.1–23. In addition, see Ronald A. Cass, "The Perils of Positive Thinking: Constitutional Interpretation and Negative First Amendment Theory," *UCLA Law Review* 34 (1987): 1405–91, and Keith Werhan, "The Liberalization of Freedom of Speech on a Conservative Court," *Iowa Law Review* 80(1994): 51–100.

CHAPTER 3: THE PROBLEM OF SUBVERSIVE ADVOCACY AND THE CENTRAL MEANING OF FREEDOM OF SPEECH

The best treatment of the evolution of subversive advocacy jurisprudence is by Harry Kalven, Jr., in his posthumously published *A Worthy Tradition: Freedom of Speech in America* 119–236 (New York: Harper & Row, 1988) (Jamie Kalven, ed.). For an argument justifying the First Amendment protection of subversive advocacy, see Steven D. Smith, "Radically Subversive Speech and the Authority of Law," *Michigan Law Review* 94 (1995): 348–70. The leading argument that subversive advocacy should not be protected by the First Amendment is to be found in Robert H. Bork's "Neutral Principles and Some First Amendment Problems," *Indiana Law Journal* 47 (1971): 1–35, pp. 23–35. The classic treatment on the general interrelationship between free speech and unlawful action is Kent Greenawalt, "Speech and Crime," *American Bar Foundation Research Journal* (1980): 647–785, which was updated and expanded in Greenawalt's *Speech, Crime, and the Uses of Language* (New York: Oxford University Press, 1989).

The classic discussion of the World War I decisions is by Zechariah Chafee, Jr., *Free Speech in the United States* 36–108 (Cambridge: Harvard University Press, 1967), which was originally published in 1941. For especially illuminating analyses of Justice Holmes's subversive advocacy opinions, see Yosal Rogat and James M. O'Fallon, "Holmes: A Dissenting Opinion – The Speech Cases," *Stanford Law*

Review 36 (1984): 1349–406; G. Edward White, *Justice Oliver Wendell Holmes: Law and the Inner Self*, Ch. 12 (New York and Oxford: Oxford University Press, 1993). Richard Pollenberg's exceptional history of the *Abrams* case, *Fighting Faiths: The Abrams Case, the Supreme Court, and Free Speech* (New York: Viking, 1987), provides a memorable and poignant account of the case, and a vivid evocation of the First Red Scare. For a general treatment of the free speech issues during periods of war, see Thomas I. Emerson, "Freedom of Expression in Wartime," *University of Pennsylvania Law Review* 116 (1968): 975–1011.

Not surprisingly, the Smith Act prosecutions of the 1950s, and the *Dennis* decision in particular, generated a wide range of legal commentary. Nathaniel L. Nathanson, in "The Communist Trial and the Clear-and-Present-Danger Test," *Harvard Law Review* 63 (1950): 1167–75, wrote before the Supreme Court's consideration of *Dennis* to urge the application of the Holmes-Brandeis version of the clear and present danger test. John A. Gorfinkel and Julian W. Mack, in "Dennis v. United States and the Clear and Present Danger Rule," *California Law Review* 39 (1951): 475–501, disagreed with all of the justices opinions in *Dennis*. They believed that the various positions of those in the majority were insufficiently attentive to free speech values, while the dissenting positions of Justices Douglas and Black were overly protective of speech. They would have drawn the boundary of First Amendment protection at the point a group begins to plan a conspiracy to overthrow the government. Carl A. Auerbach, "The Communist Control Act of 1954: A Proposed Political-Legal Theory of Free Speech," *University of Chicago Law Review* 23 (1956): 173–220, believed that the clear and present danger test, even as revised in *Dennis*, was too protective a standard to assess the constitutionality of the application of the Smith Act to the Communist Party USA. He argued that the First Amendment categorically allowed the suppression of totalitarian movements in a democratic society because if such a movement came to power, it would deny to all the freedom of speech as well as other democratic freedoms.

Brandenburg has generated considerable commentary as well. Hans A. Linde, "'Clear and Present Danger' Reexamined: Dissonance in the *Brandenburg* Concerto," *Stanford Law Review* 22 (1970): 1163–86, argued that the test is insufficiently protective of First Amendment values. For the strongest contemporary defense of the clear and present danger test as a constitutional measure for subversive advocacy, see Martin H. Redish, "Advocacy of Unlawful Conduct and the First Amendment: In Defense of Clear and Present Danger," *California Law Review* 70 (1982): 1159–200.

CHAPTER 4: THE CENTRAL ORGANIZING PRINCIPLES OF FREE SPEECH JURISPRUDENCE

The Categorization Principle

Frederick Schauer has written the strongest defenses of the categorization principle. See his articles, "Speech and 'Speech'—Obscenity and 'Obscenity': An

Exercise in the Interpretation of Constitutional Language," *The Georgetown Law Journal* 67 (1979): 899–933, and "Categories and the First Amendment: A Play in Three Acts," *Vanderbilt Law Review* 34 (1981): 265–307. For a philosophical examination of the role of categories in free speech analysis, see Thomas M. Scanlon, Jr., "Freedom of Expression and Categories of Expression," *University of Pittsburgh Law Review* 40 (1979): 519–50. For an early, important criticism of the categorization principle, see Harry Kalven, Jr., "The Metaphysics of the Law of Obscenity," *Supreme Court Review* (1960): 1–45. For a relatively recent scholarly exchange on categorization, see Larry Alexander, "Low Value Speech," *Northwestern University Law Review* 83 (1989): 547–54, Cass R. Sunstein, "Low Value Speech Revisited," *Northwestern University Law Review* 83 (1989): 555–61, and Frederick Schauer, "The Aim and the Target in Free Speech Methodology," *Northwestern University Law Review* 83 (1989): 562–68.

For an excellent article arguing for a strategic understanding of the First Amendment that restricts the ambit of constitutional coverage in order to maximize protection for expression at the core of freedom of speech, see Vincent Blasi, "The Pathalogical Perspective and the First Amendment," *Columbia Law Review* 85 (1985): 449–514. For strong disagreements with Blasi's argument, see George C. Christie, "Why the First Amendment Should Not Be Interpreted from the Pathological Perspective," *Duke Law Journal* (1986): 683–94, and Martin H. Redish, "The Role of Pathology in First Amendment Theory: A Skeptical Examination," *Case Western Reserve Law Review* 38 (1988): 618–31.

The Content Distinction Principle

For a historical development of the content distinction principle, see Paul B. Stephan III, "The First Amendment and Content Discrimination," *Virginia Law Review* 68 (1982): 203–51. The most important, formative articles conceptualizing the content distinction principle are John Hart Ely, "Flag Desecration: A Case Study in the Roles of Categorization and Balancing in First Amendment Analysis," *Harvard Law Review* 88 (1975): 1482–508, and Kenneth L. Karst, "Equality as a Central Principle in the First Amendment," *University of Chicago Law Review* 43 (1975): 20–68. The leading explanation and justification of the content distinction principle is Geoffrey R. Stone, "Content Regulation and the First Amendment," *William and Mary Law Review* 25 (1983): 189–252. Perhaps the best, recent exploration of the implications and reach of the content distinction principle is Elena Kagen, "Private Speech, Public Purpose: The Role of Government Motive in First Amendment Doctrine," *University of Chicago Law Review* 63 (1996): 415–517. In that wide-ranging article, which bristles with insight, Kagan argues that the design of First Amendment doctrine is best explained as an effort to ferret out illicit governmental motives for restricting speech.

The leading article critical of the content distinction principle is Martin H. Redish, "The Content Distinction in First Amendment Analysis," *Stanford Law Review* 34

(1981): 113–51. Eugene Volokh, echoing John Hart Ely and Justice Anthony Kennedy, has argued that categorization should substitute fully for the strict-scrutiny, ends-means analysis the Court now uses as a default method for analyzing content-based restrictions. Eugene Volokh, "Freedom of Speech, Permissible Tailoring and Transcending Strict Scrutiny," *University of Pennsylvania Law Review* 144 (1996): 2417–61. The legal historian Morton Horowitz has portrayed the content distinction principle as the central device by which the Burger and Rehnquist Courts have "*Lochner*ized" the freedom of speech. He criticizes the contemporary Court's overriding commitment to content neutrality for blocking legislative efforts to "level the playing field" so that those who lack economic resources and social standing may still have a voice in political debate. Morton J. Horowitz, "The Constitution of Change: Legal Fundamentality Without Fundamentalism," *Harvard Law Review* 107 (1993): 30–117. Susan H. Williams has argued that disparate impact, rather than discriminatory purpose, should trigger a finding that governmental law or action is based on content and thus subject to strict scrutiny. See her "Content Discrimination and the First Amendment," *University of Pennsylvania Law Review* 139 (1991): 615–730. For my critique of the Court's handling of content-neutral restrictions, see Keith Werhan, "The *O'Brien*ing of Free Speech Methodology," 19 (1987): 635–79.

CHAPTER 5: THE CODIFIED FIRST AMENDMENT

Provocative Speech

Hostile Audiences

The best review of the Court's approach to what Harry Kalven has labeled "reflexive disorder" is Harry Kalven, Jr., *A Worthy Tradition: Freedom of Speech in America* (New York: Harper & Row, 1988): 77–118. Kalven's survey of the case law is characteristically thorough and thoughtful.

Fighting Words

For a careful analysis of the fighting words problem, as well as related free speech issues, see Kent Greenawalt, *Fighting Words: Individuals, Communities, and Liberties* (Princeton: Princeton University Press, 1996). Greenawalt argues that fighting words are properly considered unprotected speech because their purpose is to cause harm rather than to communicate ideas. Mark C. Rutzick, "Offensive Language and the Evolution of First Amendment Protection," *Harvard Civil Rights-Civil Liberties Law Review* 9 (1974): 1–28, provides an excellent comparison of the *Chaplinsky* and *Cohen* decisions, emphasizing the differences in judicial sensitivity to free speech values manifested in the two opinions.

The Court's decision in *Cohen v. California* is something of a paradox in First Amendment jurisprudence. While the dispute may seem trifling—involving as it did the right of a teenager to wear a jacket with an expletive printed on its back—the Court's opinion in the case was both thoughtful and groundbreaking. For that reason, it has generated considerable commentary. William Cohen, "A Look Back at *Cohen v. California*," *UCLA Law Review* 34 (1987): 1595–1614, provides an illuminating look at the factual context, legal arguments and litigation strategy in the *Cohen* case. Cohen, who is not the same Cohen involved in the case, also recounts the precedential significance of the Court's decision. Daniel A. Farber, "Civilizing Public Discourse: An Essay on Professor Bickel, Justice Harlan, and the Enduring Significance of *Cohen v. California*," *Duke Law Journal* (1980): 283–303, examines the Court's denial of state authority to enforce a legal level of civility in public discourse.

Hate Speech

The problem of hate speech has generated an enormous literature in recent years. Some scholars have argued that a fairly broad definition of hate speech should be created as a distinct category of unprotected speech. Particularly influential arguments for this view are by Richard Delgado, "Words that Wound: A Tort Action for Racial Insults, Epithets, and Name-Calling," *Harvard Civil Liberties-Civil Liberties Law Review* 17 (1982): 133–81, and Mari J. Matsuda, "Public Response to Racist Speech: Considering the Victim's Story," *Michigan Law Review* 87 (1989): 2320–81. These arguments emphasize the harm caused by hate speech to its victims, imposing, in Matsuda's language, "a psychic tax . . . on those least able to pay." Another prominent argument supporting a broad governmental power to restrict hate speech holds that the constitutional right to equal protection of the laws guaranteed by the Fourteenth Amendment provides a compelling and sufficient justification for any diminution of free speech caused by laws prohibiting hate speech. An important exposition of this view is Charles R. Lawrence, III, "If He Hollers Let Him Go: Regulating Racist Speech on Campus," *Duke Law Journal* (1990): 431–83.

A number of scholars have resisted the call for legitimating government regulation of hate speech beyond the boundaries set by conventional free speech jurisprudence. Some have argued that such regulation amounts to government censorship of a disfavored point of view. See, e.g., Charles Fried, "The New First Amendment Jurisprudence: A Threat to Liberty," *The University of Chicago Law Review* 59 (1992): 225–53, and Nadine Strossen, "Regulating Racist Speech on Campus: A Modest Proposal?," *Duke Law Journal* (1990): 484–573 (responding to the Lawrence article, cited in the previous paragraph). Others have argued that responding to hate speech by governmental silencing rather than by debate and persuasion is likely to prove unsuccessful, and perhaps even dangerous for those whom such restrictions would protect. See Henry Louis Gates, Jr., "Let Them Talk: Why Civil Liberties Pose No Threat to Civil Rights," *The New Republic*, Sept. 20 & 27, 1993: 37–49; Kenneth L. Karst, "Boundaries and Reasons: Freedom of Expression and the Subordination of Groups," *University of Illinois Law Review* (1990): 95–149; and Robert C. Post, "Racist Speech, Democracy, and the First Amendment," *William and Mary Law Review* 32 (1991): 267–327.

Finally, in an especially eloquent exploration of the problem of hate speech, with a special emphasis on the *Skokie* litigation, Lee Bollinger has argued that a strong

First Amendment protection of hate speech serves the important societal value of cultivating a spirit of tolerance by requiring that members of society tolerate even the most intolerable speech and speakers. Lee C. Bollinger, *The Tolerant Society: Freedom of Speech and Extremist Speech in America* (New York: Oxford University Press, 1986). For a view that Bollinger's position is naïve, see Kenneth Lasson, "Racial Defamation as Free Speech: Abusing the First Amendment," *Columbia Human Rights Law Review* 17 (1985): 11–55.

For an article exploring the free speech implications of hate-crime laws such as was involved in *Wisconsin v. Mitchell*, as well as a criticism of that decision, see Steven G. Gey, "What if *Wisconsin v. Mitchell* Had Involved Martin Luther King, Jr.? The Constitutional Flaws of Hate Crime Enhancement Statutes," *The George Washington Law Review* 65 (1997): 1014–70. For an article justifying more severe punishment for hate crimes than for parallel crimes, see Frederick M. Lawrence, "The Punishment of Hate: Toward a Normative Theory of Bias-Motivated Crimes," *Michigan Law Review* 93 (1994): 320–81.

Sexual Expression

David Cole has written a provocative analysis of a broad range of the Supreme Court's First Amendment jurisprudence concerning sexual expression. David Cole, "Playing by Pornography's Rules: The Regulation of Sexual Expression," *University of Pennsylvania Law Review* 143 (1994): 111–77. He argues that laws in this area reflect a governmental determination to "keep[] sex out of the public sphere." Such a project, of course, is in serious tension with the freedom of speech, and Cole argues that "the regulation of sexual expression cannot be justified under traditional speech doctrines." Vincent Blasi has used the example of sexual expression (specifically, nude dancing) to explore the implications of varying conservative legal theories for First Amendment protection. See his "Six Conservatives in Search of the First Amendment: The Revealing Case of Nude Dancing," *William and Mary Law Review* 33 (1992): 611–63.

Obscenity

For an excellent history of obscenity regulation in the United States written from a constitutional legal perspective, see Margaret A. Blanchard, "The American Urge to Censor: Freedom of Expression Versus the Desire to Sanitize Society—From Anthony Comstock to 2 Live Crew," *William & Mary Law Review* 33 (1992): 741–851. For a lively history of obscenity regulation in the United States, written with special attention to the perspectives of writers and other artists, see Edward de Grazia, *Girls Lean Back Everywhere* (New York: Random House, 1992). For a history of the Comstock era, which includes an excellent account of the national debate Comstock's efforts generated on the meaning of freedom of speech in the nineteenth century, see David M. Rabban, *Free Speech in its Forgotten Years* (Cambridge: Cambridge University Press, 1997): pp. 23–76.

Harry M. Clor's *Obscenity and Public Morality: Censorship in a Liberal Society* (Chicago: University of Chicago Press, 1969) is a leading defense of anti-obscenity laws. Harry Kalven, Jr.'s "The Metaphysics of the Law of Obscenity," *Supreme Court Review* (1960): 1–45, is the classic critique of what he labeled "the two-level speech theory" of *Roth*, and indeed, of the categorization method in general. Kalven also recognized that the *Roth* approach would place a heavy burden on the definition of obscenity, and presciently, that the definitional question would prove exceedingly difficult for the justices to administer. The leading defense of *Roth*'s "two-level theory," as well as its application to obscenity, is to be found in the work of Frederick Schauer, especially his "Speech and 'Speech'—Obscenity and 'Obscenity': An Exercise in the Interpretation of Constitutional Language," *The Georgetown Law Journal* 67 (1979): 899–933. Schauer has offered the important, if controversial, justification for the unprotected status of obscenity on the ground that such expression is not "designed to appeal to the intellectual process," but rather "to produce a purely physical effect." Schauer argued, "Thus the refusal to treat pornography as speech is grounded in the assumption that the prototypical pornographic item on closer analysis shares more of the characteristics of sexual activity than of the communicative process." For a debate on the soundness of this justification for obscenity regulation, as filtered through the work of Cass Sunstein, see Paul Chevigny, "Pornography and Cognition: A Reply to Cass Sunstein," *Duke Law Journal* 1986: 420–32, and Cass R. Sunstein, "The First Amendment and Cognition: A Response," *Duke Law Journal* 1986: 433–37.

The appropriate role of morality in obscenity jurisprudence, not surprisingly, has generated considerable scholarly attention. Louis Henkin argued early on that states outlaw obscenity, at bottom, because legislators regard such expression as sinful. Louis Henkin, "Morals and the Constitution: The Sin of Obscenity," *Columbia Law Review* 63 (1963): 391–414. For Henkin, the constitutional issue over obscenity was "whether the state may suppress expression it deems immoral,"and his article is a thoughtful critique of anti-obscenity law as "morals legislation." In a defense of anti-obscenity laws that the Court prominently quoted in *Paris*, Alexander Bickel argued that the primary value of such laws was in their authoritative statement of the moral norms of the community. Alexander M. Bickel, *The Morality of Consent* 73–76 (New Haven: Yale University Press, 1975). By contrast, David A. J. Richards, in his "Free Speech and Obscenity Law: Toward a Moral Theory of the First Amendment," *University of Pennsylvania Law Review* 123 (1974): 45–91, drew on his "moral theory" of the freedom of speech to challenge the *Paris/Miller* resettlement of obscenity jurisprudence.

Cass Sunstein has thoughtfully analyzed the obscenity problem in the light of the broader First Amendment commitment to viewpoint neutrality. Cass R. Sunstein, "Pornography and the First Amendment," *Duke Law Journal* (1986): 589–627. Sunstein blends Schauer's justification of anti-obscenity laws, feminist theory, and his view that "the central concern" of the freedom of speech is the protection of political speech to justify a particular version of pornography regulation.

The feminist-inspired, "anti-pornography" alternative to conventional anti-obscenity laws has generated an extraordinary amount of scholarship. For a recent compilation of scholarship on this issue, see Drucilla Cornell, ed., *Feminism and Pornography* (Oxford: Oxford University Press, 2000). The pioneering work, and the dominant voices, in support of this alternative come from Andrea Dworkin and Catherine A. MacKinnon. See, e.g., Andrea Dworkin, *Pornography: Men Possessing Women* (New York: E. P. Dutton, 1989); Catherine A. MacKinnon, "Pornography, Civil Rights, and Speech," *Harvard Civil Rights-Civil Liberties Review* 20 (1985): 1–70. Nadine Strossen has emerged as a leading opponent of the Dworkin-MacKinnon position, arguing from a feminist perspective that it is censorship rather than pornography that harms women. See her *Defending Pornography: Free Speech, Sex, and the Fight for Women's Rights* (New York: Scribner, 1995), and "A Feminist Critique of 'the' Feminist Critique of Pornography," *Virginia Law Review* 79 (1993): 1099–1190. In addition, the friend-of-the-court brief filed by feminist legal scholars who opposed the anti-pornography law at issue in *Booksellers* is available in print, see Nan D. Hunter and Sylvia A. Law, "Brief Amicus Curiae of Feminist Anti-Censorship Taskforce, et al., in *American Booksellers Association v. Hudnut*," *University of Michigan Journal of Law Reform* 21 (1988): 69–135.

For a brief, yet effective, defense of the judicial rejection of the anti-pornography alternative that draws on conventional free speech doctrine, see Geoffrey R. Stone, "Anti-Pornography Legislation as Viewpoint-Discrimination," *Harvard Journal of Law & Public Policy* 9 (1986): 461–80. Cass R. Sunstein challenged this conventional thinking in his influential essay, "Neutrality in Constitutional Law (With Special Reference to Pornography, Abortion, and Surrogacy)," *Columbia Law Review* 92 (1992): 1–52. Sunstein argued that the apparent viewpoint discrimination in anti-pornography laws actually furthers equality by reversing "systematic sources of social disadvantage" experienced by women. Catherine A. MacKinnon also emphasized an equality rationale for the style of anti-pornography law she champions in her post-*Booksellers* book, *Only Words* (Cambridge: Harvard University Press, 1993). Robert C. Post responded thoughtfully to such equality-based arguments in his "Cultural Heterogeneity and Law: Pornography, Blasphemy, and the First Amendment," *California Law Review* 76 (1988): 297–335.

Child Pornography and the Border Security of Protected Sexual Expression

Ironically, the application of the First Amendment to child pornography, which has become a significant ingredient of contemporary free speech jurisprudence, has received far less attention by legal scholars than has the legitimacy of feminist inspired anti-pornography laws, which has never gained a foothold in the jurisprudence. Amy Adler is the most noteworthy exception to this scholarly neglect. She has written thoughtful and provocative companion pieces on the issue of child pornography (see "The Perverse Law of Child Pornography," *Columbia*

Law Review 101 (2001): 209–73, and "Inverting the First Amendment," *University of Pennsylvania Law Review* 149 (2001): 921–1002). In the former essay, Adler argued that child pornography laws reinforce the problem of sexual abuse of children because they induce the community to sexualize children. In the latter article, she examined the potential of the child pornography exception to First Amendment protection to alter the American understanding of free speech. Frederick Schauer's "Codifying the First Amendment: New York v. Ferber," *The Supreme Court Review* 1982: 285–317, by contrast, focused less on the issue of child pornography per se. He evaluated the Court's decision in *Ferber* to create a new unprotected category of speech as a "significant milestone on the road toward elaborate codification of the First Amendment."

Channeling Non-obscene Sexual Expression

Frederick Schauer has written perhaps the most thoughtful analysis of the wisdom of creating "subcategories" of less than fully protected speech. See his "Categories and the First Amendment: A Play in Three Acts," *Vanderbilt Law Review* 34 (1981): 265-307, pp. 282–96. Schauer critiqued the *Young* decision in "The Return of Variable Obscenity?," *Hastings Law Journal* 28 (1977): 1275–1304.

Commerical Speech

The Supreme Court's decision to extend First Amendment protection to commercial advertising has been controversial, and free speech scholars are divided on the legitimacy of the Supreme Court's approach. Martin H. Redish offered a leading argument for the protection of commercial speech before the Court itself came to that position (see Martin H. Redish, "The First Amendment in the Marketplace: Commercial Speech and the Values of Free Expression," *George Washington Law Review* 39 (1971): 429–73). For a more recent, brief, and lively defense of protecting commercial speech, see Alex Kozinski and Stuart Banner, "Who's Afraid of Commercial Speech?," *Virginia Law Review* 76 (1990): 627–53. (Alex Kozinski is a Circuit Judge on the Ninth Circuit Federal Court of Appeals.)

The leading work in opposition to the Court's protection of commercial speech is Thomas H. Jackson and John Calvin Jeffries, Jr., "Commercial Speech: Economic Due Process and the First Amendment," *Virginia Law Review* 65 (1979): 1–41. Jackson and Jeffries argue that commercial advertising is better categorized as an economic or commercial practice, which typically is subject to pervasive governmental regulation, rather than as constitutionally protected speech. C. Edwin Baker, "Commercial Speech: A Problem in the Theory of Freedom," *Iowa Law Review* 62 (1976): 1–56, is also an important article critical of protecting commercial speech. Baker argues that commercial speech does not implicate the values of individual liberty and self-realization to the degree necessary to justify First Amendment protection.

Robert Post, "The Constitutional Status of Commercial Speech," *UCLA Law Review* 48 (2000): 1–57, is an excellent analysis of the contemporary controversy over the appropriate First Amendment position of commercial speech. Post defends the Court's decision to define a middle level of First Amendment protection for commercial speech, but he criticizes the *Central Hudson* test as indeterminate.

Finally, Steven Shiffrin, "The First Amendment and Economic Regulation: Away from a General Theory of the First Amendment," *Northwestern University Law Review* 78 (1983): 1212–83, provides a broad and probing analysis of the potential application of commercial speech doctrine to economic expressive activity beyond commercial advertising.

Symbolic Expression

The Court's decision in *O'Brien* was instantly recognized as a significant decision, and it generated thoughtful commentary (see Dean Alfange, Jr., "Free Speech and Symbolic Conduct: The Draft-Card Burning Case," *The Supreme Court Review* (1968): 1–52; Louis Henkin, "On Drawing Lines," *Harvard Law Review* 82 (1968): 63–92, pp. 76–82; Lawrence R. Velvel, "Freedom of Speech and the Draft-Card Burning Cases," *University of Kansas Law Review* 16 (1968): 149–79).

Since the *O'Brien* decision, scholars have tackled the challenging problem of fashioning an appropriate First Amendment approach to symbolic expression. Thomas Emerson has argued that symbolic conduct is characterized by the intertwining of a speech element and a conduct element, and that First Amendment protection should be limited to instances in which the speech element predominates (see Thomas I. Emerson, *The System of Freedom of Expression* (New York: Random House, 1970): pp. 79–90). For important challenges to Emerson's approach, see John Hart Ely, "Flag Desecration: A Case Study in the Roles of Categorization and Balancing in First Amendment Analysis," *Harvard Law Review* 88 (1975): 1482–1508, and Louis Henkin, "On Drawing Lines," cited in the preceding paragraph. Melville Nimmer emphasized the requirement that symbolic expression actually communicate a message to an audience (see his "The Meaning of Symbolic Speech Under the First Amendment," *UCLA Law Review* 21 (1973): 29–62). For a more recent analysis of what distinguishes conduct as communicative, and thus as "speech," see Peter Meijes Tiersma, "Nonverbal Communication and the Freedom of 'Speech'," *Wisconsin Law Review* (1993): 1525–89.

On the importance of the *O'Brien* decision in the evolution of free speech methodology, especially the content distinction principle, see Dean Ely's article on "Flag Desecration," cited in the preceding paragraph, and my article, Keith Werhan, "The *O'Brien*ing of Free Speech Methodology," *Arizona State Law Journal* 19 (1987): 635–79.

CHAPTER 6: THE PROCEDURAL FIRST AMENDMENT

For an influential identification and analysis of the procedural dimension of free speech jurisprudence, see Henry P. Monaghan, "First Amendment 'Due Process,'" *Harvard Law Review* 83 (1970): 518–51.

The Public Forum Doctrine

Harry Kalven, Jr., coined the term "public forum" in his seminal article, "The Concept of the Public Forum: Cox v. Louisiana," *The Supreme Court Review* (1965): 1–32. Kalven argued for a broad, robust right of citizens to "commandeer" public places for expressive activity. Geoffrey R. Stone's "Fora Americana: Speech in Public Places," *The Supreme Court Review* (1974): 233–80, is another important elaboration of the public forum principle. As counterpoints, see Lillian R. Bevier, "Rehabilitating Public Forum Doctrine: In Defense of Categories," *The Supreme Court Review* (1992): 79–122, which as the title suggests, defends the categorical doctrine of *Greer* and *Perry*, and Robert C. Post, "Between Governance and Management: The History and Theory of the Public Forum Doctrine," *UCLA Law Review* 34 (1987): 1713–1835, which defends the Court's reluctance to strictly review denials of speaker access to non-public forum property because of the necessity of providing sufficient managerial discretion to the government custodians of such property. Other leading articles on the public forum doctrine include Ronald A. Cass, "First Amendment Access to Government Facilities," *Virginia Law Review* 65 (1979): 1287–1355, and Daniel A. Farber and John E. Nowak, "The Misleading Nature of Public Forum Analysis: Content and Context in First Amendment Adjudication," *Virginia Law Review* 70 (1984): 1219–66.

My discussion of the public forum doctrine in the text drew from my writings on the subject, which include, Keith Werhan, "The Supreme Court's Public Forum Doctrine and the Return of Formalism," *Cardozo Law Review* 7 (1986): 335–437, and Keith Werhan, "The Liberalization of Freedom of Speech on a Conservative Court," *Iowa Law Review* 80 (1994): 51–100, pp. 76–85.

The Prior Restraint Doctrine

Thomas I. Emerson, "The Doctrine of Prior Restraint," *Law and Contemporary Problems* 20 (1955): 648–71, provides the classic argument that prior restraints of expressive activity are more threatening to free speech values than are subsequent punishments for the same activity. Vincent Blasi, "Toward a Theory of Prior Restraint: The Central Linkage," *Minnesota Law Review* 66 (1981): 11–93, provided the best account of the case against prior restraints since Emerson. Not all free speech scholars accept the distinction between prior restraints and subsequent punishment, however. John Calvin Jeffries, Jr., "Rethinking Prior Restraint," *Yale Law Journal* 92 (1983): 409–37, has argued that any such distinction is incoherent and should be abandoned. For commentary on the question, see Stephen R. Barnett, "The Puzzle of Prior Restraint," *Stanford Law Review* 29 (1977): 539-60; William T. Mayton, "Toward a Theory of First Amendment Process: Injunctions of Speech, Subsequent Punishment, and the Costs of the Prior Restraint Doctrine," *Cornell Law Review* 67 (1982): 245–82; Martin H. Redish, "The Proper Role of the Prior Restraint Doctrine in First Amendment Theory," *Virginia Law Review*

70 (1984): 53–100; and Marin Scordato, "Distinction Without a Difference: A Reappraisal of the Doctrine of Prior Restraint," *North Carolina Law Review* 68 (1989): 1–35.

For a lively and thoughtful rendering of *Near v. Minnesota*, an important decision in the evolution of prior restraint doctrine, see Fred W. Friendly, *Minnesota Rag: The Dramatic Story of the Landmark Supreme Court Case That Gave New Meaning to Freedom of the Press* (New York: Random House, 1981). The *Pentagon Papers* case has generated two thoughtful book-length treatments, Sanford J. Unger, *The Papers & the Press: An Account of the Legal and Political Battle over the Pentagon Papers* (New York: Dutton, 1972), and David Rudenstine, *The Day the Presses Stopped: A History of the Pentagon Papers Case* (Berkeley: University of California Press, 1996).

The Overbreadth Doctrine

The leading work on the overbreadth doctrine is Henry Paul Monaghan, "Overbreadth," *The Supreme Court Review* (1981): 1–39. Monaghan argues that the overbreadth doctrine should not be understood as an exception to the general requirement of litigant standing, which is the conventional view, but rather that the doctrine simply affirms that no one can be lawfully punished pursuant to an unconstitutional statute. Richard H. Fallon, Jr., "Making Sense of Overbreadth," *Yale Law Journal* 100 (1991): 853–908, and Martin H. Redish, "The Warren Court, the Burger Court, and the First Amendment Overbreadth Doctrine," *Northwestern University Law Review* 78 (1983): 1031–70, also are leading treatments of the doctrine.

The Vagueness Doctrine

The classic article on the vagueness doctrine was written by Anthony G. Amsterdam when he was a law student, Note, "The Void-for-Vagueness Doctrine in the Supreme Court," *University of Pennsylvania Law Review* 109 (1960): 67–116. John Calvin Jeffries, Jr., "Legality, Vagueness, and the Construction of Penal Statutes," *Virginia Law Review* 71 (1985): 189–245, provides another excellent analysis of the doctrine.

Table of Cases

A

Abrams v. United States, 250 U.S. 616 (1919)
American Booksellers Association v. Hudnut, 771 F.2d 323 (7th Cir. 1985), affirmed, 475 U.S. 1001 (1986)
Arcara v. Cloud Books, Inc., 478 U.S. 697 (1986)
Arkansas Educational Television Comm'n v. Forbes, 523 U.S. 666 (1998)
Ashcroft v. American Civil Liberties Union ___ U.S. ___, 124 S. Ct. 2783 (2004)
Ashcroft v. American Civil Liberties Union, 535 U.S. 564, 122 S. Ct. 1700 (2002)
Ashcroft v. The Free Speech Coalition, 535 U.S. 234, 122 S. Ct. 1389 (2002)

B

Bachellar v. Maryland, 397 U.S. 564 (1970)
Bantam Books, Inc. v. Sullivan, 372 U.S. 58 (1963)
Barron v. Baltimore, 32 U.S. (7 Pet.) 243 (1833)
Beauharnais v. Illinois, 343 U.S. 250 (1952)
Bigelow v. Virginia, 421 U.S. 809 (1975)
Brandenburg v. Ohio, 395 U.S. 444 (1969)
Bridges v. California, 314 U.S. 252 (1941)
Broadrick v. Oklahoma, 413 U.S. 601 (1973)
Brown v. Louisiana, 383 U.S. 131 (1966)
Brown v. Oklahoma, 408 U.S. 914 (1972)
Butler v. Michigan, 352 U.S. 380 (1957)

C

Cantwell v. Connecticut, 310 U.S. 296 (1940)
Central Hudson Gas & Electric Corp. v. Public Service Comm'n of New York, 447 U.S. 557 (1980)
Chaplinsky v. New Hampshire, 315 U.S. 568 (1942)
City of Ladue v. Gilleo, 512 U.S. 43 (1994)
City of Littleton v. Z.J. Gifts D-4, ___ U.S. ___, 12 S. Ct. 2219 (2004)

City of Los Angeles v. Alameda Books, Inc., 535 U.S. 425 (2002)
City of Madison Joint School District v. Wisconsin Public Employment Relations Comm'n, 429 U.S. 167 (1976)
City of Renton v. Playtime Theatres, Inc., 475 U.S. 41 (1986)
Claiborne Hardware Co. v. NAACP, 458 U.S. 886 (1982)
Clark v. Community for Creative Non-Violence, 468 U.S. 288 (1984)
Coates v. City of Cincinnati, 402 U.S. 611 (1971)
Cohen v. California, 403 U.S. 15 (1971)
Collin v. Smith, 447 F. Supp. 676 (N.D. Ill. 1978), 578 F.2d 1197 (7th Cir. 1978)
Commonwealth v. Davis (1895)
Corfield v. Coryall, 6 Fed. Cas. 546 (C.C.E.D.Pa. 1823)
Cornelius v. NAACP legal Defense and Educational Fund (1985)
Cox v. Louisiana, 379 U.S. 536 (1965)
Cox v. New Hampshire, 312 U.S. 569 (1941)
Curtis Publishing Co. v. Butts and Associated Press v. Walker, 388 U.S. 130 (1967)

D

Davis v. Massachusetts, 167 U.S. 43 (1897)
Debs v. United States, 249 U.S. 211 (1919)
DeJonge v. Oregon, 299 U.S. 353 (1937)
Dennis v. United States, 341 U.S. 494 (1951)
Doubleday & Co. v. New York, 335 U.S. 848 (1948)
Dun & Bradstreet, Inc. v. Greenmoss Builders, Inc., 472 U.S. 749 (1985)

E

Edwards v. South Carolina. 372 U.S. 229 (1963)
Erznoznik v. City of Jacksonville, 422 U.S. 205 (1975)
Ex Parte Jackson, 96 U.S. 727 (1877)

F

Federal Communications Commission v. Pacifica Foundation, 438 U.S. 726 (1978)
Feiner v. New York, 340 U.S. 315 (1951)
Fiske v. Kansas, 274 U.S. 380 (1927)
44 Liquormart, Inc. v. Rhode Island, 517 U.S. 484 (1996)
Freedman v. Maryland, 380 U.S. 51 (1965)
Frohwerk v. United States, 249 U.S. 204 (1919)

G

Garrison v. Louisiana, 379 U.S. 64 (1964)
Gertz v. Robert Welch, Inc., 418 U.S. 323 (1974)
Ginsberg v. New York, 390 U.S. 629 (1968)
Ginzburg v. United States, 383 U.S. 463 (1966)
Gitlow v. New York, 268 U.S. 652 (1925)
Gooding v. Wilson, 405 U.S. 518 (1972)
Grayned v. City of Rockford, 408 U.S. 104 (1972)

Greater New Orleans Broadcasting Ass'n v. United States, 527 U.S. 173 (1999)
Greer v. Spock, 424 U.S. 828 (1976)
Gregory v. City of Chicago, 394 U.S. 111 (1969)

H

Hague v. Committee for Industrial Organization, 307 U.S. 496 (1939)
Hamling v. United States, 418 U.S. 87 (1974)
Hartzel v. United States, 322 U.S. 680 (1944)
Heffron v. International Society for Krishna Consciousness, 452 U.S. 640 (1981)
Herndon v. Lowry, 301 U.S. 242 (1937)
Hess v. Indiana, 414 U.S. 105 (1973)

I

International Society for Krishna Consciousness v. Lee, 505 U.S. 672 (1992)

J

Jacobellis v. Ohio, 378 U.S. 184 (1964)
Jenkins v. Georgia, 418 U.S. 153 (1974)
Jordan v. DeGeorge, 341 U.S. 223 (1951)
Joseph Burstyn, Inc. v. Wilson, 343 U.S. 495 (1952)

K

Kingsley Int'l Pictures Corp. v. Regents of the University of the State of New York, 360 U.S. 684 (1959)
Konigsberg v. State Bar of California, 366 U.S. 36 (1961)
Kovacs v. Cooper, 336 U.S. 77 (1949)

L

Lakewood v. Plain Dealer Publishing Co., 486 U.S. 750 (1988)
Lee v. International Society for Krishna Consciousness, 505 U.S. 830 (1992)
Lewis v. City of New Orleans, 408 U.S. 913 (1972)
Lovell v. Griffin, 303 U.S. 444 (1938)

M

Martin v. City of Struthers, 319 U.S. 141 (1943)
Masses Publishing Co. v. Patten, 244 Fed. 535 (SD.N.Y. 1917), rev'd, Masses Publishing Co. v. Patten, 246 Fed. 24 (2nd Cir. 1917)
Members of City Council v. Taxpayers for Vincent, 466 U.S. 789 (1984)
Memoirs v. Massachusetts, 383 U.S. 413 (1966)
Metromedia, Inc. v. City of San Diego, 453 U.S. 490 (1981)
Miller v. California, 413 U.S. 15 (1973)
Mills v. Alabama, 384 U.S. 214 (1966)
Minneapolis Star & Tribune Co. v. Minnesota Commissioner of Revenue, 460 U.S. 575 (1983)
Monitor Patriot Co. v. Roy, 401 U.S. 265 (1971)

N

Near v. Minnesota, 283 U.S. 697 (1931)
Nebraska Press Ass'n v. Stuart, 427 U.S. 539 (1976)
New York v. Ferber, 458 U.S. 747 (1982)
New York Times Co. v. Sullivan, 376 U.S. 254 (1964)
New York Times Co. v. United States, 403 U.S. 713 (1971)
Noto v. United States, 367 U.S. 290 (1961)

O

Ohralik v. Ohio State Bar Ass'n, 436 U.S. 447 (1978)
Osborne v. Ohio, 495 U.S. 103 (1990)

P

Palko v. Connecticut, 302 U.S. 319 (1937)
Paris Adult Theatre I v. Slaton, 413 U.S. 49 (1973)
Patterson v. Colorado, 205 U.S. 454 (1907)
Perry Education Ass'n v. Perry Local Educators' Ass'n, 460 U.S. 37 (1983)
Police Department of Chicago v. Mosley, 408 U.S. 92 (1972)
Pope v. Illinois, 481 U.S. 497 (1987)
Posadas de P.R. Assocs. v. Tourism Co., 478 U.S. 328 (1986)

R

R. A. V. v. City of St. Paul, 505 U.S. 377 (1992)
Redrup v. New York, 386 U.S. 767 (1967)
Roe v. Wade, 410 U.S. 113 (1973)
Rosenberger v. University of Virginia, 515 U.S. 819 (1995)
Rosenbloom v. Metromedia, 403 U.S. 29 (1971)
Rosenfeld v. New Jersey, 408 U.S. 901 (1972)
Roth v. United States, 354 U.S. 476 (1957)
Rubin v. Coors Brewing Co., 514 U.S. 476 (1995)

S

Sable Communications of California, Inc., v. Federal Communications Commission, 492 U.S. 115 (1989)
Scales v. United States, 367 U.S. 203 (1961)
Schenck v. United States, 249 U.S. 47 (1919)
Schneider v. State, 308 U.S. 147 (1939)
Shaffer v. United States, 255 F. 886 (9th Cir. 1919)
Simon & Schuster, Inc. v. Members of the New York State Crime Victims Board, 502 U.S. 105 (1991)
Slaughter-House Cases, 83 U.S. (16 Wall.) 36 (1873)
Smith v. Collin, 439 U.S. 916 (1978)
Smith v. Goguen, 415 U.S. 566 (1974)
Smith v. United States, 431 U.S. 291 (1977)
Spence v. Washington, 418 U.S. 405 (1974)
St. Amant v. Thompson, 390 U.S. 727 (1968)
Stanley v. Georgia, 394 U.S. 557 (1969)

State v. Blyth, 226 N.W.2d 250 (Iowa 1975)
Stromberg v. California, 283 U.S. 359 (1931)

T

Taylor v. Mississippi, 319 U.S. 583 (1943)
Terminiello v. City of Chicago, 337 U.S. 1 (1949)
Texas v. Johnson, 491 U.S. 397 (1989)
Thomas v. Chicago Park District, 534 U.S. 316 (2002)
Thornhill v. Alabama, 310 U.S. 88 (1940)
Turner v. Williams, 194 U.S. 279 (1904)

U

United States v. Carroll Towing Co., 159 F.2d 169 (2nd Cir. 1947)
United States v. Dennis, 183 F.2d 201 (2nd Cir. 1950)
United States v. Eichman, 496 U.S. 310 (1990)
United States v. Grace, 461 U.S. 171 (1983)
United States v. O'Brien, 391 U.S. 367 (1968)
United States v. Playboy Entertainment Group, Inc., 529 U.S. 803 (2000)
United States v. Reidel, 402 U.S. 351 (1971)
United States v. United Foods, Inc., 533 U.S. 405 (2001)

V

Valentine v. Chrestensen, 316 U.S. 52 (1942)
Village of Skokie v. National Socialist Party of America, 373 N.E.2d 21 (Ill. Sup. Ct. 1978)
Virginia v. Black, 538 U.S. 343 (2003)
Virginia State Board of Pharmacy v. Virginia Citizens Consumer Council, 425 U.S. 748 (1976)

W

Ward v. Rock Against Racism, 491 U.S. 781 (1989)
Watchtower Bible and Tract Society of New York v. Village of Stratton, 536 U.S. 150 (2002)
Watts v. United States, 394 U.S. 664 (1969)
Whitney v. California, 274 U.S. 357 (1927)
Widmar v. Vincent, 454 U.S. 263 (1981)
Wisconsin v. Mitchell, 508 U.S. 476 (1993)
Wolston v. Reader's Digest Ass'n, 443 U.S. 157 (1979)

Y

Yates v. United States, 354 U.S. 298 (1957)
Young v. American Mini Theatres, Inc., 427 U.S. 50 (1976)

Index

ABOUT THE AUTHOR

KEITH WERHAN is the Geoffrey C. Bible and Murray H. Bring Professor of Constitutional Law at Tulane Law School. He specializes in Constitutional Law, the First Amendment, and Administrative Law, and has written widely in those areas. Professor Werhan entered the practice of law in Washington, D.C., first with a private law firm and later with the U.S. Department of Justice.

LaVergne, TN USA
17 June 2010
186533LV00003B/3/P